A Modern Jewish Perspective on the Gospel of John

A Modern Jewish Perspective
on the **Gospel of John**

—————— Jesus, God, "the Jews," and the Devil ——————

Charles David Isbell

RESOURCE *Publications* · Eugene, Oregon

A MODERN JEWISH PERSPECTIVE ON THE GOSPEL OF JOHN
Jesus, God, "the Jews," and the Devil

Resource Publications
An Imprint of Wipf and Stock Publishers
199 W. 8th Ave., Suite 3
Eugene, OR 97401

www.wipfandstock.com

PAPERBACK ISBN: 978-1-6667-3750-9
HARDCOVER ISBN: 978-1-6667-9701-5
EBOOK ISBN: 978-1-6667-9702-2

06/06/22

Contents

Preface

BECAUSE THIS BOOK IS not a verse-by-verse commentary, many parts of the Gospel of John are left untreated. The eleven essays included here are organized around broad themes that the author of John chose as the basis for his opinions about numerous issues that were significant and often controversial in the formative years of what grew to become the Christian religion. Accordingly, each essay reviews multiple teachings written by John, sometimes derived from a closely organized and tightly structured narrative, but often scattered in different sections throughout the Gospel. As each essay is considered, readers should compare the opinions presented here with the words of John in their own Bible that have prompted those opinions.

The sequence of the essays found here is designed to lead readers through opening questions about John and then through a series of issues that are deemed to be essential to an understanding of his gospel. I have tried to avoid technical jargon, but sometimes the subject matter calls for details to be studied carefully as a necessary component of grasping what is important and what is not. The parts of each essay that are technical usually involve linguistic *minutiae*. But detailed linguistic analysis is sometimes necessary because the Gospel of John was written in (common) Greek, not the language that Jesus used to study Scripture (Hebrew) or his mother tongue that he used in teaching and day-to-day conversation (Aramaic).

Except where otherwise noted, I have used my own translation of the Greek text of John, the Greek rendition of the Septuagint (LXX), the standard Masoretic Text (MT) of the Hebrew Scriptures, and all the Aramaic phrases under discussion. There are several excellent versions available for readers who are working from an English translation of these ancient texts. Wherever my English rendition differs from the version a reader normally uses for study, it is recommended that two or three different published versions be consulted for comparison.

Abbreviations

BCE   Before the Common Era

CE   Common Era

DSS   Dead Sea Scrolls

LXX   Septuagint

MT   Masoretic Text

NT   New Testament

OT   Old Testament

TB   Babylonian Talmud

Reference Works, Commentary Sets, Dictionaries, Encyclopedias

ABD   *The Anchor Bible Dictionary*. 6 vols. Edited by David Noel Freedman. New York: Doubleday, 1992.

AG   Walter Bauer, Frederick W. Danker, W. F. Arndt, and F. W. Gingrich. *Greek-English Lexicon of the New Testament and Other Early Christian Literature*. 3rd ed. Chicago: University of Chicago Press, 2000.

CBQ   *Catholic Biblical Quarterly*

EJ   *Encyclopaedia Judaica*. 22 vols. Jerusalem: Keter, 1971–1972.

HTR   *Harvard Theological Review*

IDB   *The Interpreter's Dictionary of the Bible*. 4 vols. Edited by George Arthur Buttrick. Nashville: Abingdon, 1962.

IDBSup   *The Interpreter's Dictionary of the Bible, Supplementary Volume*. Edited by Keith Crim. Nashville: Abingdon, 1976.

JBQ	*Jewish Bible Quarterly*
JBL	*Journal of Biblical Literature*
JNES	*Journal of Near Eastern Studies*
MR	*Midrash Rabbah.* 10 vols. Edited by H. Freedman and Maurice Simon. Translated by H. Freedman et al. 3rd edition. New York: Soncino, 1983.
NIV	*The Holy Bible: New International Version.* Grand Rapids: Zondervan, 1978
NIB	*The New Interpreter's Bible.* 12 vols. Nashville: Abingdon, 1994.
RBL	*Review of Biblical Literature*
SHERM	*Socio-Historical Examination of Religion and Ministry.*
TDNT	*Theological Dictionary of the New Testament.* 10 vols. Edited by Gerhard Kittel and Gerhard Friedrich. Translated by Geoffrey W. Bromiley. Grand Rapids: Eerdmans, 1964-76.
TDOT	*Theological Dictionary of the Old Testament.* 15 vols. Edited by G. Johannes Botterweck and Helmer Ringgren. Translated by Geoffrey W. Bromiley et al. Grand Rapids: Eerdmans, 1974-2004.

Scripture Abbreviations

Hebrew Bible / Old Testament / The (Jewish) Scriptures:

Gen	Judg	Neh	Song	Hos	Nah
Exod	Ruth	Esth	Isa	Joel	Hab
Lev	1–2 Sam	Job	Jer	Amos	Zeph
Num	1–2 Kgs	Ps (*pl.* Pss)	Lam	Obad	Hag
Deut	1–2 Chr	Prov	Ezek	Jonah	Zech
Josh	Ezra	Qoh	Dan	Mic	Mal

New Testament:

Matt	Acts	Eph	1–2 Tim	Heb	1–2–3 John
Mark	Rom	Phil	Titus	Jas	Jude
Luke	1–2 Cor	Col	Phlm	1–2 Pet	Rev
John	Gal	1–2 Thess			

Introduction

THIS BOOK IS WRITTEN for readers of the Gospel of John who are troubled by its incendiary language aimed at the Jews, by historical inaccuracies in the text, by the differences between John and the other canonical gospels (Mark, Matthew, Luke), or by various other kinds of textual complexities it presents. The eleven essays in the following chapters are my attempt to grapple with actual questions posed to me over a period of more than forty years by Jewish colleagues, synagogue congregants, lecture audiences, and university students who found the Gospel of John to be both puzzling and uncomfortable. Broadly speaking, they are designed to engage thoughtful readers from every religious background, to encourage their questions, and to suggest plausible answers to the questions raised by problems in the text of John. Because there is no central authority to broadcast *the* Jewish position and because of their commitment to the idea that "iron sharpens iron" (Prov 27:17), other Jewish scholars may offer competing answers to the issues addressed here. Christian scholars may choose different questions and find answers leading down an alternate path. Individual readers of all faiths should articulate their own questions and frame their own responses. My answers are intended to assist in their efforts and to encourage the kind of honest engagement with the gospel text that produces a clearer understanding of John's true worth in defining Christianity for the world.

John Among the Gospels

The early Christian Church produced at least twenty-one gospels, each of which portrays Jesus of Nazareth as a compelling and unique historical figure. Only four of the twenty-one were accepted into the official canon of early Christendom, and the process of eliminating more than eighty percent of the candidates was influenced by multiple factors. First, the non-canonical works that appeared soon after the death of Jesus suffered from a variety of shortcomings. Some were focused too narrowly on only one aspect of

1

the life and teachings of Jesus, or on some minor theological nuance not widely shared in early Christendom, or on blatantly magical deeds that had neither plausibility nor connection with the *spiritual message* of Jesus as it was perceived by the church at large.[1]

Second, because they expected Jesus to return from heaven at any moment after his resurrection, his closest disciples apparently felt no sense of urgency to write about him. Responding to the "Great Commission" of Matthew 28:19–20, they were too busy *preaching* their message about him at multiple sites targeted for missionary activity in their endeavor to go into "all the world" spreading the faith they believed Jesus had taught them.

Third, had there been an official stenographer present to hear Jesus speak and to write down his words with precision and exactitude as the disciples heard them in Jerusalem and the Judean hillsides, much of that material would have been of local interest only, not likely to have been of significance in a message delivered outside the homeland of Jesus. And because the sphere of his ministry was limited to Judea, early Jewish Christians were surely influenced by the Judean aversion to written literature out of concern that it might be viewed as an extension of what came to be known as the "Old Testament" (OT). Because of this hesitancy to produce written works that might be viewed to be in competition with sacred Scripture, oral discussion and debates among early Jewish sages were not set into writing until well into the third century CE when the Mishnah was published.[2]

Finally, the disciples were not literary men either by background or by profession.[3] Thus, although apostolic authority would come to be viewed by the church as essential to the authenticity of a gospel, the fact is that none of the four canonical gospels was written by one of the twelve original apostles.[4]

During the time that elapsed between the crucifixion of Jesus ca. 33 CE and the appearance of Mark, the earliest canonical gospel (ca. 70 CE), potential authors interested in the life of Jesus had almost four decades to reflect on his reputation as a healer, miracle worker, and teacher. This interlude witnessed the transition of the early Church from a small Jewish

---

1. Ehrman, *Lost Christianities* offers a helpful summary of the non-canonical gospels and some of the reasons why they were excluded from the official New Testament canon.

2. 220 CE is the usual date given. Instead of the abbreviations BC ("Before Christ") and AD (*Anno Domini*, "in the year of the Lord"), the more neutral CE ("Common Era") and BCE ("Before the Common Era") are used throughout.

3. Acts 4:13 describes Peter and John as "uneducated (*agrammatoi*) and ordinary men" (*idiōtai*).

4. The authorship of John is discussed further in Essay I.

sect to a predominately Gentile membership, and it allowed time for those newer Christians to digest the impact of Jesus' life on peoples and territories outside of Judea. It also indicated the wisdom of publishing his story in a language (*koiné* Greek) far more widely known in the world than the Aramaic dialect Jesus had spoken in this lifetime.

From the time of Mark's publication until the appearance of the Gospels of Matthew and Luke, another fifteen to twenty years elapsed, time for additional reflection that once again broadened the lens through which the life of Jesus might be viewed. Luke's assessment of numerous non-canonical gospels is spelled out in the opening chapters of his gospel (Luke 1:1–4), where he notes that "many" narratives pertaining to the life of Jesus had already been written, each claiming connection with the traditions about Jesus handed down by eyewitnesses. The differences among these numerous documents led Luke to assert that his work was an "orderly account" resulting from careful research and evaluation of these multiple sources.

By the time of John late in the first or early in the second century CE, Jesus had become far more than simply a miracle worker, and John's portrait is clearly more detailed and theologically oriented than any previous work. John's multi-dimensional Jesus is a loyal and loving friend to Lazarus and his sisters. He is the teacher whose skill and patience with his disciples are unparalleled and whose openness to outsiders and foreigners, including Roman officials and a lowly Samaritan woman, is startling. "To these qualities, John adds Jesus' tender acceptance of children, his focus on both physical and spiritual wellness, and his concern for the hungry and the needy. Ultimately, John's Jesus faced death with bravery and equanimity, willingly offering his own life for the benefit of others. To borrow the word picture of John, Jesus is indeed the 'Good Shepherd.'"[5] But John's Jesus is even more. In John, Jesus has become the quintessence of eternal light,[6] and some scholars believe the elevation of Jesus to the status of divinity is directly traceable to the Fourth Gospel.[7]

John and "the Jews"

But when modern Jews read John's narration of a two-sided dispute between "the Jews" and Jesus, they hear John quoting Jesus citing "your law" against his opponents (John 10:35), giving the impression that "the Jews" in John are opposed by Jesus the Christian who disavows his own Jewish

5. Isbell, *Essays*, 18.

6. John's brilliant encomium about light and life in the opening chapter is matchless.

7. This concept is discussed at length in Essay XI.

heritage. In fact, Gentile readers of John "often . . . think of Jesus more as a Christian than as a Jew!"[8]

While such a perception may seem normal to a non-Jew, for Jewish readers, it produces a heavy black cloud hanging over the portrait of a loving Jesus painted elsewhere in the Fourth Gospel. That cloud is the Johannine depiction of "the Jews," a sorry and despicable bunch that began to despise Jesus early in his life, tried repeatedly to murder him, and ultimately framed him with false accusations in a Roman court that led to his death. Thus, although John's hostile depiction of "the Jews" has remained a fixture in the minds of *Christians* of all denominations and theological iterations for two millennia, it is not surprising that *Jewish* readers of the gospel have found it difficult to discover the comfort and inspiration that the Jesus of John offers to Christian readers.

How can modern Jewish rabbis and scholars of religion explain to Jewish readers of John the harsh and judgmental narratives in John? Would John's disdain for a modern Jewish reader be the same attitude he exhibited towards "the Jews" of his day? Would John label twenty-first century Jews as children of the devil? Many of John's stinging words of condemnation do indeed appear to be applicable directly to modern Jewish readers. But many honorable Christian readers also are uncomfortable enough with this Johannine tendency to disavow its extreme supremacist rhetoric. As a result, modern New Testament (NT) scholars have posited numerous theories designed to soften the hammer blows of this anti-Jewish sentiment that suffuses the entire Gospel of John. But despite the level of their education in other fields, readers who lack academic training in NT scholarship may find it impossible to navigate the troubled waters of modern NT *theories* that are difficult to square with a plain sense reading of the text itself.

To heighten his implication that Jesus the Christian and "the Jews" are enemies, John draws his picture of "the Jews" in detail. Taken seriously as it is written, modern readers learn John's conviction that "the Jews" denied the clear witness of their own Scriptures to the correct understanding of Jesus. With the proper "spin," John's Jesus may be imagined arrogating to himself the personal name of the God of the Jewish Scriptures, and this led to the idea that "the Jews" had turned their backs on God Himself. Worse still, this Jewish denial was deliberate and purposeful, arising from willful spiritual blindness exacerbated by hard and unbelieving hearts and minds. And, according to John, these hard-hearted, unbelieving Jews cruelly and violently *expelled* early Christians from their synagogues.[9] Ultimately, of course, "the

---

8. Brown, *Community*, 40–41.

9. Essay V explores this concept in detail.

Jews" used false testimony as an illegitimate way to have Rome do what they lacked the legal authority to do—to put Jesus to death on a cross. Each of these Johannine assertions is challenged in the essays that follow.

Wrestling With the Problem Texts in John

In attempting to address issues of this nature with congregants and students, rabbis and professors of Judaism are required to deal with the historical inexactness of the Gospel of John and to point out the numerous instances where John depicts late first-century events as having occurred during the life of Jesus, where John's misunderstanding of history is undeniable, or his grasp of Jewish belief and *praxis* is misinformed. Christian scholars have long noted these problems in interpreting John, and scholarly acknowledgement of their presence in the text has spawned many an interesting theory about how and why such misrepresentations were made in the first place. But the typical modern reader cannot be expected to master the details of NT literary criticism as a precondition to reading and restructuring what the author said plainly. In other words, the average reader of John, Jewish or Christian, should be permitted to engage John without the scholarly patina that has accrued in the wake of numerous theories about the deep meanings that might be possible via *theoretical* readings of John's text.

There are two particularly troublesome examples of such theoretical explanations. The first is that the text of John should be read on two levels historically, parts of it reflecting the lifetime of Jesus in the first one-third of the first century CE, but other parts reflecting the final decade of that century during which the Gospel of John was composed. This means that the individual interpreter is free to move a troublesome text from one historical period to another. But a two-level John text is a theory derived from the imagination of modern scholars, not from the text that John wrote.

The second theoretical key assumed by interpreters of John is the idea that "the Jews" does not always mean "the Jews." Ultimately, some NT scholars speculate that seven different definitions of the term must be applied before one can understand what John was saying. This too is a theory that exists in the mind of the interpreter, not in the text of John.

Given all the theories employed to explain some of the more troublesome passages in John, it is not surprising that John is misread literally by some and imagined to be impossibly obtuse by others. But virtually all readers of John agree that the Fourth Gospel was and remains a major source of contention between Christians and Jews. Parlous theories do not solve the problems involved in reading John, and it is not difficult to understand why

Jewish reactions to John can appear to be as negative and dismissive to John as John is towards Jews. On the other hand, Christian readers can either retreat to the intellectual bunker of literalism or try to ignore the plain teachings of the author himself by studying theoretical reconstructions instead of analyzing the text that John wrote. In either case, Jews and Christians are left so far apart that rapprochement appears impossible. It is important to know when and why this chasm began to form.

The Myth of a Common Tradition

It is demonstrably true that the faith systems of Christians and Jews are and always have been radically different. The incomparable rabbi and academic scholar Jacob Neusner framed it this way: "The conceptions of a Judeo-Christian tradition that Judaism and Christianity share is simply a myth in the bad old sense: a lie."[10] This is true, Neusner argued, because "neither religion has a theory of the other framed in terms that the outsider can share."[11] And this means that Judaism and Christianity were "each speaking within precisely the same categories but *so radically redefine the substance of these categories* that conversation with the other became impossible."[12]

Christianity simply redefined the substance of the categories of faith they borrowed from Judaism, but those redefinitions are not difficult to discover. In the first place, early Christians assumed that they could define Judaism via their own etic ("outsider") interpretations of the Hebrew Scriptures.[13] In the process, the foundational categories that Jewish sages had employed in the construction of their faith system were immediately dismissed by early Christianity as inconsequential and incorrect. Said another way, Judaism was dubbed the "old" covenant, and a "new" covenant was deemed necessary for Christianity from the outset. In search of that "new" covenant, early Christians seized on the phrase coined by the prophet Jeremiah.[14] But Christian interpreters quickly steered the *term* coined by Jeremiah into a radical ninety-degree turn away from the prophet and *his understanding of the term* he had chosen.

For example, "Jeremiah notes twice that the new covenant of which he speaks was to be a covenant for and with *Israel and Judah*, and he makes no

10. Neusner, *Jews and Christians*, ix.

11. Neusner, *Jews and Christians*, ix-x.

12. Neusner, *Jews and Christians*, 5, emphasis added.

13. Isbell, "Emic or Etic."

14. "Behold, days are coming," declares Yahweh, "when I will make a new covenant with the House of Israel" (Jer 31:31).

mention of Gentiles. Instead, Jeremiah 31:33 speaks of engraving upon the hearts of *Israelites* and *Judahites* the principles of the old covenant."[15] The post-biblical sages who created the fundamental rabbinic explanations of Scripture that became the Mishnah–Tosefta–Talmud followed Jeremiah's lead, and they also declined to reshape the Israelite-Judahite covenant to include Gentiles. For them, consonant with Jeremiah's original expression, the "new covenant" was interpreted as "an internalization, an actualization, a faithful and total assimilation of the principles of old that were deemed to be eternally true and valid for the children of Abraham, Isaac, and Jacob."[16]

By contrast, the ninety-degree turn that took early Christian thinkers down a decidedly different path interpreted the words of the prophet as a call for the radical reconstruction of the entire system of Jeremiah's Judaism. The Christian "new covenant" was defined as universal in scope, reaching far beyond the world of Jeremiah, Jews, and Judaism. But this *re*construction required a radical *de*construction and Christianity did not shrink from the task, jettisoning major components of the "old" covenant to prepare the way for the "new." The apostle Paul became the chief architect of this deconstruction.[17]

The "New" vs. the "Old"

What began as a small fissure quickly widened into a chasm so vast that the two faith systems were quite unable to understand each other or work together productively. To be sure, both systems recognized the need for a new covenantal structure. But once Christianity redefined Judaism and "new covenant" to suit themselves, it was clear that no attempt would be made to understand what Jeremiah had meant. In other words, Christianity retained the *category* of "new covenant" but gave it a *definition* that was unrecognizable to Jews. The result was tragic. The rabbis believed the assertion of Deuteronomy 30:11–14, that each person has the power to choose life and good instead of death and evil. But Paul determined he absolutely could *not* make such a choice. Then, having denied the assertion of Deuteronomy, Paul leapt to the conclusion that only by the insertion of Jesus into the mix could reconciliation with God become possible.[18]

---

15. Isbell, "Essays," 21.

16. Isbell, "Essays," 21.

17. Isbell, "Saul the Sadducee?" "Paul and Judaism."

18. See his anguished inner struggle articulated in Romans chapter seven, especially verse 18b: "I *want* to do what is good, but I *cannot*."

One additional result of these two different interpretative pathways was (and is) a shared vocabulary with radically different definitions and perceptions of what a divine-human relationship entailed.

> Well before the dawn of Christianity, Judaism had already started the oral process that would ultimately yield its written "Mishnah."[19] The title of the work itself ("Repetition") implies that its function in Judaism was comparable to the role that would come to be played by the New Testament in Christianity. In both cases, that role was to reshape the ancient Scriptures for service to modernity, preserving basic values but presenting them in different cultural and temporal dress. "Judaism" thus became not the religion of the Hebrew Scriptures or the Christian Old Testament, but the system carved out by sages who lived after their biblical literature had been completed, and who had witnessed the destruction of virtually all aspects of their daily lives. With no king, no nation, and no Temple, much of the Hebrew Scriptures became indecipherable or inapplicable. The work of the Jewish sages (ca. 100 BCE-200 CE) was to mine the core values presented by the narratives of Scripture, strip them of time-bound and event-specific clothing, and re-issue them as timeless and abiding truths that served the needs of their modernity.[20]

To this day, the false premise of a shared Judeo-Christian tradition makes it difficult for Jews and Christians to understand each other's sacred texts. Neusner was correct. The two systems still share numerous categories, but the vastly differing definitions of those categories make each side sound foreign to the other.

A Path Forward

The essays that follow do not solve every troubling aspect of these differences, and they cannot answer every objection by one side about the definitions chosen by the other side to explain the contradictory perceptions of shared theological concepts. They are designed to serve as one way to address some of the more significant subjects that the thoughtful study of John raises in the minds of all who read his gospel seeking to learn about Christianity or simply to broaden their own understanding of one of the most influential

19. The Mishnah was not formally published until ca. 220 CE, but it includes rabbinical debates that began as much as one hundred years before the birth of Jesus.

20. Isbell, "Essays," 22.

Christian texts of all time. Because these essays are offered to persons who are troubled by what they read in John and who wonder why the gospel has chosen to depict "the Jews" and so much of their faith in such a negative fashion, it is my hope that the answers presented here will help readers to think clearly about their own religious faith and *praxis*. Each reader must ask how the NT writer framed his answers to the great issues of his/her own life. Then each one must determine whether and to what extent subsequent and modern scholars of John have been faithful to those answers.

At the end of that process, two additional questions must be asked: (1) How do the answers given by John impact the moral and social values reflected in a modern society that is so heavily dominated by Christian culture? (2) Do the answers of John reflect my own values and judgment?

Jewish readers must decide whether each essay isolates the gist of the problem being addressed and whether appropriate and adequate responses are being offered about the passages in John that are the most troubling. And they might even question whether John offers anything at all of value for a Jewish reader. Christian readers should ask whether their own response to John requires re-examination or whether they are satisfied with the way John describes Jews and others who do not share his view of Jesus. All readers must decide if each essay proceeds in a fair and unbiased way even when they do not agree with the analysis presented here.

Along the way, perhaps the two sides can come to understand each other a bit better. If there is indeed only one God, perhaps it is not surprising that he should have more than one "child." If then, neither Judaism nor Christianity is the only child of God, the words of Psalm 133:1 may acquire fresh relevancy: "Behold, how good and pleasant it is for brothers [and surely sisters too!] to dwell together in unity."

Ken yehi ratzon. "May it be God's will."

I. Opening Questions

As noted in the INTRODUCTION, there are specific questions that demand answers for modern readers of the Gospel of John. In this initial essay, the first four of these questions are: [A] When was the Gospel composed? [B] Who wrote the Gospel of John? [C] Was the author of John an apostle, perhaps even an eyewitness to the life and teachings of Jesus? [D] Why is his perspective so radically different from that of the three earlier ("Synoptic") gospels? As a corollary to the identity and perspective of John, Essay II will discuss an additional issue that has been raised by recent NT scholars: was John Jewish, a Samaritan, or a "Jewish-Christian"? How would more precise information about his identification have impacted the 2000-year history of Johannine interpretation?

When Was the Gospel of John Written?

It is widely held by NT scholars that the Gospel of John was written in the latter decade of the first or the first decade of the second century CE: scholarly opinions about a more specific date generally range from 90 to 110 CE.[1] Catholic Johannine scholar Raymond Brown includes a detailed survey of the latest dates for John to have been written, concluding that "the positive arguments seem to point to 100-110 as the latest plausible date for the writing of the Gospel, with strong probability favoring the earlier limit of 100."[2] Brown also posits the writing of an earlier "first [i.e., partial] edition" to be dated "somewhere between 70 and 85 (a dating which is very much a guess)."[3] This general timeframe falls well beyond the lifetime of Jesus and raises a serious difficulty facing interpreters of the Fourth Gospel—most of

---

1. For a concise overview of the authorship question, see Burkett, *Introduction*, 214–222. Earlier periods of scholarship included attempts to date John as late as 170 CE. But the evidence for such a late date fails to convince current Johannine scholars.

2. Brown, *Gospel According to John* (i–xiii), Lxxxiii.

3. Brown, *Gospel*, Lxxxvi.

the incidents reported as involving Jesus clearly occurred not between Jesus and those who opposed him during his lifetime, but rather between the generation of Jews and early Christians that lived almost seventy-five years after the death of Jesus. John's historical revisionism of these kinds of events receives further examination in later essays.

Who Wrote the Gospel of John?

Modern readers, Jew and Gentile alike, typically approach the Fourth Gospel with the assumption that it was authored by an original apostle. Although the Gospel of John was written anonymously and includes no decisive internal indication of its authorship, early Church tradition attributed it to John the son of Zebedee, a prominent member of the original band of twelve apostles. This John was also widely presumed to be the mysterious "beloved disciple" standing near the mother of Jesus at the time of the crucifixion (John 19:26).[4] Obviously, an eyewitness account about Jesus from an original apostle would have carried a lot of weight in early Christendom.

Some early challenges to this view of authorship came from a group of heterodox Christians in Asia Minor ca. 200 CE, who thought the Gospel of John could not have been authored by an apostle. Instead, they ascribed the gospel to Cerinthus, a "Jewish Gnostic and an opponent of John."[5] Because of their discomfort with the Johannine doctrine of the Logos as the word made "flesh," which offended their belief that anything material is evil, the group came to be known as the "Alogi," a play on the word "illogical" and the Johannine use of *Logos*.[6] Despite their opposition, the confidence of the Church in the biblical, if not strictly apostolic, authority of John remained unshaken in most parts of Christianity until modern times.

Conservative Christian scholars have consistently maintained that the early Church was correct to ascribe the gospel to the apostle John, and they have appealed often to the idea that it is mathematically feasible to assume that John the apostle could have lived and traveled with Jesus while still in his twenties and then remained alive into his nineties, i.e., long after the crucifixion. Further, as perhaps the last surviving apostle to have known Jesus personally, this John might well have had not only the physical stamina but also the motivation to have written and published a book that late in his life.[7]

4. Additional references to the beloved disciple occur in John 13:23; 20:2; 21:7, 20.

5. Frend, *The Rise of Christianity*, 143.

6. A convenient survey of the Alogi is available in Schaff, *Dictionary*, 34.

7. The bibliography on the subject is enormous, and impossible to survey in a

From the opposite end of the theological spectrum, a comparable suggestion of the apostolicity of John's author was made by Shelby Spong, the most liberal Episcopal bishop since James Pike.[8] The sub-title of his book is *Reading the Bible with Jewish Eyes*. But readers soon discover that Spong does not have Jewish eyes. His book on the subject falls into the category of special pleading for the sake of different-ness in and of itself. Accordingly, he offers little by way of scholarly advancement.

While such positions derived from Christian extremism may be discounted, there is an additional factor that may have influenced the early Church to single out John the son of Zebedee as the gospel author. The Gospel of Mark records an occasion when Jesus dubbed John and his older brother James the "sons of thunder" (Mark 3:17). Early Church scholars surely knew of this nickname, and they also would have known why such a sobriquet would have been accurate. For example, Mark again, the earliest of the four canonical gospels, describes an occasion when the apostle John accosted a man who was unknown to the other disciples, forbidding the stranger to cast out demons in the name of Jesus because, "he was not one of us" (Mark 9:38). And according to Luke, when James and John learned of a Samaritan village that refused to welcome Jesus because he was heading for Jerusalem,[9] the two brothers sought permission to call down fire from heaven to destroy its inhabitants (Luke 9:51–56). In ascribing the Gospel of John to such a person, perhaps the early Church might have presumed that lashing out repeatedly against "the Jews" represented a predictable reaction from the man who was known to have classified people in terms of "us" vs. "them," and once had been willing to destroy an entire Samaritan village over a perceived social slight. In other words, the Apostle John's reaction to "the Jews" who dared to disagree with him might have seemed plausible to the early Church based on his attitude to the would-be missionary for Jesus who was "not one of us" or the Samaritans in the village that failed to provide appropriate hospitality to Jesus. Regarding "others," John the Apostle proved to be completely intolerant.

Nonetheless, the early Church was determined to connect each of the four canonical gospels closely to an apostle-author. No other apostle could have been a more plausible choice as the author who had written the consistently negative attitude to "the Jews" in the Fourth Gospel. Thus,

---

reasonable space. Two extreme fundamentalist, and frankly non-scholarly, examples are by Lizorkin-Eyzenberg and Roberson. A moderate and well-informed defense of authorship by John the son of Zebedee was presented by Earle, Blaney, and Hanson, eds, *Exploring the New Testament*, 188–191.

8. Spong, *Liberating the Gospels*.

9. Samaritans and Judeans did not associate with each other. See John 4:9.

linking the Fourth Gospel with an original "son of thunder" would not have required a huge leap.[10]

Modern mainstream NT scholars almost unanimously reject this identification of the author of the Fourth Gospel as John the son of Zebedee who traveled with Jesus in the original group of his apostles. First, the Apostle John was not known to have lived in Ephesus (where the gospel probably was published). Second, one reading of Mark 10:39 can be taken to mean that John the Apostle might have been martyred some thirty years before the composition of John the Gospel. In 10:39, John and his brother James, having requested special seats flanking Jesus in the world to come, were treated to an enigmatic explanation from Jesus disallowing their request. A purely speculative inference by some early Christian scholars was that Jesus was implying that James and John would not live long enough for their request to be granted.[11] A third point of difficulty pertains to the degree to which the Fourth Gospel includes Christological theological development far beyond that attested in the three Synoptic versions.

For all these reasons, almost all mainstream NT scholars prefer to think of the Fourth Gospel as an anonymous work, while they continue to refer to its author simply as "John," and the book as the "The Gospel of John" as a matter of custom and convenience.

Is the Gospel of John an Eyewitness Account?

A major aspect of the early Church tradition that acclaimed John the son of Zebedee as the author of the Gospel of John was attraction to the idea of a gospel author who had been an "eyewitness" to the life and works of Jesus. This claim appears first in the pages of the gospel itself.[12] Although he doubts that "the beloved disciple" mentioned in these texts was the Apostle John, son of Zebedee, Professor Richard Bauckham has written a powerful defense of the idea that John is "the one [i.e., *only*] Gospel that was actually written by an eyewitness."[13] His method is spelled out in minute detail, and his erudition

10. Of course, these "sons of thunder" references are not intended to argue — nor should they be taken as any sort of definitive proof — that John the son of Zebedee authored the Gospel of John.

11. Burkett, Introduction, 215.

12. See the references in note 1 above.

13. Bauckham, *Jesus and the Eyewitnesses*, especially chapters 14 and 15. Bauckham believes that the beloved disciple was the author of the Gospel of John. He views this John as a historical person, but a "less prominent disciple, not one of the Twelve and not so widely known in the early Christian movement as the leading members of the Twelve were" (550).

is evident in the examination he offers of virtually all relevant information re. the issue. In fact, Bauckham may be correct that multiple eyewitnesses contributed important information to the author of John, whether John himself had been an eyewitness or not. But Bauckham's claim raises serious questions that demand answers, the first of which is simply stated: Would not an eyewitness, or multiple eyewitnesses for that matter, have overridden the historical revisionism that suffuses the entire Gospel? There is virtually unanimous agreement among NT scholars that multiple incidents cited by John as linked directly to the life and times of Jesus refer instead to events that occurred decades after his death and resurrection.[14] If the author of John was an eyewitness, and if he relied upon the eyewitness accounts of others who had been present with Jesus in the early first century CE, this blatant revision of time and sequence would be unforgiveable.

Four incidents demand attention: [1] Could there have been an eyewitness to the actual moment when John describes "the Jews" as having expelled a healed former blind man? The acid test of the expulsion theory based on John 9 is an incident in the Jerusalem *Temple*, not an unnamed synagogue somewhere.[15] In the foundation story, the healed man speaks clearly and forcefully about his new-found sight, holds a positive opinion of Jesus that he shares openly, and is himself a recognized member of the worshiping community. Yet after what John refers to as his ignominious expulsion, he utters no expression of sorrow about his treatment at the hands of people who had known him all his life. Would such a man not have become a permanent member of the new group that grew to become the Johannine Community? Yet not a word from the former blind man has been preserved.

As Essay V explains, the only evidence we have about the functioning of a Jewish curse against apostates (*birkat ha-mînîm*) makes no mention of a theological dispute akin to that endured by the blind man whom John insists was violently expelled merely for being grateful that Jesus had healed him. Everything known about the later synagogue ritual relates the *berakhah* in question to the position of service *leader* only; Jewish worshipers who held heretical positions were not allowed to dominate (lead) the service of worship. Any presumed eyewitness to the incident of miraculous healing recounted in John chapter nine would have included people who knew the former blind man personally.[16] In the interest of truth and authenticity, would not such witnesses stand and explain that whatever may have

14. Many of these events will be discussed in later essays.

15. "Expulsion" is discussed in detail in essays V and VI.

16. But note that no Temple service leader could have been a blind person (see Lev 21:18), a fact of which John probably was unaware.

happened to the blind man healed by Jesus in the Temple had nothing at all to do with the split between Jews and Christians that did not occur until at least seventy years after the death of Jesus? If everyone who had been present to witness the healing of the blind man by Jesus had then refused to speak the truth, the conclusion would be that John was not the only early Christian hater of Jews, that anti-Judaism was more widely spread through early Christianity than Bauckman *et al* are willing to concede. Someone ["John"], whoever it was, falsely linked a spectacular fictitious episode directly to the time of Jesus. And this Johannine account went to extremes to portray "the Jews" in the most negative fashion imaginable by describing them as opposing Jesus in person and persecuting a recipient of his healing. And no eyewitness rose to oppose his portrayal.[17]

[2] An eyewitness (or "earwitness") to the repeated refrain that "the Jews" sought repeatedly to murder Jesus would carry a lot of weight. But the text of John includes not a scintilla of such evidence.

[3] Any eyewitness to the life of Jesus who lived long enough to contribute to the Gospel of John also surely would have witnessed the gradual devolution of the Sadducees as the dominant power group in Judaism and the rise of the Pharisees replacing the Sadducees as the political and ritual leaders. What is more, to have been a disciple of Jesus and to have survived long enough to pen John, the author himself also would have experienced these other salient aspects of first century Palestinian Jewish history as an eyewitness. At the least, he would have witnessed the Roman siege of Jerusalem, the destruction of the Temple, and the promotion of the Pharisees over the Sadducees. These events brought the Pharisees into political favor with the Romans and religious leadership among Jews, both for the very first time forty years *after* the death of Jesus. Yet the Gospel operates under the mistaken assumption that in the time of Jesus, "the Pharisees" were the party in charge of all Jewish political and theological matters.

[4] What evidence could an eyewitness give about a cleansing of the Temple that evinces no basis in reality?[18] If Jesus had done to the Temple what John alleges, every Jew throughout Jerusalem and beyond would have been outraged, and such a callous and disrespectful act would surely have been included in the indictment of Jesus brought by the Jews to Pilate. This did not happen!

Clinging to the idea of any eyewitness testimony to the life of Jesus is one way to argue for at least a modicum of historical plausibility for

17. Similarly, as essay VIII makes clear, no early Church leader or scholar raised a single word of objection to the anti-Judaism of John when the Gospel was under consideration for canonicity 400 years later.

18. See the discussion of this incident in essay VIII.

"John." But the historical unreliability of the Gospel remains after every eyewitness claim has been considered.

John is not about history, but ideology leading to a theology fashioned almost three-quarters of a century after the death of Jesus. What appears in John is not a series of contextual markers for the life of Jesus, but a gauntlet thrown down about a Johannine (and now modern Christian) definition of the nature and significance of Jesus. To argue that the Gospel is based on trustworthy eyewitness accounts is to insult the honest reader and divert attention away from its essential Jesus-ology.[19]

The Unique Perspective of the Gospel of John

Even a cursory examination of the Gospel of John uncovers facts that are startling, the most obvious of which is the difference between John and the gospels of Mark, Matthew, and Luke. It is universally recognized that all three of these other canonical gospels share the same basic point of view, a "synoptic" perspective. And NT authority Bart Ehrman has noted correctly that, "despite the important and significant differences among the Synoptic Gospels, they are much more similar to one another than any one of them is to John."[20] Ehrman has also provided a succinct and clearly written summary of these differences, reminding readers that not only does "John" *include* numerous stories about Jesus that are absent from the Synoptic Gospels, but conversely, that "John" *omits* some of the most important episodes in the Synoptic Gospels, narratives without which the first three gospels would scarcely be recognizable. In addition, *the person of Jesus* is portrayed by "John" in a manner radically different from the Jesus of the Synoptics.[21]

It is difficult to understand fully why this is true. Partial differences may be explained as due to different authors, writing in different locations, armed with different levels of Greek literary skill, or seeking to influence specific kinds of people or audiences. And some of the differences may be due to the passage of time between the writing of the latest of the three

---

19. I mean no disrespect by avoiding the more common word, "Christology." "Christ" is not a name, but a title, an anointed one (a messiah, Hebrew משיח). The *name* of the person whom the NT wished to designate as "messiah" was Jesus. Accordingly, only if one assumes that Jesus was the messiah is it accurate to speak of Christology with respect to Jesus of Nazareth. I do not make that assumption.

20. Ehrman, *New Testament*, 137. Smith, *John Among the Gospels* and Kysar, *John, the Maverick Gospel*, have authored comprehensive treatments on the subject.

21. Ehrman, *New Testament*, 137–141. Raymond Brown has also addressed some of these differences in *Epistles*, 80–81. Burkett, *Introduction*, 216–19, has a more concise and well-written summary of the issues.

Synoptic Gospels (Luke) in ca. 80–85 CE, and the writing of John perhaps fifteen or twenty years later.[22]

During this time, in response to the shifting composition of its membership, the emerging Church continued to mature and change from a small Jewish base to a larger and more diverse membership in which Jews were quickly becoming an ever-smaller minority. Added to this changing demographic makeup was the fact that Jerusalem began to be rivaled and then surpassed as *the* center of Christian influence during the period. This occurred initially in Antioch, where the name "Christian" was first applied to the young group (Acts 11:26), and then to an even greater extent in Rome.

But these changes in time, demography, location, linguistic skill, and circumstance cannot account fully for the vast difference between the Gospel of John and the Synoptic Gospels, and there is a dominant and recurrent theme in this Fourth Gospel that must be added to all other partial explanations. From beginning to end, the writings of John are posted in the shadow of an ongoing struggle between synagogue and church, Jew and Christian. It may even be accurate to say that the author of John was more concerned with demonstrating that Christians and Jews had begun to be at war with each other early in the life of Jesus than it was with depicting the late first century community of his readers in a harmonious relationship with members of other Christian communities. In fact, in addition to its differences with the Synoptic Gospels, the people for whom the Gospel of John is widely believed to have been composed, the Johannine Community, appear to have been at odds with the community that followed the leadership of Peter,[23] as well as being "relatively isolated from other streams of Christian thought such as the Pauline."[24] Whether there was an actual "Johannine Community" or not, the message of the gospel does appear to have been written with a limited and very specific readership in mind.[25]

Raymond Brown was one scholar who had no doubts about a "Johannine Community," and he was convinced that they were quite an insular group. Based on this assumption, Brown issued a startling claim, arguing that the Gospel of John "articulates no demand to love all human beings or to

22. For the dates of all four canonical gospels later than those followed by most NT scholars, see Freed, *The New Testament*. Freed suggests a date for John between 90 and 120 CE. He also cites copious bibliography for various positions on the dating of the four.

23. Burkett, *Introduction*, 225–226.

24. Kysar, *John, the Maverick*, 173.

25. Adele Reinharz has questioned the existence of this "Community" in *The Gospel of John and Jewish-Christian Relations*, 14. The fact that there is no direct evidence about such a community is troubling. But it is useful to retain it as a working hypothesis.

love one's enemies—only true believers in Jesus are the children of God and, therefore, brothers."[26] If true, this concept offers at least a partial explanation of the animosity to "the Jews" in John's Gospel whose views of Jesus were unacceptable to John and thus to Brown. These Jews were caustically dubbed by Brown, "Jewish Christians of inadequate christology."[27]

That solemn debates about Jesus-ology may have existed in the early Church should not be doubted. But it would seem odd that the Gospel famous for its statement that God "so loved *the world* that he gave His one and only son . . . to save *the world* through him" (John 3:16-17) would have developed into a community that would love only its own insider members to the exclusion not only of theologically "inadequate" Jews, but also the rest of the entire world, Christian and non-Christian alike. Brown was aware of this objection from John chapter three, but remained unmoved by it, concluding by doubling down on his position: "it is not clear that the Johannine God loves the sons of darkness."[28] His stance thus began with the claim that Johannine Christians need love only each other and no one else before expanding to the view that John's *God* also rations his love to exclude those with inadequate theology.[29]

Readers of John must face honestly the kinds of questions that John and his followers raise. The initial question should be this: Did John believe that "outsiders" need not be loved or valued? If Brown was wrong, and John really does not teach that, readers may have no need to re-evaluate their own beliefs in the matter.

But if Brown was correct, two additional questions must be answered. Has this Johannine perception of "others," so universally observed in modern *secular* society, also infiltrated modern religious life? Is this perception of John the position that persons of faith should approve and accept in their own *religious* institutions?

---

26. *Epistles*, 85. Brown appends the defense of this position as his own on pp 269–273.

27. *Epistles*, 270.

28. *Epistles*, 272.

29. This contention of Brown is treated in greater detail in essay XI.

II. Modern Scholarship and The Gospel of John

FOR 2,000 YEARS, CHRISTIANITY has relied on the Gospel of John in search of answers to many of the great questions of Christian faith. As a corollary to the background and perspective of John, this essay addresses the discussions of recent John scholars that have probed more deeply into John from another angle: was John Jewish, a Samaritan, or a "Jewish-Christian"? And how would more precise information about his identification have impacted the 2,000-year history of Johannine interpretation? Above all, does any specific view of John's identity, Jewish or Christian, change what his gospel means to readers in the twenty-first century?

The Fourth Gospel has been one of the most studied books of the New Testament for two millennia, and the past one hundred years have witnessed an explosion of books and articles on John that is perhaps unmatched since the gospel first appeared. These works include scholarly treatises, serious exegetical textual analyses, theological and historical surveys, analyses of literary form, function, and context, and numerous essays on Jewish-Christian relationships from the time of John to the present day. Works written by Christian clergy interested in the homiletical (sermonic) value of John have also burgeoned. Sadly, books by poorly trained (or untrained) fundamentalist non-scholars who bring more heat than light to the subject also have rolled off the presses.

Writings of various depth and value have come from authors who represent divergent religious viewpoints, among them Catholic, Southern Baptist, mainline Protestant, fundamentalist Protestant, and Jewish. Some of these NT scholars seek anodyne positions, partially to avoid even the appearance of anti-Judaism in themselves, while others appear anxious to initiate controversy and attack the slightest perceived error. The one issue with which they all are concerned is the enduring value of the Gospel of John.

But with only a few notable exceptions, Johannine scholars have worked from a Christian perspective to define the issues that they deem significant for a Christian pathway of religious life. Chief among those issues is the definition of Jesus of Nazareth: Who was he? Was he the messiah? Was he divine? Was his life predicted in the Jewish Scriptures?

Jewish readers of John are thus expected to respond to questions of interest and concern to Christian readers. Consequently, the initial burden of the Jewish reader of John often must be to examine these Christian questions addressed in John and reframe them into a format that has relevance for Jewish life and faith. It should not be surprising that offering a *Jewish* response to issues framed in a *Christian* laboratory can be controversial. But the effort must be made, nonetheless.

Noted Jewish Johannine scholar, Professor Adele Reinhartz has offered a masterful work from the perspective of a Jewish reader of John. But as she herself notes, she is a highly skilled specialist in Johannine studies and not the ordinary Jewish reader. "Much as I might try, I do not come to this text as a first-time, 'naïve' reader, but as a longtime professional reader. My readings of the Fourth Gospel have been informed by my Jewishness but they have also been filtered through and refined in the field of Johannine studies."[1] In search of a different focus, the assumption in the essays being presented here is that the vast majority of Jewish readers of John are unlikely to possess the undoubted technical skill and extensive scholarly background that Reinhartz brings to her reading of John. An alternate question is thus required: Can the *average* Jewish reader, someone not involved in the ofttimes obtuse scholarly wrangling about what John meant by what he said, trust his or her ability to read John and understand his meaning?

Speaking once again as a Jewess, Reinhartz expresses this concern bluntly. "What, after all, beyond the gap in time and place, is to distinguish those Jews whom the Johannine Jesus reviles as unbelieving descendants of the devil, blind, sinful, and incapable of understanding their own scriptures, from ourselves and the Jews around us? Can we continue to read and appreciate a text that expresses its point of view through the denigration of the Other? These questions cut to the core of what it means to be a Jew reading this difficult text."[2]

Christian readers of John face a serious question as well: Are the issues chosen for debate among John scholars the most important issues about which honorable readers of all faiths need to know? In other words, while Jewish readers may need to reframe the issues that are debated in John about Judaism, Christian readers may feel the need to ask whether John's approach to anti-Jewish bias is acceptable to them. Both Jews and Christians may ask

1. Reinhartz, *Befriending the Beloved Disciple*, 15.

2. Reinhartz, *Befriending the Beloved Disciple*, 15.

whether John's teachings about other important issues are appropriate for them and their faith community.

The Jewishness of John and the Dead Sea Scrolls

The first issue confronting every reader of the Gospel of John is the definition of "the Jews" as it is used by the author. Early Christians who presumed that the gospel author had been a Jewish apostle of Jesus, also presumed that every word in John came from the mouth of God rather than from a human author. Over time, thoughtful Christian interpreters, who knew that a human author had been involved in the composition of John, typically presumed that the human author (even if he were not the apostle John) had been guided by God as he wrote. For centuries, that meant, among other things, that the Gospel of John was viewed as a fully authentic and historically accurate picture of Jews in the time of Jesus. As attention shifted to the influence of John on Christian thought, scholars came to realize that for the Gospel of John to have earned a hearing outside of the narrow confines of Palestinian Judaism, it must have been meaningful to a target audience far more diverse than Jews alone. Accordingly, beginning in the nineteenth century, modern scholars began to emphasize the Hellenistic character of John. This idea was buttressed by the fact that John was written in Greek and referred exclusively to the Greek translation of the Jewish Scriptures.

The discovery of the Dead Sea Scrolls in the mid-twentieth century prompted many NT interpreters to shift from this virtually universal scholarly view of the Hellenistic character of John to embrace the idea that "The discovery of the Dead Sea Scrolls has demonstrated the Jewish character of John."[3] This is at best an overstatement. The supposed parallels between the Dead Sea Scrolls (DSS) and John are limited in number, and many proposed parallels can be found not only in the Scrolls and in the gospel, but also in Hellenistic literature,[4] in a form of Zoroastrian dualism,[5] and in early Egyptian theological texts.[6] In multiple significant ways, the community that produced the DSS and the community for which the Gospel of John was

---

3. Burkett, *Introduction*, 215.

4. The classic work by C. K. Barrett, *The New Testament Background*, provides a dizzying array of background material from the world of Hellenism.

5. Isbell, "Zoroastrianism and Biblical Religion," *Jewish Bible Quarterly* 34/3 (2006) 143–154.

6. In this category are the Egyptian idea of an incarnate god, a novel creator force (as the *Logos* was the intermediate creating force in John chapter 1.), and a deity who is unique from all others, cited often as a fourteenth-century BCE proto-monotheistic impulse. A convenient and worthy survey is Redford, *Akhenaton, the Heretic King*.

composed were radically different. With remarkable brevity, noted Jewish NT scholar, Michael Cook has offered a succinct statement that illustrates the wide gap between the NT and the Dead Sea community that featured "belief in two messiahs, depreciation of women, ultra-strict legalism, and militaristic imagery."[7] The following may be added to Rabbi Cook's short list.

1. Linguistically, the DSS are written in classical Hebrew by a conservative Jewish sect, while John is in the *Koiné* Greek used by common people in regions that range far beyond the NT world of Jesus and the first disciples.

2. Except for Old Testament figures, there is no overlap between the cast of characters in the scrolls and the New Testament. For example, neither Jesus nor John the Baptist appears in the Dead Sea literature, although Jesus presumably visited John the Baptist, who lived in an area of the wilderness around the Jordan river that was not far from the Dead Sea Scroll caves (see Luke 1:80; 3:3).

3. The writers of the DSS appeared to have no interest in proselytizing among non-Jews and certainly no impulse to attract all the nations of the world to their membership, while the goal of early Christianity was to spread its message to the entire world.

4. Socially, via attention to strict regulations about "purity," members of the Dead Sea community kept themselves apart from more traditional Jews, while the Johannine community sought early on to loosen restrictions imposed by Jewish purity regulations. This Johannine separation from other Jews was caused by their distinct definition of Jesus as a divine-human messiah rather than a dispute about Jewish law and *praxis*.

5. While Dead Sea members emphasized and practiced different, often minor, tenets of Judaism, and while both they and the Johannine community offered criticism of specific aspects of normative Judaism, the Dead Sea community did not attack "the Jews" with explicit charges denying their relationship with Abraham or accusing them of being offspring of the devil.

6. The DSS authors did not claim that they had been cast out of Judaism violently by their fellow Jews, and

7. they did not claim that "the Jews" were seeking the death of a leader or a master teacher outside of their group like Jesus, who was teaching his disciples perfectly acceptable Jewish legal and theological concepts.

7. Cook, *Modern Jews Engage the New Testament*, 315, note 11.

8. The greatest difference between the two communities is that the Dead Sea community did not create a worshiping body of members who fashioned a specific human teacher into a superhero who was pre-existent, omniscient, incapable of error, and ultimately more authoritative than God Himself.[8]

Despite these differences, and despite repeated attacks on Jews, their worship, their history, and their relationship with God, the idea that the author of the Fourth Gospel was himself Jewish has recently returned to the fore among NT scholars, including those with impeccable credentials. One of the clearest expressions of this theory was sharply articulated by Professor Gail R. O'Day: "The Gospel of John was thus written by a Jewish Christian for and in a Jewish Christian community that was in conflict with the synagogue authorities of its day (represented in the Gospel as 'the Pharisees' or 'the Jews')."[9] Professor O'Day, the author of this "no room for debate" statement, was a highly skilled biblical scholar who knew a good bit about Judaism and who clearly was not herself anti-Jewish. But her decision to describe the author of John as a "Jewish-Christian" is problematic. Many modern Jewish authorities agree that a Jew who converts voluntarily to another religious faith can no longer be recognized as a Jew. Regardless of how the question may be viewed *halakhically* (legally), as a *practical* matter, by converting to a different faith system, not simply by having studied with a non-traditional teacher like Jesus, but by joining voluntarily with a group of people who separated themselves out of Judaism because of basic theological and social differences, a person could choose to opt out of Judaism.

In other words, by the process of becoming a Christian, a Jewish-born John would have ceased *practicing* and *thinking* as a Jew.

Surely the harshest criticism of any religious system comes from someone who has become disenchanted with the faith of his/her birth and left it voluntarily. For this reason, before John may be titled a "Jewish Christian," readers should consider whether a disgruntled former Jew is a competent source from which to learn about the faith he once prized but now has rejected and which he can no longer view objectively. He may have been capable of explaining to another person why he left Judaism, but it would have been virtually impossible for him to understand and articulate why other Jews stayed. If John had understood Judaism as his co-religionists did, he would not have left. Because his perception of Judaism would not have matched that of Jews who remained faithful to their understanding of Judaism, once John left, anything he says about Judaism is of little help in understanding

8. I.e., by defining both God (the "Father") and himself.

9. O'Day, *John*, 506.

Judaism. Said bluntly, if indeed he was an ex-Jew himself, John might be cited as an authority on ex-Jews, but not on Judaism. At best, he was only a former Jew who stood outside of Judaism (an "apostate") and had chosen to become a Christian.[10] To speak of John accurately is not to portray him as a "Jewish-anything," but as a former Jew.[11]

Still, on the question of a Jewish author of John, Professor O'Day's confidence was absolute. For her, John is a written record of "conflicts between two different groups of first-century Jews: the community of the Fourth Gospel (Christian Jews) and the synagogue authorities."[12] Concomitantly, "it is language spoken by one group of Jews to another, not by Gentile Christians about Jews."[13] In sharp contrast to O'Day's assertion, Professor Amy-Jill Levine correctly grasped the implications of blaming the Jews for the language of John: "The Jewish community preserved the prophetic literature, not the Gospel of John. To tell the [Christian] congregation [or the typical modern Jewish reader] that John is simply speaking the way Jews speak with each other, as Jeremiah or Ezekiel spoke to the children of Israel is, in effect, to state that 'the Jews' are to blame for John's rhetoric."[14] Such a presumption is simply wrong.

Still, O'Day was so fervent in her belief on the matter that she issued a stern warning: "To appropriate this language into the modern situation of Jewish-Christian relations without attending to the inseparability of this language from the social world of Johannine Christians is unethical at best, tragic at worst."[15] Her idea that John's Gospel reflects nothing more than an inner Jewish disagreement, or as Robert Kysar terms it, a "family feud!"[16] is a theory that requires examination, even at the risk of being labelled "unethical" or "tragic."

---

10. The term "Jewish Christian" is problematic in the same way that Paul's "spiritual body" (*sōma pneumatikon*) is. Both are essentially meaningless. One may be either a Christian or a Jew, but not both simultaneously.

11. A divorcee is no longer a husband or a wife, but an "ex." Similarly, even if the author of John was or ever had been Jewish, when he left Judaism, he was no longer a "Jewish" anything.

12. O'Day, *John*, 507. Were this accurate, O'Day would be omitting 95 percent of the Jews then alive in her analysis. This overly simplistic explanation of "the Jews" is examined further below.

13. O'Day, *John*, 507.

14. Reinhartz, ed., *The Gospel of John and Jewish-Christian Relations*, 95-96.

15. O'Day, *John*, 507.

16. Kysar, *Voyages with John*. See especially his chapter, "The Expulsion from the Synagogue: The Tale of a Theory," 237–245. Elsewhere in this volume, Kysar presents a useful review of twentieth century scholarship on John.

Just a Family Feud?

At best, the Johannine side of the squabble must have been written by a dyspeptic ex-Jew, an apostate. As noted in Essay I, one does not acquire the sobriquet "son of thunder" for no reason.[17] So, it is important to remember that the Gospel of John was written for the Johannine Community which, by the time of John's writing, was deeply committed to its own brand of *Christian* theology. They were not a Jewish community trying to understand Judaism, they were a Christian community attempting to define their own faith in *opposition* to Judaism. To that end, the focus of the entire book of John was to define Jesus-ology as Christology.

It is also important to note that upon reading John, his very first interpreters, early Christians, all of whom had committed themselves to Jesus as the messiah, immediately felt at liberty to direct his gospel language openly against *all* Jews.[18] O'Day's commitment to John appeared to dictate that she somehow must link the origin of the anti-Jewish orientation of the Fourth Gospel to some indisputable outside influence rather than simply to the author himself. Her theory has the look of an attempt to shield John from responsibility for the interpretations offered by succeeding generations of post-Johannine Christian interpreters. But John wrote words that are largely unsupported by honest appraisal of first century Judaism. His interpreters merely read his words, took them to heart, and applied them broadly to all Jews in every generation.

There is more. If the objective is to interpret John directly, rather than backwards through the two millennia of exegetical patina contributed by his subsequent interpreters, the simplicity of John's language argues against the idea that the author was a Jew writing for Jews. How is it accurate to assume that in a supposed *Jewish* debate, one side of the debate was inextricably linked with what O'Day identified as the "social world of Johannine Christians?" A person who has abandoned Jewish religious faith and exited the social world of Judaism to enter the social world of Christianity is in fact an outsider who no longer thinks or writes as a Jew. Consequently, a dispute between the "social world of Johannine Christians" and the social world of Judaism is not an "inner-family squabble."

While O'Day was careful to say that John's attacks were not from *Gentile* Christians, it is fair to ask how it dilutes John's virulence to assume that it is acceptable for an author to attack "the Jews" because he himself had

17. Although the Apostle John, an original "son of thunder," is not considered to be the author of the Fourth Gospel, whoever did write it surely qualified as a member of the "sons of thunder" club.

18. See Appendix D.

once been Jewish before deciding to become a *Christian*. In fact, by the time of John's writing, the "social world of Johannine Christians" included only a small minority of former Jews. At best, then, John and a minority portion of his original audience in the late first or early second century, along with his early interpreters, represented a coterie of apostates, ex-Jews, and a few committed Christians anxious to attack openly all Jews who dared to disagree with them. Their side of the argument being presented against "the Jews" in John was framed from "the social world of Johannine Christians." The side of their opponents was framed from the world of Judaism. This was not an argument between two groups of Jews.

No! By the time of the argument presented by John, this was anything but a simple Jew vs. Jew affair. Anyone born Jewish who remained in the Johannine community at the time of John had long since ceased believing and living as a Jew. And most of the members of the Christian community that now became involved in John's negative portrayal of and opposition to "the Jews" had never been Jews to begin with. In short, even if he had been born Jewish, by the time of the battle between Jews and Christians with which he was concerned, the author of the Gospel of John entered the fray as a Christian theologian. Here the succinct notation of William Nicholls is helpful: "It is not legitimate to study Judaism from the standpoint of Christian theology."[19]

Even an ex-Jew with a modest grasp of Judaism would have known that the Pharisees were still only a minority group during the lifetime of Jesus. By the time that John was writing near the end of the first century CE, the Pharisees had grown from a small movement into an organized party and had consolidated their influence over Jewish law and worship. But when Jesus was alive, "the Pharisees" were not "the Jews," and they were not the "leaders" of Judaism as John portrays them. By the dawn of the second century, with the demise of the Sadducees and the fading fortunes of all other Jewish sects, the Pharisees had become virtually the only Jews remaining. Therefore, by lumping together the Pharisees and the Jews, and then by portraying the Pharisees as committed enemies of Jesus, John indicted *all* Jews.

According to John, Jesus tried to cinch a point in an argument against "the Jews" by claiming that he had existed since before the time of Abraham (John 8:58). This would make Jesus about 1800 years old, and would explain why, unlike Matthew and Luke, John did not offer a birth narrative for Jesus. But it is impossible to imagine that a Jewish author would have perceived a messiah in such a manner.

---

19. Nicholls, *Christian Antisemitism*, xxv.

John's Jesus also speaks to "the Jews" by referring to "your law," a disdainful and dismissive way of expressing the idea that "your" law does not belong to "me" and should have no bearing on "my" theology.[20] Surely, in an argument about "law," both sides in an internal *Jewish* debate would assume ownership of the law in question, and both sides would come to the battle determined to assert their own interpretation of that law. When John has Jesus disassociate himself from Jewish law, the effect is to portray Jesus as a Christian opponent of the Jews rather than as a Jewish teacher with whom other Jews might have meaningful dialogue.[21]

This "us" vs. "them" attitude is evident throughout John. It is difficult to imagine how the negative "them" language directed repeatedly against "the Jews" represents nothing more than a family spat. But Jews as "them," not "us" underscores the fact that John never openly identified either Jesus or himself as a Jew. If a Jewish Jesus had been challenging only Jewish *leaders*, surely he would have said, "*our* leaders" at least once. He did not. In the apt words of William Nicholls once again, the author of John, "feels no identification with the Jewish people and views them from a distance from which their internal distinctions and differences are no longer significant. He sees them in a uniformly hostile light."[22]

In contrast, Paul, the apostle to the Gentiles, offered radically different interpretations of biblical texts and quarreled often with other Jews.[23] Paul's disagreements with other Jews *were* family squabbles. John's were not. His criticism of "the Jews" indicates an author who was immediately at ease with the process of speaking ill of all Jews as Other.

It is not difficult to imagine an *ex post facto* argument that would run exactly as John put it. First, John highlighted the situation of early Christian and Jewish animosity that was current at the time of his writing. Second, he retrojected the origin of that animosity all the way back to the time of Jesus. Third, out came his *tour de force*: pinning the origin of every complaint of his late first century Christian community back onto "the Jews" of sixty to eighty years earlier using retrojection and revisionism. A fair reading of John thus reveals an author who was desperate to opine about a current reality as if it were decades old. And in this scenario, no Jew could be acceptable

20. This passage should be compared with John 7:51, where Nicodemus, in a dispute about Jesus with other members of the Sanhedrin, called for his fellow judges on the court to consider "*our* law" in their deliberations.

21. Even conservative Catholic scholar Raymond Brown was forced to admit that such a reference demonstrated a strangeness that non-Jewish readers would be likely to miss. See Brown, *Community*, 40.

22. Nicholls, *Christian Antisemitism*, 167.

23. Isbell, "Saul the Sadducee? A Rabbinical Thought Experiment," 85–119.

to the Johannine Community.[24] In other words, for John, there was no such thing as a "Jewish Christian." His world was Gentile, his community were Gentile, and those who did not fit in that world were "the Jews." Accepting the revision of history that John used to create his portrayal of "the Jews" requires a willing suspension of disbelief.

The ideology presented in John is clearly Christo-centric rather than Theo-centric as would be expected in a debate involving Jews on both sides.[25] In addition, the points John chose for debate far too often fit a Roman or Hellenistic (or even Zoroastrian) context to sustain the idea that John was doing nothing more than writing the saga of some Jews involved in a petty squabble.

The church fathers, who were decidedly not Jewish, had no difficulty in using John to denigrate Judaism. Their denigration did not require the Gentile rephrasing of what they read in a New Testament gospel written by a supposedly Jewish author. All they needed to do was to take seriously the clear meaning of what they were reading. Both the language and the historical revisionism of John provided the perfect foundation for the case these fathers prosecuted against the Jews of the second century and beyond. This was true among the initial interpreters of John, and it has remained true for two millennia.

Over one hundred years ago, the great Jewish scholar Kaufmann Kohler surveyed the voluminous Christian literature based upon the teachings of the New Testament and denominated John not merely an anti-Jewish author, but "the father of anti-Semitism."[26] Almost seventy-five years ago, Rabbi Samuel Sandmel phrased it this way: "In its utility for later Jew-haters, the Fourth Gospel is pre-eminent among the New Testament writings."[27] Fifty years after World War II, William Nicholls, a former Anglican priest, held Christian teaching as exemplified in John at least partially responsible for anti-Semitism as well as Hitler's "final solution."[28]

These multiple objections leave only one plausible conclusion. Only if John were looking at Judaism from the outside, and if he were writing for a

---

24. Essay III addresses this issue in greater detail.

25. Thompson, *The God of the Gospel of John*, has argued that John is Theocentric rather than Christocentric. Her argument is not convincing. Whenever John speaks of God, it is always God in terms of Jesus, and Jesus takes and retains center stage throughout the gospel. John's burden is always about the connection of Jesus to God; he speaks repeatedly about how God must be redefined with reference to Jesus. In other words, it is Jesus who is being defined, not God.

26. "John, Gospel of," *Jewish Encyclopedia* 9: 251.

27. Sandmel, *Jewish Understanding of the New Testament*, 269.

28. Nicholls, *Christian Antisemitism*, xxvii and *passim* throughout the book.

majority *Christian* readership, would his style and his extremely poor grasp of Jewish culture and belief go unchallenged.

Professor O'Day was certainly correct to focus on social and historical context. But no amount of "theological and historical imagination when reading John"[29] can alter the fact that John does not employ the insider language that a Jew, even an ex-Jew, would use to zero in on the true nature of the differences between Christianity and Judaism during an all-Jewish debate. There can be no denial that the language of John, taken at face value and read as one would read any other document, bristles with anti-Jewish rhetoric; no denial of the historical reality that what began as John's anti-Jewish language morphed easily and rapidly into full-blown anti-Semitism that has endured over the 2,000-year odyssey of Johannine interpretation; no way to avoid the fact that the Johannine perspective of "the Jews" was (and still is) preached in the church; no honest denial that these negative messages based on John immediately received (and continue to receive) full-throated approval when they are preached to Christian congregations around the world.[30]

At its core, then, the problem with the O'Day theory is the implication that since the trouble was started by a Jewish author, that makes it all OK. Sure, Christian interpreters have interpreted John to the world as a hateful and disdainful speaker about everything Jewish. But that's OK too because they were only agreeing with John, himself a Jew. Here it must be asked: How does the theory of Professor O'Day (and almost all other mainstream NT scholars who follow her lead) advance the prospect of Jewish-Christian dialogue that offers respect for and from both sides? How does such an idea erase a single hateful word from the Gospel of John? How does it explain why John has become the most beloved book in all of Christendom?

Final Thoughts on the Jewishness of John

The false presumption that John himself was a Jew is not an improvement on a battle that has raged for two thousand years. If that battle is to end, it is essential that the search for a winner must end for the simple reason that if a winner is demanded, so too must be a loser. The anti-Jewish vitriol of the Fourth Gospel cannot be denied, and the appropriate solution cannot be simply to explain it all away with the idea that "the Christians did not start it." The essays presented in this volume are an attempt to take a necessary first

---

29. See her plea for scholarly "historical-critical presuppositions" in *John*, 507.
30. On this issue, see further Essay VIII.

step towards a more balanced solution. And that first step can be nothing less than honest acceptance of the fact that the language of John is toxic.

It appears to me as a practicing Jew that the author of the Fourth Gospel was not and never had been a practicing or knowledgeable Jew. But his initial religious affiliation is of little consequence in the larger context of his book. Even if it be conceded that John was once a Jew, there can be little doubt that his anti-Jewish opinions immediately met with over-whelming acceptance among his *Christian* audience as the second century dawned. There is also no doubt that this acceptance has continued apace for two millennia. And there is absolutely no doubt that the words of John are as distasteful and as hurtful to Jews living in the twenty-first century as they were 2000 years ago.[31] Grotesque historical revisionism has never been an acceptable scholarly method. Incendiary language is not a valid literary genre for a sacred text. The raw negativity that marks John's Gospel should never have been the order of any era, and it does not belong in the sacred literature of any religion.[32]

Here John stands. He said what he said. The only choice left to his modern readers is whether to join in his parade of vituperation or to dis-avow it categorically.

"The Jews" in John and the Theories of Two Modern Scholars

As the previous paragraphs illustrate, the scholarly world has long wres-tled with the Johannine portrayal of "the Jews," and over the past one hun-dred years or so, numerous interpretations of the term have been offered to soften the impact of the sledgehammer blows of anti-Jewish rhetoric trumpeted by John.

NT scholar J. Louis Martyn, former Professor Emeritus of the esteemed Union Theological Seminary in New York, offered to the scholarly world a theory that proposed to solve the problem of John's historical revisionism. Contrary to the common fundamentalist practice of reading John as liter-ally true and historically accurate in every detail, Martyn acknowledged that many passages in John cannot be accepted as accurately portraying events in the life of Jesus. Instead, they reflect the late first century era in which the gospel was written. So, beginning with the conviction "that the Gospel was written for an existing community,"[33] Martyn did not ignore the historical

31. Freedmann, *Antisemitism in the New Testament*.

32. This idea will be explored in more detail in essay VIII.

33. Reinhartz, *Cast Out*, 115.

gap between John's Jesus and John's Gospel. But since many of the narratives in John are set in an early first century context, seventy or seventy-five years before the "existing community" for whom John was writing, this interval in time must be acknowledged and bridged. Martyn was convinced that reading John as a "two-level drama"[34] bridges that gap.

Martyn's theory requires modern readers of John to ascertain on which level each passage should be understood. Level "A" is a "surface" level story that is set in the time of Jesus although it did not occur until much later, while Level "B" passages "reflect actual experiences of the Johannine community."[35] Of course, the proposed theory cannot alter the fact that the early church, operating without benefit of Martyn's tiered literary structure, had begun immediately to take John quite seriously at face value.

The Gospel of John claims eyewitness testimony as the basis for its description of Jesus and his opponents living in the first one-third of the first century (19:35; 21:24).[36] But when NT scholars acknowledge that the *Sitz im Leben* ("life situation") of the era in which the Gospel was *written*, in the final decade of the first century, was far removed from the lifetime of Jesus, John research demands a wide array of interpretative shifts. In the wake of Martyn's two-level theory, the way current scholars have interpreted the Johannine depiction of "the Jews" has been to trace the development of a "Johannine community" from the time of Jesus to the end of the first century. But neither Martyn nor any other scholar can erase the fact that John repeatedly linked late first-century events directly to Jesus.

Martyn's colleague at Union, Professor Raymond Brown, a brilliant scholar who was unabashedly and ideologically Catholic,[37] was also clearly aware that all four NT gospels, especially including John, "tell us primarily about the church situation in which they were written, and only secondarily about the situation of Jesus which *prima facie* they describe."[38] Thus, the Gospel of John may provide first-hand or eye witness insight into the final decade of the first century CE, but only secondhand information about the life and career of Jesus. The trick is to know what is primary

34. Martyn, *History and Theology*, 2003.

35. Martyn, *History and Theology*, 46.

36. See the discussion in Essay I.

37. To underscore the importance Catholic ideology played in Brown's work, it is helpful to recall the description of Brown and two of his NT colleagues offered by Bishop Spong: "Each of these men is a brilliant researcher, but none of them will draw the conclusions to which their research clearly leads them if it violates the official teachings of the church they serve." Spong sees this as "their lack of intellectual courage." See *Liberating the Gospels*, 15.

38. Brown, *Community*, 17.

(90–110 CE) and what is secondary (30–33 CE). "We have no evidence to support J. L. Martyn's theory of a two-stage narrative."[39] But Martyn and Brown remained convinced that they could determine the proper tier for each episode in John.

Brown went further. Taking the hypothesis of Martyn as his starting point, he became determined to define a "high" Christology that could be shown to have emanated from John, and which he noted was, "very familiar to traditional Christians because it became the dominant Christology of the church."[40] According to Brown, "the Jews" in John's drama opposed not only Jesus, but also the Christology later to be adopted by the church. But since John insists that Jewish opposition began during the lifetime of Jesus, all the modern scholar need do is switch tiers and the text becomes intelligible. Unfortunately for Brown's theory, there was no "church" either in the lifetime of Jesus or at the time of John's writing.

But Jewish opposition continued to grow until it became a major problem for Christians living decades later than Jesus. Since virtually none of the Jews alive in the time of Jesus still would have been alive when the Gospel of John was written, Brown decided that the Jews in the Gospel of John describes not a single group, but multiple classes of people who are "enemies" of Jesus at various times and who exhibit different levels of opposition.[41]

For Brown, again building upon the tiers of Martyn, the historical context for the composition of the Gospel of John had to be the church situation that was experienced by a distinct group of Christians, the *Johannine* community.[42] While this community may have begun during the lifetime and ministry of Jesus, the Gospel that features its hero, (John, the disciple whom Jesus loved) was not composed until some seventy to seventy-five years after Jesus' death. During that interval, the community grew and expanded; during that time also, the opposition to the Johannine followers of Jesus came from sources that were in constant flux.

But the author of the Fourth Gospel had no hesitation in ascribing directly to Jesus an opinion about a situation that occurred long after his death. This testifies to the fact that he and the members of his community were confident that they alone understood the mind of Jesus.

39. Levine, "Christian Privilege," 93.

40. Brown, *Community*, 45.

41. In *Community*, 25–58, Brown's position is spelled out in much greater detail than the brief summary presented here.

42. Reinhartz, *Cast Out*, 122, has raised a serious challenge to this idea, noting the lack of conclusive evidence of such a separate community.

"The Jews"

Although the phrase "the Jews" appears to be essentially synonymous with "the enemies" in the Gospel of John, Brown argued that just as the shifting context of John demanded two different literary tiers, "the Jews" could signify more than a single group or sub-group of individuals. This multi-level, variegated meaning of the Jews also came to mean that the same term ("the Jews") could describe accurately either one among multiple groups of Jews or a concatenation of ideas from the same group as time elapsed. The specific group to which the term refers in John must be teased out with reference to the circumstances in which the Johannine community found itself in the context of a particular late first century narrative rather than to the circumstances of the relationship between "the Jews" and Jesus during his lifetime.

In this manner, John and his community could justify a late first century idea as having originated with Jesus decades earlier and then entrusted to them via the Paraclete.[43] The plausible explanation of Burkett is that belief in the Paraclete ("Advocate" or "Holy Spirit") sent to earth to comfort believers in the absence of the now ascended Jesus left the Johannine community with, "no need to limit their ideas about Jesus to what the earthly Jesus might have said. They could justify a new portrait of Jesus by regarding it as a new revelation from the Paraclete"[44]

The way in which Brown layered the meaning of "the Jews" is intriguing. Initially, during the lifetime of Jesus, some Jews accepted the basic claims of Jesus to messiahship, what Brown refers to as a "Low Christology."[45] For them, Jesus could be son of God, a miracle worker, and perhaps even a Davidic messiah. Some members of this group were the former disciples of John the Baptist who left their teacher to follow Jesus because they viewed him as the Messiah rather than John.[46]

---

43. See John 14:15–21; and note in verse 26 the assertion that after the departure of Jesus from the earth, this third member of the Trinity, "the Advocate, the Holy Spirit, will teach you all things."

44. Burkett, *Introduction*, 227. On the existence and characteristics of a Johannine Community, see Culpepper, *The Johannine School*.

45. Much of this and the following paragraphs are summarized from Brown, *Community*, 25–58.

46. Brown adopts the stance of the church that Jesus was the Son (a second member of the Trinity) of God and that he was also the divine Messiah. Greek manuscripts of NT books like John do not distinguish capital letters from lower case ones as is done in English. The church custom of capitalizing both words is ecclesiastical rather than biblical, and Brown simply starts with the church stance and reads it back into John.

Next, a second group of Jews joined themselves to the nascent community, carrying with them a belief about Jesus that was more developed and nuanced than that of the first group. Although Acts 8:5 notes that the first time the Christian message had been brought to Samaria was after the death of Jesus, Brown posits quite a different story about the evangelization of the Samaritans. He suggests (theoretically?) that this second group of Jews in the lifetime of Jesus (who presumably would later become part of the "Johannine community") had earlier participated in the evangelization of some Samaritans, whom they brought into the proto-Johannine community as well. A story in John chapter 4 describes a brief encounter between Jesus and an adulterous Samaritan woman who reported to the citizens of her town that Jesus had revealed to her that he was the messiah. Her report caused many Samaritans to become believers (John 4:39), after which other villagers heard Jesus teaching in person, and "many more became believers" (John 4:41). Burkett notes that "such a story would have been most meaningful to a community engaged in such a mission,"[47] and thus it was an evangelism story chronicling a situation much later than the lifetime of Jesus. Nonetheless, John depicts Jesus as the starring actor in the narrative to beef up its *gravitas*.

Brown continued to argue that at roughly this same time, perhaps ten to fifteen years after the death of Jesus, this second set of Jews and their Samaritan converts began to be convinced of the pre-existence and ultimately the divinity of Jesus, establishing a trend that led to a "High Christology." Here are to be located the first steps in the direction of the Christology that was later codified into official church doctrine. Brown characterized these Jews as understanding Jesus "against a Mosaic rather than a Davidic background."[48] Not surprisingly, Brown was unable to clarify exactly how pre-existence and divinity could be identified as "Mosaic" (Judaism rooted in the traditional teachings of Moses) or Davidic (the beloved but clearly flawed great former king of Israel). And he remained unconcerned that nowhere in the "Jewish Scriptures" does either of these characteristics of a messiah find expression.

Brown also declined to address the way in which "High Christology" Jews could have been working from a "Mosaic background," while at the same time they evinced no respect for Mosaic (traditional) Judaism. To the contrary, he argued that these "High Christology" Jewish believers had little respect for the Jerusalem Temple and the rituals of traditional Judaism, believing that Jesus Christ/God had made them irrelevant. For

---

47. Burkett, *Introduction*, 224.
48. Brown, *Community*, 166.

Brown, these were the Johannine Christians whom traditional practicing Jews forced out of the synagogues by cursing and embarrassing them with a caustic prayer known as the *birkat ha-mînîm*. But as will be explained in essay V, the prayer to which Brown was alluding was not introduced earlier than the final quarter of the first century, and it was not directed against Christianity until well into the second century.[49] Still, Brown argued, it was these "High Christology" Jews who, expelled from the synagogues, "saw 'the Jews' as children of the devil."[50] But Brown does not acknowledge that "High Christology" Jews who were angry at being expelled from the synagogues were not the ones who accused "the Jews" of being children of the devil. This accusation was something that John attributes directly to Jesus in 8:44: "You belong to your father the devil."

At best, this curious literary peregrination of Brown fails to account for a major weakness of the Gospel of John. Despite the special pleading of Brown, to make his reconstruction work, "John" had been forced to tie directly into the lifetime of Jesus a situation and an incident that occurred only long after Jesus had died and returned to the heavens. Brown did not address the question of how such a historical revisionism could have been regarded as an advantage to late first-century Christians. But apparently, asserting that sometimes "the Jews" did not truly mean "the Jews" made everything better for Brown. It is in such instances that Brown's theory joins Martyn's two-tiered narrative as a classic example of a final refuge for the truly desperate: sometimes John does not mean what it says. This adage marks much subsequent Christian interpretation of John.

By the final decade of the first century CE, when the Gospel of John was set into writing, the supposed Johannine community had been developing for more than seventy years from a simple to a more complex theological society. According to Brown, at different times along the way, "the Jews" in the Gospel of John might refer to Jewish Christians whose Christology was not exalted enough to satisfy the group leadership and their hero, "the disciple whom Jesus loved." To make this detail of his theory work, Brown had to interpolate a word that is not in the NT text itself. Note for example this mischaracterization: "In John 8:31–34 Jesus addresses Jews who had (inadequately) believed in him . . . "[51] But John 8:31 refers simply to "the Jews who had believed in him." The word "inadequately" is not found in any Greek manuscript of John; it was nothing less than Brown's personal interpolation necessary to sustain his theory.

49. Essay V discusses the *birkat ha-mînîm* in detail.

50. Brown, *Community*, 166.

51. Brown, *Epistles of John*, 82.

In fact, the word "[in]adequate" was an obsession with Brown.[52] And since he believed that the trouble between Jews and Christians was nothing more than "a battle over christology,"[53] it should not be surprising that Brown felt it necessary to argue that the Greek word (*messias*, "messiah") was also multi-tiered. In each case, the clue to the appropriate tier was Brown's personal view of "adequacy." In John 1:41, Andrew used the term messiah referring to Jesus, but Brown argued that "it was not an adequate grasp of his identity. Nor is it adequate on the lips of Martha in John 11:27."[54] But since the Gospel of John was written "so you may believe that Jesus is the Messiah" (John 20:31), "the term *can be* an adequate description of Jesus."[55] Not always, but sometimes it *can be*. The trick, of course, is to determine when messiah means messiah and when it does not.

Thus, "the Jews" in John might sometimes refer to the Samaritans who were not real Jews anyway,[56] the Mosaic anti-Temple "High Christology" believers in Jesus, or the actual bad guys (Jewish leaders) who did not believe in Jesus at all and were determined to murder him. The trick, once again, is to determine to which group "the Jews" is alluding in each narrative.

In the wake of the controversy about Temple worship and high versus low Christology, Brown appeared to argue that Jews *in the time of Jesus* introduced the previously noted harsh prayer designed specifically to force Jewish Christians out of the synagogues. It cannot be repeated often enough that the Gospel of John has little, if any, credibility as "history" for honest readers. The facts that Brown was certain that Jews had begun violent expulsions of Christians from synagogues in the time of Jesus, that they had already begun to murder Christians by the time the Fourth Gospel was composed, and that a sinister plot to murder Jesus was hatched early in his public career are simply not believable.[57]

Final Thoughts on Modern Scholars and "the Jews"

To the persons who read it beginning as early as the dawn of the second century, the Gospel of John was the word of God. Of course, this was also an era when non-Jewish Christians had become a sizeable majority in the Johannine

52. Brown, Community, 73–81 contains Brown's extended argument describing "The Jewish Christian Churches of Inadequate Faith."

53. Brown, *Community*, 43.

54. Brown, *Community*, 44.

55. Brown, *Community*, 44.

56. Note John 4:9: "Jews do not associate with Samaritans."

57. Essay III discusses the "plot to kill Jesus" which Brown took as factual.

community. For Brown's theories to hold water, it is necessary to believe that everyone on all sides of these late first-century theological disputes lacked the sophistication of modern analysts to realize that many times "the Jews" did not mean "the Jews," "messiah" was not always "messiah," belief in Jesus was sometimes "inadequate," and "John" really was not anti-Jewish even though he used the most anti-Jewish rhetoric in the New Testament.[58]

Two things are clear. First, Martyn, Brown, and their followers among current Christian scholars of John have signaled their unwillingness to deal with the commonsense interpretation of John's own words. Second, the theories proposed about the best way to avoid admitting that John was virulently anti-Jewish often produce more confusion than clarification.

---

58. Brown's reconstructions are fascinating, but his involvement in the question of "John" and the history of anti-Semitism, surveyed in Essay VI, has faced numerous scholarly challenges.

III. "The Jews" as the Enemy in the Gospel of John

Preliminary Remarks

ALTHOUGH THERE IS NO indication that the author of John had read or knew about them when he began to compose his gospel, Mark, Matthew, and Luke already had pointedly fingered the Jews as guilty of opposing and even killing Jesus by convincing Rome to do the deed for them. As noted in Essay II, a widely held perception among NT scholars has been that these Jewish enemies were always Jewish *authorities,* never the common people. Average Jews are believed to have opposed Jesus only when they were incited to do so by their leaders. This is an admirable position taken by those who perhaps wish to distance themselves from the centuries of post New Testament violence and persecution inflicted on ordinary Jews.[1]

In pursuit of their efforts to soften the anti-Judaism of John, NT scholars have seized John's numerous references to "the Jews" (Greek *hoi Ioudaioi*) as an opportunity to translate a simple description by the gospel author in multiple ways.

Yet the decision to render *hoi Ioudaioi* as anything other than "the Jews" is not translation. It is ideology expressing a position that does not arise from the testimony of the gospels themselves. The goal of NT translation must be to express in a second language what the original Greek text *says.* It is not designed to offer what a translator thinks it *should mean* to support a pet theory.

What is more, the determination to translate Greek *hoi Ioudaioi* in multiple ways other than "the Jews" sells the Fourth Gospel author short. When John wished to describe Jewish authorities specifically, he knew that the Greek word *archontes* ("leaders" or "first ones") was readily at hand

---

1. See for example the passionate expression of uneasiness with the anti-Judaism of "John" by Kysar, *John, the Maverick*, especially, "The Jews' in the Fourth Gospel," 80–84.

(John 7:26). This indicates clearly that when John chose *hoi Ioudaioi* in other stories, he did so purposely. And in such cases, it is difficult to deny that "the Jews" is meant to describe Jews in general, *all* Jews. Of course, as Professor Amy-Jill Levine has remarked a bit mischievously, "these authorities are still Jews."[2] In addition, as Levine also has noted, "had the Jewish population wanted to combat their leaders, they had the power to do so."[3] In this light, it is hardly a complimentary portrayal of "the Jews" to conclude that gospel writers indicted only a few Jewish authority figures as the bad guys while erroneously depicting all ordinary Jews as little more than mindless dupes of their leaders.

Jewish Enemies in the Synoptic Gospels

All four gospel accounts deem it self-evident that the absolute worst Jewish opponent of Jesus was not an authority figure of any kind, but the man who betrayed him for money, Judas Iscariot. John (6:64) is confident that Jesus knew Judas was a betrayer from the first, but the other three gospel accounts offer no reason to doubt either that Jesus' initial appraisal of Judas was positive or that Judas held a similarly positive evaluation of Jesus and his mission. Although all the gospel lists of the original twelve typically place Judas last, the fact that he was the group treasurer indicates that until his betrayal became known, no one of his fellow apostles had cause to distrust him. As a result, the three gospel writers who preceded John viewed the betrayal by Judas as a major shift in attitude whose cause could not be ascertained or understood.

But there is no reason to believe that Judas was different in any appreciable way from his peers who were described in Acts 4:13 as "uneducated (*agrammatoi*) and ordinary men (*idiōtai*)." It is difficult to understand how any reader could view such a man as a Jewish "authority." But even though ordinary, uneducated Judas could not have been a Jewish "authority," John still found a way to argue that the father of "the Jews" ("the devil") became personally involved in the scheme of his offspring ("the Jews") by prompting one of his children (Judas) to betray Jesus (13:2).[4]

When the Synoptic narratives move beyond the despicable action of Judas to describe the trials and crucifixion of Jesus, three significant facts emerge.

2. Levine, "Christian Preaching," 94.

3. Levine, "Christian Preaching," 94.

4. In both 8:31 and 13:2, John uses the Greek word *diabolus* to describe "the "devil." In John 6:70, John has Jesus label Judas himself a *diabolus*.

First, Mark (15:11) and Matthew (27:20) do in fact blame "the chief priests and the elders" for manipulating the people, while Luke 23:35 notes that when Jesus was on the cross, "the chief priests and the scribes stood by, vehemently accusing [Jesus]," without claiming that they incited others to do so.

Second, Mark, Matthew, and Luke repeatedly lumped together two groups of Jews (Sadducees and Pharisees) that were fierce opponents who would not have agreed to work together under any circumstance. In numerous episodes, the gospel authors declined to define either the precise character of these two disparate groups or the radical theological and ideological differences that separated them from each other. The simple designation of "leaders" does not advance understanding of the kind of Jewish opposition faced by Jesus and his followers,[5] and this lack of precision creates the impression that all Jews in any leadership capacity, along with their non-leader followers, were staunchly opposed to Jesus. However, linking early first century CE Sadducees and Pharisees together in any unified politico/theological action is not credible, and only an author ignorant of first century Jewish sects and parties could have joined together indiscriminately such radically disparate groups.

Third, even with the active participation and urging of the Jewish authorities, the Synoptic Gospels note multiple actions that involved more than Jewish leaders. The infamous rant, "his blood be on us and on our children," was a cry said pointedly to have come from "all the people" (Matt 27:23). Similarly, readers are told clearly by Luke that, "They all cried out together, 'away with this man; release Barabbas to us'" (Luke 23:18). Even more telling is the assertion by both Mark (15:29) and Matthew (27:39) that while Jesus was on the cross between the two thieves: "Those who passed by derided him," followed by the notation that "the chief priests also mocked him" (Mark 15:31; Matt 27:41). Thus, in this scene, the order is first the people, and then the authorities.[6]

Jewish Enemies in John

By contrast with the Synoptic Gospels, the Gospel of John makes it clear from the outset that the Jewish opponents of Jesus included more than merely the authorities: "he came to his own homeland and his own people did not

---

5. We will note below the statement of Josephus that indicts "leading men" (Sadducees) of such opposition.

6. Luke 23:35 is slightly different: "The people stood by, watching, but the rulers scoffed at him."

accept him" (John 1:11).[7] Thus, Raymond Brown correctly observes that "the Jews" in John, "include Jewish authorities but cannot be confined to them."[8] In fact, it is readily apparent that whenever John says "the Jews," it is consistently a negative term intended to target an entire group (leaders *and* people) for abuse and blame. It is also clear that the resultant unbalanced depiction of "the Jews" lacks historical validity.

These two theses may be tested in another way. Professor Bart Ehrman made the important point that ancient historians, who lacked contemporaneous notes or recordings, "quite consciously *made the speeches up themselves*."[9] With respect to the Gospel of John, it is obvious that John is placing on the lips of Jesus speeches he himself has composed. For this reason, it is impossible to learn from the Gospel of John what *Jesus* thought of "the Jews." The words we read are from the mind of an author writing in the final decade of the first century rather than from Jesus speaking in the late twenties or early thirties of that same century. In this manner, John is claiming that his personal late-century animosity to Jews originated in the time of Jesus.

Because he is also portraying a Jesus who viewed "the Jews" as "other," it is fair to ask whether John perceived Jesus himself to be authentically Jewish. First, as noted in Essay II, it is difficult to understand why Jewish Jesus would have referred to the sacred Jewish Torah as "*your* law" (John 10:34) or "*their* law" (John 15:25) instead of "*our* law." But the salient point here is that whenever John depicts "the Jews" as opposing Jesus he is also depicting Jesus as opposed to "the Jews" and all things Jewish. When this is considered, it is not implausible to think that a reader might perceive the two sides as bi-polar opposites coming from two different ethnic groups and two different religions: "the Jews" vs. the Christians led by Jesus.

Second, it is hard to imagine Jesus reminding his disciples, Jews all, of something he had said to "the Jews" (John 13:33).

Third, it is also impossible to imagine that Jesus would have described those who hated him as "the world" before ripping from its context a verse

7. In Greek, the neuter plural of *idios* (*ta idia*) means something like "[his] own things," i.e., the things that were part of the world that "the *Logos*" had created, thus [his] own country or homeland. This is followed by the masculine plural form of the same word (*hoi idioi*), used as a substantive, "[his] own people."

8. Brown, *Introduction to the New Testament*, 339, note 13. This is a welcome switch from Brown's earlier contention that "the Jews" is used in John to designate Jewish religious authorities only. See his *Gospel According to John*, lxxi.

9. Ehrman, *New Testament*, 117, emphasis added. Ehrman's notation serves to introduce his understanding of the speeches attributed to various individuals by Luke writing the Book of Acts. He also illustrates his point with extra-biblical examples to show that he is describing a widespread literary phenomenon in the ancient world.

that had no referential connection to him as a way of affirming that "*their* law" (not *mine!*) declares: "they hated me without a reason" (15:25). "They hated me without a reason" appears to be a loose translation of a statement from two Psalms: 35:19 and 69:4.[10] But haphazardly appropriating the generic function of a verse from an OT Psalm of Lament does not advance the narrative and it is far from a complimentary example of Jesus as an exegete. This is especially true since immediately after placing this clear third person reference to Jews on the lips of Jesus, John quickly tried to explain that Jewish Jesus and all his Jewish disciples were not part of that Jewish world (John 15:18–25). It is equally clear that John was also making up the speeches attributed to the Jews whom he wished to depict as opposing Jesus. In other words, the Gospel of John does not present the views of Jesus, actual Jews, or anyone else who was Jewish. Instead, it presents the opinion of a non-Jewish gospel writer who created a speech that allowed him (John) to define for his readers the words and opinions of "the Jews" whom he considered his own enemy at the time of his writing, seven or eight decades after the lifetime of Jesus. The idea of forming one's definition about a group of people solely from information given out by their enemies is a concept that will be examined in more detail below.

"The Jews" and a Plot to Kill Jesus

One of the hallmarks of the Gospel of John is its repetition nine times of a sinister Jewish murder plot against Jesus. In this way, John makes clear his identification of the enemies of Jesus ("the Jews") and clarifies the depth of their depravity as so complete that it includes murder. Even casual readers of the Fourth Gospel are aware of the passion plot in John. It begins with the description of "the Jews" remanding Jesus to the custody of Pilate and tagging him as a "criminal" (18:30), refusing to retain him for judgment by Jewish law alone (18:31a), and explaining that they had "no right to execute anyone" (18:31b). Dissatisfied with Pilate's initial decision, "I find no basis for a charge against him" (18:38), "the Jews" remained upset when Pilate had Jesus merely flogged but not executed (19:1). The second confession of Pilate that he could find "no basis for a charge against him" (19:2) not only failed to satisfy their thirst for blood, but also prompted

10. It should be noted with respect to 35:19, that a few verses later (35:28) the same author promises, "My tongue will declare your righteousness, your praises all day long." Thus Psalm 35 is not looking forward to the time of Jesus, it is the expression of grief at circumstances common to almost everyone, including acquaintances who speak false and hurtful things, gloat over our failures, and seem to enjoy our troubles.

a specific shout of "Crucify, Crucify" (19:6a). Yet a third iteration of "no basis for a charge against him" (19:6b) from the compassionate (!) Pilate likewise had no effect.[11]

"The Jews" then tried another tactic, warning Pilate that he would be considered unfriendly to Caesar unless he relented and acceded to their demand that Jesus be crucified. "Finally," John notes, after repeated calls for execution of the man whom they could not convict by their own law, "Pilate handed him over to them [i.e., "the Jews"] to be crucified" under Roman law (19:16). But this statement is patently false, as the Fourth Gospel itself notes. It was not "the Jews" but the Roman soldiers who took charge of Jesus and did the dirty deed (19:16, 23). Still, John makes clear his belief that *responsibility* for the death of Jesus belonged to "the Jews" alone.

John's indictment of "the Jews" at this juncture is not surprising. Long before the passion narrative appears late in his gospel, readers had been assured repeatedly that a sinister Jewish plot to kill Jesus had been hatched almost from the beginning of his earthly career. By including this murder plot idea in multiple different locations and vignettes, John does not limit the charge of murderous Jews plotting against Jesus to a single scene in his passion narrative. Instead, he scatters the idea of a Jewish murder plot throughout his entire gospel, inserting it awkwardly and often when unrelated to the primary story being told. Nine times, John repeats the scheme that he insists had been hatched early in the life of Jesus.[12] His drumbeat becomes ever louder as the narratives pile up, one by one repeating the baseless claim.

Sometimes the Jewish plot to kill Jesus includes people who believed in him, and the common scholarly attempt to limit the identity of the plotters only to Jewish "authorities" or "leaders" is belied by John's own words. Throughout the chapters preceding the passion narrative, the idea of a murder plot against Jesus had been nothing less than John's wild conspiracy theory spun from the yarn of imaginary ignorant witnesses. Finally, nearing the end of his gospel, John manages to pin the death of Jesus on "the Jews." But from a literary perspective, the passion plot is not only unsurprising, it is also merely the culmination of an idea planted and cultivated repeatedly by its author throughout the Fourth Gospel.

The first reference to a Jewish murder plot against Jesus appears in John chapter 5. In the process of healing an invalid, Jesus instructed the man to pick up his mat and walk (5:8). Spotting the man carrying his mat,

---

11. John was apparently unaware that "the administration of Pilate was characterized by corruption, violence, robberies, ill treatment of the people, and continuous executions without even the form of a trial." See Singer and Broydé, "Pilate, Pontius," *Jewish Encyclopedia* V: 34.

12. See John 5:18; 7:1, 19–25; 8:37, 40, 59; 10:31; 11:53; 12:10.

"the Jews" reminded him that it was unlawful to carry a mat on Shabbat (5:10). He responded by informing his Jewish critics that his healer (5:11) had instructed him to carry his mat, and they asked who that healer was (5:12). Since Jesus had slipped into a crowd, the former invalid had no idea of the identity of his benefactor (5:13). However, a short time later, when Jesus and the man met inside the Temple, "the Jews" put two and two together and concluded that Jesus had been the healer. Because the healing had occurred on Shabbat, "the Jews began to persecute Jesus" (5:16) and Jesus defended himself with a cryptic response: "My Father is still working and I am working also" (5:17).

John's description of the instantaneous Jewish reaction to this statement by Jesus is both puzzling and lacking in context: "They tried all the more to kill him; not only had he violated Shabbat, but he had even called God his Father, making himself equal with God" (5:18). Although there has been no hint of such a plot in any earlier narrative, the phrase "all the more" implies that there had been at least one prior effort to kill Jesus. The reason John gives for this impulse to murder Jesus is the erroneous idea that Jews believed claiming to be a son of God was a sin equivalent to claiming to be the equal of God.[13]

Closely following the narrative in John chapter 5, chapters 6–8 include a hodgepodge of interesting vignettes that are "disconnected and hard to follow."[14] After the discourse on his body and his claim to be "the bread of life" (John 6:48), Jesus spoke about his flesh and blood in a manner that "the Jews" found confusing (6:52). So difficult was his lesson about eating his flesh and drinking his blood (6:54) that Jesus realized some members of his audience were grumbling (6:61). Jesus also knew that "there are some of you who do not believe" (6:64), and "many of his disciples turned back and followed him no longer" (6:66). Jesus then held a private conference with the inner circle of his disciples during which Peter affirmed that he and his fellow apostles *had* "believed" and had no desire to seek any other teacher (6:68–69). At this same private meeting, Jesus also referred to his future betrayer (6:70–71), and the episode ends.

In this manner, throughout chapter 6, a clear distinction is made between these two points of view represented in the audience of Jesus: (a) Some Jews included in his own inner circle of followers were believers; and (b) other Jews in that same circle were non-believers. Both the believers and the non-believers were Jews studying with Jesus ("disciples") and there are no Jewish *leaders* described among the audience on either side. Jesus is not in Jerusalem

---

13. These accusations are treated at length in Essay IV.

14. Burkett, *Introduction*, 231.

but in the synagogue in Capernaum (6:59). When some of the non-believers left (6:66), the believers remained. And since even the ones who left were described as among the students ("disciples") of Jesus, they clearly were not Jewish authorities. Jesus then returned to Galilee.

This is the context drawn by John before he makes the astounding announcement that Jesus could no longer travel around in Judea, "because *the Jews* sought to kill him" (7:1).

John offers no explanation for this announcement. Jesus had just noted that there were some Jews who did *not* believe (6:64), leaving the clear implication that other Jews in his audience *did* believe. In fact, Peter makes that affirmation specifically (6:68). When a later episode revealed the willingness of "the chief priests" to kill Lazarus as well as Jesus (John 12:10) readers are left with the impression that "the Jews" were already on the hunt not only for Jesus but also for other possible targets who might be affiliated with him even as a friend.[15] Would Peter and the other apostles who believed in Jesus enough to stick with him as their teacher have been targeted for murder along with Jesus? John does not connect the dots at this juncture, but his earliest readers who linked their late first-century controversy with Jews (seventy years after the death of Jesus) all the way back to these multiple mentions of a murder plot against Jesus easily might have concluded, based on the situation faced by Lazarus only a short time later, that the plot against Jesus included *his followers*.

Chapters seven and eight also tilt back and forth between two different groups: (a) those strange bedfellows ("chief priests and Pharisees") who sought to arrest him (7:30, 45), and (b) those who "marveled" at Jesus' erudition (7:15) but remained silent because they feared "the Jews" (7:13). Because members of the second group were themselves Jewish, and it is nonsensical to state that "the Jews" were silent because they feared "the Jews," many scholars imagine that "the Jews" in this context includes only leaders and no average folk. But as the larger narrative advances, it becomes clear once again that John is not limiting his indictment to leaders only.

Initially, Jesus continued teaching an audience that still included both (a) those "who did not understand" (8:27) and also (b) many others who "believed in him" (8:30). But beginning with John 8:31–59, an abrupt and peculiar switch begins to occur. The narrative develops as a dialogue between Jesus and "the Jews who believed in him," and we might expect a pleasant conversation or a teaching dialogue between Jesus and some of his believers. The Gospel of Mark, after noting that many hearers of Jesus

---

15. Lazarus was not an "apostle," but certainly a beloved friend, as John 11:36 makes clear.

would have difficulty understanding his teachings couched in the language of parables, added what might serve as a description of this type of private meeting chronicled in John: "When he was alone with his own disciples, he explained everything" (Mark 4:34). John does not record this specific observation, but in his narrative, there is no indication of hostility at the outset of his account of a discussion between Jesus and his disciples. Jesus and these *Jewish believers* (sic!) converse back and forth: they were asking questions and he was answering patiently.

Then abruptly, with no clue from the text as to what triggered his outburst, the narrative has Jesus interject an aggressive, adversarial tone into the dialogue by returning to the accusation that first had been leveled against "the Jews" in 7:1. This time, John uses Jesus as his mouthpiece to accuse some members of his audience directly: "*you* want to kill me" (8:37). It is startling to note that the people at whom Jesus aimed this accusation were "the Jews who believed in him" (8:31), again surely not Jewish "leaders." And it is telling that in neither John 7:1 nor 8:37 is any legitimate justification offered for John's accusation that even the Jews who did believe in Jesus were determined to murder him. Brown's explanation that their belief was "inadequate" misses the point. What confronts readers of John throughout is only the solemnly repeated assurance that it was "the Jews" who desired the death of Jesus.

This, then, is the impassioned way in which John insists that the desire to murder Jesus extended all the way to those Jews whom readers might logically assume were the good guys, believers. First, John has Jesus say that even believing Jews "want to kill me" (8:37) and then he has him repeat the charge in 8:40: "You are looking for a way to kill me." Finally, John has Jesus attack "the Jews" with the accusation that the "father" of all Jews is not God, as they presume, but "the devil" (8:44). Here it is necessary to recall the notation in Essay II of the explanation by Raymond Brown that "High Christology" Jews had become members of the Johannine Community, and they were the people who "saw 'the Jews' as children of the devil."[16] How strange it seems that in defense of his multi-level interpretation of "the Jews," Brown pointed to the Jews who had the highest estimation of Jesus as the source of the vilest anti-Jewish slur anywhere in John's Gospel.[17]

But here at last John furnishes his explanation for why "the Jews" wanted Jesus dead. Since the father of "the Jews" was the devil, "a murderer from the beginning" (8:44), it should come as no surprise that "the Jews"

---

16. Brown, *Community*, 166. And see note 47 in Essay II.

17. Brown overlooks the fact that John 8:44 attributes the accusation to Jesus himself.

(the children of the devil) would want to murder Jesus. The crux of the argument is clear. John needs his readers to think that *all* Jews wanted to carry out the wishes of their father (the devil).

This is the picture John paints—all Jews, even the believers whose faith in Jesus was not "high" enough, were willing to commit murder over a minor theological dispute. And since the devil is not only the father of "the Jews" but also "the father of lies," the Jews themselves are "liars" (8:55) who can never admit that they are determined to murder an innocent man. To prove John's point, these same "Jews who believed in him" (8:31), became angry at his claim to be older than Abraham, and "picked up stones to throw at him" (8:59).[18] Although modern scholars seem determined to unravel this muddled picture of "the Jews" by positing multiple groups that are being described at various times by the same phrase, it appears on its face that for "John," there simply were no good Jews.

Rabbinic Debate in the Time of John

The written evidence of rabbinic debates of the general era (100 BCE–200 CE) should make it impossible to believe that murder would have been the choice of Jewish scholars or of Jewish disciples who disagreed with Jesus about a point of theology, no matter how erroneous they deemed his position to be.[19] Even within the pages of the Bible itself, different points of

18. Throwing rocks at a person is not the same thing as attempting to execute him by "stoning," a procedure rabbinically ordained in the Mishnah but surely unknown to John. The ritual required first, that a formal trial be held and second, that the accusing witnesses in that capital trial be directly involved in the act of execution. Although the specific method of "stoning" was not codified until the Mishnah (ca. 220 CE), these requirements are based on Deut 13:10: "your hand [which the rabbis determined referred to the chief witness] shall be the first against him, and the hands of the other people thereafter." Deut 17:7 repeats this procedure after first ascertaining that at least two witnesses have testified under oath that they saw the actual criminal offense. Rabbinic law follows this injunction almost literally, but it adds the specific stipulation that the procedure take place within narrow boundaries. First, the condemned person was to be placed on a platform at least twice his own height. Second, the chief witness was to throw or shove the convicted man off the platform to the ground. Third, if the fall to the ground and the almost certain concussion did not bring death instantly, the second witness was to slam a heavy stone directly into his chest. Fourth, if these two actions did not suffice, additional trial witnesses would throw stones at the prostrate body until death ensued (Sanh 6:4; 4; 45a ff; *Sifra Emor* 19; *Sifre Num* 114; *Sifra Deut* 89, 90, 149, 151). John appears not to know the difference between throwing rocks and the official legal procedure of "stoning." His description here of an attempt to "murder" Jesus is not believable for knowledgeable readers.

19. Sadducees and Pharisees did seek to destroy each other; their fights were not simply over theological differences, but about political power and influence flowing

view are legion. As early as the opening chapters of its first canon, Jewish literature has never portrayed an ideological monolith. Genesis includes contradictory narratives about the order of creation, the number of animals Noah took into the ark, and the process by which the important town of Shechem came into the possession of the early Israelites.[20]

Similar examples could be multiplied easily throughout the Bible. Exodus chapter 6 ascribes the introduction of the divine name YHWH to the time of Moses, although prayer to YHWH is attested fifty chapters earlier in Genesis 4:26, when Adam and Eve were still alive. Eighth century Isaiah and sixth century Jeremiah offered different responses to the military sieges of Jerusalem each witnessed. Ninth century Elisha and eighth century Amos had radically different opinions of the Jehu dynasty. The cynical book of Ecclesiastes tries to overturn the prophetic assurance that righteous folk enjoy divine protection and special favor. And the justly famous book of Job goes to great lengths to argue that suffering and loss are not the exclusive experience of the sinful, again flying in the face of the standard point of view. It is truly remarkable that the sourcebook of Judaism, the Bible, does not shy away from recording alternative and sometimes conflicting points of view. This fact should make it difficult for a fundamentalist interpreter to force the Bible to support one and only one viewpoint.

As time advanced and Judaism became more mature and reflective, the situation did not change in this respect. One need only to scan virtually any page of Mishnah–Tosephta–Gemara ("Talmud"), chrestomathies of *Midrashim* (homilies), and Jewish biblical commentaries to encounter sharply divergent views on significant theological issues. The pattern of the published accounts of the most important of these rabbinic disputes now chronicled in the Talmud is (a) to report the arguments made by all sides of a disagreement, sometimes four or more, (b) to make clear which position has the strongest backing of the rabbinic community, and (c) to move on to the next issue to be debated. No penalties are exacted from anyone deemed to be on the "wrong" side of an issue.

John's Idea About Jewish Debate

By contrast with these and innumerable other examples about actual Jewish debate over critical theological differences, the portrayal of "the Jews" in John represents the irresistible urge of an author desperate to pin the death

---

from such differences. For more on rabbinic and disagreements and debate, see examples included in Appendix D.

20. See Genesis 33:18–20 and compare Genesis 34.

of Jesus on "the Jews" rather than the Romans whose favor he needed to curry, even while he wanted desperately to portray the new faith as Jewish to the core. To accomplish his goal, John attempts to convince his audience that even believing Jews were intent on killing Jesus.

Readers of John in every age have been hard pressed to find any Jews depicted positively in the Fourth Gospel: Jesus' own brothers did not believe in him (7:5); "fear of the Jews" kept people on both sides of the argument about Jesus quiet (7:10–13); Nicodemus, himself a Pharisee and probably a member of the Sanhedrin (Jewish High Court), was insulted first by Jesus for his ignorance (3:10) and then by his peers for his reasoned response to Jesus' teaching (7:45–52); and "the Jews" refused to accept Jesus and God ("the Father") as two different witnesses (the number necessary in Jewish law) to prove a legal argument made by Jesus (8:12–18).

With reference to this last point, noted Johannine scholar Gail R. O'Day was well aware that "Jewish law held that a man's witness on his own behalf is not legally admissible evidence" and that "he must have the witness of two other men."[21] Nonetheless, she calmly noted that Jesus "meets the Pharisees' demand for two witnesses by offering himself and God," describing his offering as proof that Jesus "gives the Pharisees what they ask for."[22] But she herself had just stated quite correctly the plain fact that the testimony of Jesus "on *his own* behalf is *not* legally admissible evidence." Nevertheless, O'Day believed that "the Pharisees" in John's Gospel continued to oppose Jesus because of their "profound ignorance about the identity of God and the relationship between God and Jesus."[23] Her treatment of the passage thus appears to confirm John's claim that "they did not understand" (8:27).

But if there is in fact "profound ignorance" in the story, it is to be found in the mind of a gospel author who appears spectacularly incapable of grasping a simple legal concept. At the end of the day, no matter who Jesus was, the legal principle was clear: no one can bring admissible evidence about himself into a legitimate Jewish court via his own testimony. Surprisingly, John himself acknowledges this very principle, and quotes Jesus as equally aware of it: "If I testify about myself, my testimony is not true" (5:31).[24] So,

---

21. O'Day, *John*, 633. O'Day here cites "Jewish law" that is codified in the Mishnah, again later than the time of the Gospel of John. But, as with the ritual of stoning, it is probable that the rules of evidence in later Jewish law originated much earlier than the time of their publication in the early third century CE.

22. O'Day, *John*, 633.

23. O'Day, *John*, 633.

24. Elsewhere, John had Jesus say exactly the opposite: "Even if I testify on my own behalf, my testimony is true" (John 8:14). In both verses, English "true" is the Greek word is *alēthēs*, either "true" in a general sense or "valid" forensically.

offering himself and God as his two witnesses did not give the Pharisees what they wanted or what the unambiguous wording of Jewish law required. Their refusal to abandon the clear legal principle involved did not imply that they were guilty of "profound ignorance."

Instead of accusing the Pharisees of ignorance, an unbiased reader should recognize the handiwork of John propounding a decidedly non-Jewish view of what he thinks Jews *should* have accepted simply because it was Jesus making the offering. Yet the fact remains that the response of Jesus did not meet the Jewish legal definition of evidence. Citing only himself and God meant that Jesus offered *no* witness to his testimony. It is not difficult to understand why the Pharisees felt that John's Jesus was obfuscating the issue, just as it is quite easy to imagine a similar reaction from a modern court if a witness should attempt to prove a point simply by asserting, "God agrees with me."

John's Idea About How a Jewish Debate Ends

Ultimately, by far the two most outrageous claims of John are (a) that the undefined Jewish "authorities" (*hoi archontes*) probably *did* know that Jesus was the messiah and that was the true reason they wanted to kill him (7.26); and (b) that "the chief priests also planned to put innocent Lazarus to death" (12:10) to stop the flood of Jews who were believing in Jesus from joining his followers. It is hard to imagine two more negative portrayals of an entire group. As noted above, John 7:26 attests that when John wished to describe Jewish authorities specifically, the Greek word *archontes* was readily at hand. Even in this passage, these murderous intentions by Jewish "authorities" must be added to the murderous intentions of "the Jews" recounted throughout the gospel. But it was not the "authorities" who originated the idea of murdering Jesus. According to John, that had already been done by ordinary Jews, many of whom "believed" in Jesus. But for John, even believing in Jesus did not furnish motivation enough to resign from the murder cabal. John's condemnation of "the Jews," *all* Jews, was unrelenting and final.

IV. John and the Jewish Rejection of Jesus

Preliminary Remarks

WHILE THE IDEA IN John that "the Jews" were the quintessential enemies of Jesus *during* his lifetime is over-stated and largely false, *after* the death of Jesus, Jews by and large did reject the call to join in the company of those who were in the process of forming the Christian church. Few issues have been as contentious as the determined search to explain this Jewish rejection of the proto-*ecclesiastical* portrait of Jesus, a question that receives repeated emphasis in the typical introductory New Testament work. To understand that process, it is important to remember that "if the tradition behind John is firmly rooted in Judaism and Palestine, the presentation of that tradition has moved considerably beyond Jesus' ministry."[1]

This is a reminder that the Jesus in John is not the Jesus of the early first century. Consequently, what the Gospel of John depicts is not a reflection of Jewish attitudes toward the historical Jesus, but a reflection of Jewish attitudes toward the theological conception of Jesus that his Christian followers had begun to develop in the several decades after his death.[2] The fact that Jews rejected post-Jesus Christian claims has been explained in multiple ways. Raymond Brown offered three reasons that have been widely adopted by NT scholars: Christian "free interpretation of the Law; their proclamation of Jesus' divinity; their proselytizing, etc."[3]

However, for Jews there was—and is—a *more basic fact*: Jesus did not accomplish what Jews expected from a messiah. He made no effort to loosen the yoke of Roman hegemony and domination of Jewish life and culture before dying on a Roman cross as a common criminal. This refusal or inability to end Roman occupation and restore Judean independence was the bi-polar

---

1. Brown, *Introduction*, 370.

2. Throughout the twentieth century, NT scholars debated the issue framed as "The Jesus of History" compared to "The Christ of Faith."

3. Brown, *Introduction*, 82, note 29.

opposite of what first century Jews believed and expected to see happen under the leadership of their ideal liberator and ruler, their "messiah."

Jesus and the Jewish "Scriptures"

Two points are important with respect to the task of defining the "Scriptural" description and identification of a messianic candidate. The first point is the idea of early Christianity that the Jewish Scriptures were divinely inspired and therefore authoritative to govern life and belief. This claim is articulated plainly in a pseudo-Pauline[4] letter: "Every scripture (*graphē*) is inspired by God and is useful for teaching, for reproof, for correction, and for training in righteousness" (2 Tim 3:16). Commenting on this verse, Raymond Brown stated emphatically: "There is no doubt that 'Scripture' designates all or most of the books we [Christians] call the OT."[5]

Second, these same Jewish Scriptures were later appropriated by Christianity as the introductory part of its own official sacred texts (canon).[6] This adoption of the Jewish Scriptures explains why early Christians felt the need to prove their contentions about Jesus by citing Jewish scriptural authority that they were determined to claim as their own.

The specific exegetical processes followed by early Christians seeking to discover Jesus in the Jewish Scriptures are examined in greater detail in Essays IX and X. This essay explores the foundation of Jewish law and *praxis* furnished by those Scriptures, the sacred literature that functioned as the major influence on (a) early attempts to demonstrate the growing Christian conviction that Jesus of Nazareth was the messiah who was promised in the Scriptures; (b) Scriptural teaching supposedly supporting the Christian idea about the suffering, death, and resurrection of Jesus; and (c) the vast difference between the way Jews read and understood their own sacred literature and the use to which that literature had been put after being appropriated by Christians to support their ideology.

Modern Christian scholars have been led once again by Brown, who contributed a detailed two volume study to the idea that Jesus' life, death, and resurrection were in full conformity with the expectations of the Jewish Scriptures.[7] To the contrary however, despite the spirited assertions of various NT authors and the special pleading of their numerous modern NT interpreters,

---

4. I.E., falsely ascribed to Paul as the author who in fact was anonymous,

5. Brown, *Introduction*, 678.

6. It is more accurate to say that the Old Testament *was* the first Christian canon.

7. See his two-volume *Death of the Messiah*.

most Jewish scholars perceive this Christian assumption about Jesus in the Old Testament to be a fundamentally flawed pursuit of ideology.

But Jewish scholars are not alone in this regard. Although Brown has been followed by the largest contingent of Christian NT scholars, some prominent Christian exegetes also have been brutally honest about the matter. In her widely lauded commentary on the Gospel of Mark, Professor Pheme Perkins disputes the idea that everything anyone wants to know about Jesus was already present in the OT long before his birth and death by crucifixion. Perkins also zeroes in on the reason why such a claim was made originally and continues to be repeated: "Although there is no specific text behind the comment that the Son of Man must suffer and be rejected (v. 12c), this formulation represents a common early Christian understanding of the death of Jesus as the fulfillment of the prophetic testimony."[8]

Christian scholar Bart Ehrman underscores the first point of Perkins in greater detail: "There were no Jews prior to Christianity who believed that the future messiah was to die for sins and then be raised from the dead."[9] Furthermore, Ehrman is correct to note that "[Jesus] clearly was not the messiah anyone had expected. The earliest Christian believers were therefore compelled to insist that the messiah, *contrary to general expectation,* was to die and be raised from the dead, and they began to search their Scriptures for divine proofs of this. Thus began the *distinctively Christian* notion of a suffering messiah who died for the sins of the world and was vindicated by God in a glorious resurrection."[10]

This assessment is true. So, it is odd that Ehrman should cite approvingly the exact opposite view only six pages later in the same work: "For Paul, faith in Jesus was in complete conformity with the plan of the Jewish God as found in the Jewish Scriptures."[11] Or again, "Paul appears to have turned to the Jewish Scriptures to understand how Jesus' death was according to the plan of God."[12] These assertions by Paul are unaccompanied by the citation of any verse from the Scriptures. Yet Ehrman adds that it was "from the Scriptures, of course, [that] Paul knew of the suffering of the Righteous One of God, whom God ultimately vindicated."

---

8. Perkins, *Mark, New Interpreter's Bible,* VIII: 631. But the "early Christian understanding" was nothing like a plain sense reading of the text.

9. Ehrman, *New Testament,* 235, Box 16.1.

10. Ehrman, *New Testament,* 235, Box 16.1. Emphasis added.

11. Ehrman, *New Testament,* 241.

12. Ehrman, *New Testament,* 252.

This assessment is assuredly not true.[13] As Perkins noted just above, the idea of a *suffering* and *dying* messiah is not a Jewish or a "scriptural" notion. Despite NT efforts to link the "suffering servant" of Isaiah with Jesus, it is crucial to remember that the "suffering servant" of Isaiah chapter 53 is never called "messiah." The linkage of the two concepts (messiah and suffering) is a post-Scriptural, non-Jewish creation that became necessary after the death of Jesus when his disciples insisted that his crucifixion should not be interpreted as the invalidation of the hopes of those who had lived and studied with him. In short, the idea of a "suffering servant" is post biblical ecclesiastical ideology, not Scriptural truth.

In fact, the "Scriptures" to which the apostle Paul, Ehrman, Brown, and many others refer do indeed constitute the defining source of Jewish expectations for a messiah. But they point to the reasons why first century Jews did *not* perceive Jesus to have met those expectations. Careful study of those very "Scriptures" indicates that Jews living in the first century did not reject Jesus because they *failed* to understand him. To the contrary, they rejected him as a messiah because they understood him quite well. They knew his teachings and deeds, as well as the story asserting that he spent his life as an anointed person who would undergo the radical event of his own death for the purpose of bringing spiritual renewal to Judah. Just as surely, they knew that such a life was not in any manner consistent with the "scriptural" picture of a messianic hero who would bring *political* liberty to Israel. Delbert Burkett summarizes the issue succinctly: "Even though Judaism had not a single conception of the Messiah but a variety, Jesus seemed to fit none of them."[14]

The only non-royal, non-priestly individual identified in the "Scriptures" as a "messiah" was the Persian ruler Cyrus, the sixth century BCE, decidedly non-Jewish military genius. In the context of the expected restoration of Israel, the author of Isaiah 45:1 took careful notice of the military successes of Cyrus and, in recognition of his role as the leader who had allowed exiled Judahites to return from Babylonian captivity to their homeland in Judah, promptly identified him as the messiah of YHWH. In short, the actions of Cyrus brought a form of *political* restoration to Judah, and thus the title "messiah" was deemed appropriate by the biblical prophet.

It is necessary to ask who would have been convinced by non-existent "proofs" of the messiahship of Jesus supposedly founded upon the pillars of Jewish Scripture. Not only does no Jewish Scripture define the messiah as

---

13. Ehrman, *New Testament*, 252. This idea of the "suffering servant" is examined in detail in Essay IX.

14. Burkett, *Introduction*, 66.

someone who is destined to suffer and die for the sins of the entire world, no Jewish prophet predicts a *divine* messiah, a virgin birth, or an atoning death. Nor did Jews in the first century long for the appearance of a messiah who would be executed as a common criminal for the crime of sedition against the Roman Empire. But these yawning *lacunae* in the "Jewish Scriptures" had little meaning to those who had no awareness that the "proofs" promised in the gospels so often simply do not exist.

Why, then, the stubborn ideological insistence that Jesus was rejected by his own people to comport with supposed teachings of "the Jewish Scriptures?" And were these reasons accurate reflections of Jewish Scripture and/or tradition? The search for answers to these questions must begin with an examination of the charges against Jesus attributed to the Jews by the Synoptic Gospels before turning to the way in which John incorporates their point of view. In the case of all four gospels, elaborate conspiracy theories are woven from imaginary yarn supplied by authors with little understanding of the Jewish Scriptures or Judaism.

First False Charge: Claim to be the "Messiah" (Blasphemy)

Jesus Before the Sanhedrin

Well before the time of "John," the Synoptic Gospels had agreed that Jesus had been accused by "the Jews" of having committed multiple acts that violated Jewish law. These accusations that every Jew possessing nominal intelligence would have recognized as false were then said to have been used by the Sanhedrin (Jewish High Court) as justification for its decision that Jesus deserved the death sentence.[15] According to Mark 14:55 and Matthew 26:59, "the chief priests and the entire Sanhedrin were looking for false evidence (*pseudomartyrion*) against Jesus so they could put him to death."[16] To this end, "many false witnesses came forward," but they all failed to produce satisfactory evidence against Jesus. Finally, an anonymous someone testified: "This fellow said, 'I can destroy the temple of God and rebuild it in three days.'"

Even though the testimony of the witnesses did not agree, the high priest urged Jesus to answer their accusations. Frustrated at his refusal to respond, the high priest himself took charge of the proceedings, homing

15. See Mark 14:53–65 and parallels for the words and phrases cited in the following discussion.

16. Luke 22:66–71 shortens the accounts of Mark and Matthew, and then moves straight to the question of messiahship.

in on what he apparently considered to be the heart of the matter: "Tell us if you are the messiah, the son of God." In the earliest gospel, Mark, Jesus responded simply, "I am" (14:62). In Matthew and Luke, his answer to the high priest was ambiguous: "So you say." Mark (14:63–64) and Matthew (26:65) recount this exchange as proof that no further witnesses were necessary because Jesus had committed "blasphemy," while Luke 22:71 phrases it only slightly differently but with the same implication: "Why do we need any more testimony? We have heard it from his own lips."

Three facts are noteworthy. First, the punishment for blasphemy was execution by stoning (Lev 24:14, 16, 23). If Sanhedrin had voted to hand Jesus over for crucifixion, the Roman penalty of crucifixion instead of a legally mandated Israelite stoning would not have satisfied Jewish law. This is a detail of which the Synoptic authors appear to have been unaware and modern scholars fail to address. For this reason alone, it is highly unlikely that Jesus ever appeared before the Sanhedrin and there is ample evidence to doubt a trial before the Sanhedrin.[17] This High Court body "was considered lawfully convened only if approved by the local Roman prefect" (i.e., Pilate).[18] Third, even if the Jewish High Court had met to consider the fate of Jesus, there is no evidence anywhere in Jewish law that claiming to be a messiah was "blasphemy."[19]

"Blasphemy" and the Synoptic "Passion" Narratives

Following his supposed interrogation before the Jewish Sanhedrin, Jesus was taken to an appearance before the Roman ruler Pilate. Each gospel in turn adds more Jews to the scenes in its version of the Passion narrative. Mark has "*the chief priests*" stir up the crowd to choose Barabbas and shout, "crucify him [Jesus], crucify him" (15:6–15). Matthew notes that "*the chief priests and the elders* persuaded the people to ask for Barabbas and destroy Jesus" (27:20). Finally, in Luke's portrait, "*chief priests, rulers, and people*" (23:13) all together demand that Pilate release Barabbas and crucify Jesus (23:18). Luke also notes how Pilate's repeated judgment that Jesus was innocent was overcome by this combined group because "they were urgent, demanding with loud cries that he should be crucified" (23:23). The key

17. This was the position argued most persuasively by John Dominic Crossan, *Who Killed Jesus?*

18. Cook, *New Testament*, 42.

19. The parade example of blasphemy is the act of uttering a curse using the ineffable name of God (Lev 24:11).

phrase notes pointedly that, "their voices prevailed" (23:23b) above the voice of reason expressed by Pilate.

From a Christian perspective, any claim made by Jesus about his messiahship, his status as a son of God, or virtually any other status could not be deserving of punishment for the simple reason that even the most exalted claims he might have made would be assumed to be true. And the typical Christian perception, derived from the Synoptic Gospels themselves, is that "the Jews" (or "the high priest") viewed the claims of Jesus to be blasphemous merely because they did not consider him to be the messiah. This concept appears to be underscored by the quick movement in the Sanhedrin trial to the ultimate question of messiahship.

However, outside the Synoptic Gospels, the NT itself realizes that Jesus was not the first Jewish person to claim messiahship, and the historical record is clear that he would not be the last. Two earlier claimants (Theudas and Judas the Galilean) are named in Acts 5:33–39 by the great Jewish scholar Gamaliel. About a century later, the highly respected Rabbi Akiva proclaimed the Jewish warrior Simon bar Kokhba to be the messiah, clearly anticipating that he would lead a successful military campaign to free Jews from Roman occupation in much the way that Cyrus of Persia had ended Babylonian Exile in the sixth century BCE.[20] No charges were leveled against any of these claimants, and the idea that Jesus would be guilty of blasphemy even if he had claimed to be a messiah is something concocted out of whole cloth by the gospel writers with no basis in Jewish law, tradition, or precedent.

In fact, a fair analysis of this Synoptic idea leads to the conclusion that "technically speaking, no blasphemy had occurred."[21] And there is a specific reason for such a statement: "No profanation of the divine name[22] appears to be involved."[23] In short, depiction of a scene in which Jesus committed blasphemy is not a false Jewish charge against Jesus, but a false charge against "the Jews" trumpeted repeatedly by the authors of the Synoptic Gospels. But even though "First-century Jews by and large rejected any idea that Jesus could be the messiah,"[24] neither the gospel writers themselves nor modern Christian NT scholars can show any connection in Jewish law between claiming messiahship and blasphemy.

20. For the story of the bar Kokhba rebellion and the role played by Akiva, see Roth, *A History of the Jews*, 111–16.

21. Ehrman, *New Testament*, 67, Box 5.5.

22. The legal basis for a charge of blasphemy.

23. Chilton, "Caiaphas," 1:803. Also note his citation of Leviticus 24:15, 16; and *Sanhedrin* 7:5.

24. Ehrman, *New Testament*, 150.

John's Passion Narrative

Although he had employed the term blasphemy earlier in his gospel (John 10:33), it is noteworthy that John omits a formal Sanhedrin trial of Jesus with its emphasis on claims of messiahship equated with blasphemy. This omission also hints at the probability that no trial before the Sanhedrin occurred.

But perhaps there is an additional reason for John's omission of a formal trial of Jesus by the Sanhedrin. In terms of literary structure, the Johannine narrative here does not require any charge that would lead to the pronouncement of a death sentence. Much earlier, following the raising of Lazarus, John had already described an informal (and thus illegal and non-binding) Sanhedrin session that resulted in the consensus that Jesus needed to die (John 11:53). Perhaps like Mark, Luke, and Matthew, John also did not know that such a session, called by "the chief priests and the Pharisees" (John 11:47) would not be lawful, meaning that the Roman authority would not accept any decision from such an *ad hoc* meeting. Still, John confidently reports that the high priest Caiaphas, a Sadducee who opposed the idea of resurrection, articulated the argument that persuaded the deliberative body of the guilt of Jesus: "it is expedient[25] for you that one man should die for the people" (John 11:50). This puzzling statement of his was reported in the context of a large crowd forming to see the resurrected Lazarus, surely an unpleasant prospect for anyone who denied the resurrection. And the incident John describes occurs well in advance of the passion narrative. But regardless of when he might have said it, there is no verse in the Scriptures that teaches this concept of Caiaphas.

It must also be recalled that John's record of the incident was written more than seventy years after the fact, at a time when there were virtually no Sadducees still in existence because they had lost the final vestiges of their political influence with the destruction of the Temple in the year 70 CE. Thus, when John cited the top-ranked Sadducee giving an opinion about a non-existent verse of Scripture, not only was he recreating a scene that was more than seventy years in the past, but he was also depicting a party whose leader had been out of power for at least thirty years when John wrote about it. Even before this time, the Sadducees had been concerned chiefly with Temple ritual and its relationship to their leadership role as the priestly party.

All in all, this is surely the most ludicrous explanation for the legal necessity of the death of Jesus that one can imagine. It appears to be

---

25. The word used is *symphero*, connoting the idea of something advantageous or profitable.

nothing more than a bold attempt to have Caiaphas, who had been the top Jewish official in the land in the time of Jesus, act as a Christian prophet and predict the "saving" death of Jesus. That same statement, of course, indicts all Jews for refusing to accept this preposterous claim with no basis in Scripture, custom, or Jewish law.

This is not the only place where John portrays "the Jews" as so callous and so willing to violate their own rules that they would accept even a baseless and ridiculous excuse to murder in cold blood a man with whom they had a theological disagreement. A prime example is illustrated by the plaintive plea from Nicodemus to his brother Pharisees who served with him on the Sanhedrin: "Does our law judge a man without first giving him a hearing and learning what he has been doing" (John 7:51)? John's re-creation of their response to Nicodemus is chilling. Without debate, and with neither hesitation nor contemplation, this reasonable question from one of the High Court's own members was unceremoniously swept aside: "No prophet will arise from Galilee" (John 7:52).[26] End of discussion.

Still, if in fact *Caiaphas* had said what John imputes to him, the later appearance of Jesus before *Annas* (the father-in-law of Caiaphas), becomes a complete puzzle because of John's confused perception of the high priest (John 18:19-24). First, he states that "the high priest (Annas) questioned Jesus." Then, when Jesus' answers were deemed unsatisfactory, an irritated anonymous official slapped him and remarked, "Is this the way you answer the high priest?" Third, when Jesus was not nearly as deferential to Annas as Paul would be to Ananias in his later appearance before the Sanhedrin,[27] Annas, before rendering a decision about Jesus, apparently was left with no choice but to send him "bound to Caiaphas," his son-in-law.

In this short scene, John titles both Annas and Caiaphas "high priest" as if there were two high priests at once. That could not have been the case. Annas served as high priest from 6 to 15 CE, but he retained considerable influence in Jewish affairs after he stepped down. Caiaphas served as high priest from 18 to 36, so he would have been the formal leader of the Sanhedrin during the events depicted in the gospels. John either did not know or did not care about the relative chronology between the two men. For John, brushing aside an impossible time sequence in conflict with his argument was inconsequential. But since Caiaphas had already decided the fate

26. In later rabbinic texts, the rabbis referred to a Galilean as a *gelili shoteh*, a "stupid Galilean" (*Eruvin* 53b). Galilean rabbis were mocked because of their inability to distinguish consonants that were similar, and for this reason, a Galilean rabbi was not allowed to chant the Torah in the Temple for fear that his poor pronunciation would make his words unintelligible.

27. Acts 23:1-5, an incident discussed in Isbell, "Paul and Judaism."

of Jesus (John 11:47–50), John had no need to create a hearing before him in his passion narrative, as the Synoptic authors did in theirs.[28] In John, the only role of Caiaphas was to relay Jesus on to Pilate.

Thus, the Fourth Gospel opts not to use the charge of blasphemy to indict Jesus in its passion narrative. Surprisingly, "the Jews" who handed Jesus over to Pilate did not cite any issue of religious (Jewish) law at all. Instead, they seized upon the idea that claiming to be a king violated Roman *criminal* law: "If he were not a criminal, we would not have handed him over to you" (John 18:30).[29] This is a startling change from wrangling among Jews about theology and *sin*, to a specific charge before Pilate about the *crime* of sedition. And it is noteworthy that John depicts "the Jews," after trying to convince themselves that Jesus was guilty of a breach of Jewish law, admit openly in John that they had failed to accomplish their goal. The only option that remained was for them to remind Pilate that they were not authorized to administer a death penalty and accuse Jesus of sedition (John 18:31). Pilate understood them correctly, and his first question to Jesus was political with no theological undertone to the Roman mind: "Are you the king of the Jews" (John 18:33)?

How ironic was this final report of John that Jesus died, not because he did anything *Jewishly* wrong or sinful, but because Pilate used the *Roman* criminal charge of sedition to find Jesus guilty and sentence him to Roman crucifixion (John 19:16).

Still in all, John could not resist the temptation to depict Pilate as so compassionate that he thrice reported having found nothing criminal in Jesus, but also so weak that he went against his own judgment and caved to what John describes as an angry mob of Jews. Thus, John "goes beyond the Synoptic gospels in exculpating the Romans and blaming the Jews."[30] After repeated calls for the death of Jesus (John 18:40; 19:6, 7, 12, 15), "*Finally* Pilate handed him over to them to be crucified" (John 19:16). This was apparently the narrative that convinced Origen, the great third-century Christian theologian, to state flatly that "It was not so much Pilate who condemned him . . . as the Jewish nation."[31] Sadly, Origen's opinion has prevailed among Christians for now more than eighteen centuries.

---

28. See Mark 14:60–64 and parallels.

29. The Greek phrase is *kakon poiōn*, literally "doer of a bad thing." But *The New Jerusalem Bible* and the *New International Version* both understand that the force of this idiom describes a violation of criminal law, and they both translate correctly as quoted here, "criminal."

30. Sandmel, "Pilate," 812.

31. *Contra Celsus*, Book II: xxxiv

Second False Charge: "the son of God"[32] as Blasphemy

Even to the very last, during his version of the passion narrative, John describes "the Jews" as shouting what he apparently did not realize was a baseless and false claim: "We have a law. And according to that law, he must die because he claimed to be the son of God" (John 19:7). But if John had no idea that such a charge was false, virtually every Jew alive would have known it immediately. Instead of reflecting Jewish belief, John's choice of a second false charge reflects his background in Hellenistic (Greek) culture. "In Hellenism, Son of God indicated 'possessing divine qualities,' 'exhibiting a divine aura,' or the like."[33] Thus, since John was thinking as a non-Jew immersed in Greek culture, a claim to be the son of God might indeed imply a claim to be a divinity oneself.

But in the world of Judaism, claiming to be a son of God lacked these Hellenistic implications entirely. To the contrary, claiming to be a child of God was/is *not* a sin or a crime in Judaism at all. It was/is an idea woven into the very fabric of Jewish tradition as early as the story of the Exodus and divine deliverance from Egyptian slavery. After Yahweh instructed Moses to return to Egypt to orchestrate the Exodus, the first thing He ordered Moses to say to the Pharaoh was "Israel is my first-born son" (Exod 4:22). The word "son" is singular in *form* but collective in *function*, including every Israelite in Egypt (sons *and* daughters). The same idea is attested in Hosea 11:1: "I began to love Israel when he was still a young boy and ever since Egypt, I have called him my son." Here too, "young boy" and "son" are singular in form but collective in function, once again asserting that *everyone* in "Israel" was a child of Yahweh. Sonship also describes the relationship between God and every king of Israel (Ps 2:7).

One thing that clouds this issue for readers of the English NT is the capitalization of the word son in English translations.[34] And although the decision to capitalize "son" is an ideological one, not derived from written evidence attested in Greek NT manuscripts, to a modern reader of the English text, the capitalized "Son of God" phrase immediately conjures up a mental image of exclusivity and divinity.

In this context, the assertion that Jesus was the *"only"* son of God also calls for explanation. In addition to Exodus 4:22 and Hosea 11:1 just cited, Deuteronomy 14:1 introduces a detailed series of statements giving

32. For this section, see also "The Son of Man and the Father-Son Relationship," in Kysar, *John, the Maverick*, 51–56.

33. Perrin, *New Testament*, 49.

34. As is done with the famous declaration of John 3:16. The same ideological determination capitalizes the word messiah.

guidance for a variety of religious and social practices incumbent upon Israel. These regulations must be followed because, "You[35] are the sons [and daughters] of YHWH your deity" (14:1). This is tantamount to saying, "All of you are God's children." Then the significance of this father-child relationship is underscored one verse later with the reminder that the people of Israel must live lives of "holiness" that differ in numerous ways from the practices of all other people on earth because they have been singled out ("chosen") to be the "treasured possession"[36] of Yahweh. Because of this repeated OT emphasis on the idea that everyone in the entire nation is a child of God, John's introduction of the term *only* Son" would have been nonsensical to a Jewish audience.

But John himself presents an even more complicated difficulty in dealing with the supposed sinfulness of calling oneself a son or child of God. The Gospel of John opens with a majestic "Preface" (1:1–18) that is designed to introduce the main character of the narrative to follow. In the opening verse, that character is identified as none other than "the *logos*[37] of God" whose own origin is with God and who is himself God (or divine). The ensuing literary concatenation is brilliant: this "*logos*" was the creator of everything, and he is the personification of "life" itself (1:3), the very life that brings "light" to humanity (1:4), a light so powerful that it cannot be extinguished by darkness (1:5). This *logos* came to his own creation and was rejected by his own people (1:11).[38] But, John assures his readers, "to everyone who received him, who believed in his name, he granted authority (*exousia*) to become *children*[39] of God" (1:12).

It is difficult to understand why John apparently thought that "the Jews" viewed claiming to be a child of God as blasphemy. Either he did not know that claiming to be children of God was not blasphemous in Jewish law and life or he simply was determined to argue that claiming sonship with God was considered blasphemous by "the Jews" only when Jesus did it. Perhaps he personally subscribed to the Hellenistic idea of sonship that was foreign in Judaism. If so, that may explain why he presumed that accusing Jesus of

35. Here the Hebrew plural form *'atem* is used to signify everyone, males *and* females.

36. Hebrew *segullah* denotes a special treasure or unique heirloom reserved for a favored child. Israel is called the *segullah* of Yahweh in Exodus 19:5.

37. Usually translated into English as "word" (capitalized in Christian ideology although it, like "son" and "messiah," lacks justification in any Greek text). It is understood in Neo-Platonic thought as "pure reason."

38. See Essay III, note 7.

39. Greek *tekna* = both sons *and* daughters.

claiming sonship with God would result in a damning indictment. Whatever the case, John was clearly confused about sonship in Judaism.

There is more. John makes the claim that sonship with God is possible for everyone, but only via belief in the anonymous (to this point in the gospel) *logos*. Consequently, his opening statement overturns his own depiction of Jesus as the "only"[40] son of God. If Jesus were indeed the *only* son of God, no one else could be. But John appears to argue that being a child of God is a distinct possibility for everyone, if they achieve that designation in the manner that he prescribes. Everyone must "believe" what John is about to explain or he/she simply cannot be a child of the divine. "Only true believers in Jesus are the children of God."[41]

Assuming that his interpretation was the only possible correct point of view allowed John to leap to the conclusion that "the Jews" could know nothing about the true nature of sonship. But the fact is that John was the one who had no clue about Jewish ideas pertaining to sonship. That is why John accused "the Jews" of wrongdoing by citing a practice they never would have imagined as anything less than an expression of confidence in and gratitude for their relationship with the divine. And that is why, in the face of centuries of Jewish teaching about the Fatherhood of God and the sonship and daughter-ship of *all* His human partners, John conjured up a ridiculous charge that "the Jews" sought to impose a capital sentence on one individual, Jesus, merely for expressing confidence in his personal relationship with God. Then, based on his own pernicious misunderstanding, John appeared to be offended by another idea that existed only in his own mind, his insistence that "the Jews" would subject Jesus (and his followers) to the death penalty for daring to claim God as Father.

In sum, the issue for John could not have been that Jewish law forbade an individual to claim to be a child of God, which it absolutely did not do, and neither John nor anyone else could cite a single verse to substantiate such a claim. The issue for John was his unshakeable certainty that *Jewish* sonship to God was impossible because it was not achieved through Jesus in the manner that he prescribes.

---

40. The Greek word used in John 1:14 is *monogenes*, "unique," "the only one of its kind."

41. Brown, *Epistles*, 85.

Third False Charge: Equality with God ("Blasphemy" Yet Again)

According to John, the most serious charge leveled against Jesus by "the Jews" was that he claimed to be the equal of God, a charge that, if proven, might come close to the idea of profaning the name of God and thus might fit the technical, legal definition of "blasphemy" in Jewish law. It is fascinating to see how John portrayed the steps taken by "the Jews" in support of his contention that the teachings of Jesus led to the idea that he was claiming divinity and full equality with God for himself.

[1] John 5:18: "[He] called God his Father, making himself equal with God." For this charge to have validity, it would be necessary to demonstrate that claiming sonship was illegal, a charge just shown to be spurious. These two issues simply do not belong together. Even if claiming to be a son of God were a sin, the idea that such a claim would make a person the equal of God is nonsensical on its face. There is nothing in Jewish law or tradition to indicate that first century Jewish legal scholars, or Jewish thinkers of any era, linked these two ideas together. Why John imagined such a linkage is a total mystery.

[2] John 10:30: "I and the Father are one." This idea that Jesus and God are "one" may be viewed as John's attempt at a radical rephrasing of the most basic statement of faith in all of Judaism: "Listen, O Israel. YHWH is our deity. YHWH is *One*" (Deut 6:4). A few chapters later, John portrays Jesus praying that his disciples may be "one" as he and God are one (John 17:11), and Rabbi Michael Cook has zeroed in on the negative consequence of this concept. "The true gravity of this matter is that, by literary license, the Fourth Gospel has assigned to the historical Jesus what is after all only John's own theology. Further, insofar as John presents Jesus as the Christ ["messiah"], and insofar as the Christ and the Father are deemed by John to be 'one' (10:30; 17:11), *John has imputed his theology to God personally, thereby in effect making God appear anti-Jewish!*"[42] Sadly, soon after the Gospel of John was published, Rabbi Cook's concern became the norm in a lot of Christian preaching. Jesus became God and God became the Enemy of "the Jews."[43] But this "norm" is not grounded in the teachings of the historical Jesus. It comes from the imagination of the proto-ecclesiastical John.

On a surface level of this gospel statement attributed to Jesus, John's statement could appear to be a radical and unique claim showing Jesus identifying himself as the equal of God. The appeal to the authority of Scripture,

42. Cook, *New Testament*, 228. Italics in original.

43. A brief survey of this custom among early Christian preachers is found in Appendix D.

"Is it not written in your (sic!)[44] law (John 10:34), 'I said you are gods'?"
(Ps 82:6), seems to validate the position of Jesus with great force because it
appears to back the claim of Jesus by a citation from the Bible. But when one
reads Psalm 82, it is readily apparent that verse 6 is not talking about human
beings as if they were "gods." It is referring to the divine assembly ('adat
'el) that furnishes the context and background for the entire psalm. There
the one God is sitting in judgment over all other "gods," indicting them
for withholding justice from the weak (dal), the orphan (yatōm), and the
needy ('evyōn), while showing partiality to the wicked (resha'im).[45] These
are the beings that the Psalmist has God call "gods" before designating them
as inferior to the Most High One ('Elyon) and declaring that they will "die
like mere mortals and fall like every other ruler" (82: 6b).

The Psalmist obviously believed that the one true God could not be
killed or die like a mere mortal, a fact that is seldom noted when the Jews are
accused of having killed God. But Psalm 82 portends the death of all other
pretend "gods" who do not provide justice.

In fact, Psalm 82 in its entirety underscores the command to early
Israel: "There will be no other gods for you" (Exod 20:3). In both places,
the Ten Commandments and Psalm 82, there is no denial that other "gods"
exist. They may exist in the imagination of their followers, but they do not
bring justice, they advance wickedness, and they are not real. All gods like
this are out of bounds for Jews. When these false gods die as puny mortals,
their impotence will be revealed by the one and only true God.

Surely no first century Jewish scholar would have been persuaded by
appeal to a partial verse wrenched out of context from a psalm ("You are
gods."), and it would be disrespectful to imagine that Jesus would have said
anything so foolish. Clearly this is John attempting to prove an unprovable
point by placing a short snippet of a single verse (82:6a) on the lips of Jesus.
Had Jesus offered such an abstruse interpretation, readers familiar with
Scripture would have concluded that Jesus himself had no ability to read
a simple psalm and understand it anywhere close to correctly. Fortunately,
the gospel narrative has Jesus himself point to the real reason for the decision of "the Jews" to accuse him of "blasphemy." It is "because I said, 'I
am the son of God'" (82:36), a statement that John appeared incapable of
realizing came nowhere near to blasphemy.

---

44. Again, as noted in the Introduction, it would have been inconceivable for Jewish Jesus to have said "your law" rather than "our law." This is proof positive that nothing in the statement derives from Jesus. It is John speaking, thrashing about desperately
for a way to level a baseless charge that he can claim "the Jews" lodged against Jesus.

45. Verses 2–4.

[3] John 14:9: "I am in the Father and the Father in me." This statement, somewhat akin to "I and the Father are one," is better seen as a parallel to "My Father is working still, and I am working" (John 5:17) or "The Father is in me and I am in the Father" (John 10:38). But almost as soon as this statement is made, John notes another saying of Jesus that directly contradicts the idea that he was claiming equality with God: "The words that I say to you I do not speak on my own authority, but the Father who dwells in me does his works" (John 14:10). This is an idea repeated elsewhere in the Gospel: (a) "The son can do nothing of his own accord, but only what he sees the Father doing" (John 5:19). (b) "I can do nothing on my own . . . I seek not my own will but the will of him who sent me" (John 5:30). (c) "I have not come of my own accord" (John 7:28). No fair analyst could interpret any of these statements as Jesus claiming equality with God for himself.

[4] John 17:1: "Glorify your son that the son may glorify you." Here Jesus asks that God "glorify him," a statement no more sacrilegious than the report that when the Israelites saw the Egyptians dead on the beach, "they believed in the LORD (YHWH) *and* in his servant Moses" (Exod 14:31). Nor is it more presumptuous than the request of Elijah on Mount Carmel, praying for God to answer him rather than the prophets of Baal: "O LORD [YHWH], deity of Abraham, Isaac, and Israel, let it be known today that you are God in Israel, and that I am your servant, and that I have done all these things at Your command" (1 Kgs 18:36). In the cases of Moses and Elijah, a human partner of God received certification of his life and work, and both responded with thanksgiving and praise. There is no hint of equality with God in either narrative.

[5] John 18:38–19:7: After Pilate says three times, "I find no crime in him," "The Jews answered him, 'we have a law, and by that law, he ought to die, because he has made himself *the son of God.*" Here the issue comes full circle. "John," ignorant of the facts of Jewish law, repeatedly insists that "the Jews" judged Jesus liable for the death penalty because he said something that every Jew in the world, then and now, could say with pride and confidence. Even if some Jews had hated Jesus passionately, it does not follow that the Sanhedrin could have been persuaded to act in direct contradiction of Jewish law simply because of a disagreement framed in this manner. And the Johannine picture of Jews scuttling their own rules and leaping to the conclusion that the death penalty was warranted for a teacher with whom they had a theological disagreement is not consistent with what is known of first century Palestinian Judaism.

These first three charges illustrate one significant way in which the Gospel of John serves as the most openly anti-Jewish of the gospels. In the hands of a Jewishly ignorant author,[46] "the Jews" consistently fill the role

46. If it be objected that John was not Jewishly ignorant, the only other possibility

of enemy, opponent, "other." And John attributes to them ideas that no Jew would have imagined much less countenanced.[47]

Before leaving the question of sonship as a status unique to Jesus alone, a final point should be made. In addition to John's own "Prologue" discussed above, it is worthy of notice that the quintessential Christian prayer recorded in Matthew 6:9–13 and Luke 11:2–4 has Jesus teach his followers to address God as "Father!"[48]

Fourth False Charge: Pre-Existence

John 17:5: "Glorify me . . . with the glory that I had with you before the world was made." This statement begins as a repetition of #4 above ("Glorify your son . . . "), but it adds an ending that implies the pre-existence of Jesus. This citation of a prayer to God by Jesus matches another famous passage (John 8:58) that John puts forward as leading to the desire of "the Jews" to kill Jesus. Both passages are linked to John's insistence that Jesus claimed to have pre-existed Abraham.[49]

It seems reasonable to suppose that a claim that elicited such a violent response would be found throughout NT teachings. However, in the entire New Testament, Paul is the only other author who appears to support John's idea of the pre-existence of Jesus (see Phil 2:5–11). None of the Synoptic authors mentions it, nor is it found in I Peter, The Apocalypse (Revelation), or any other NT book. It is fair to ask the reason for the omission of a concept so important in John. One plausible explanation is offered by Bart Ehrman: "The two New Testament Gospels that speak of Jesus being conceived of a virgin (Matthew and Luke) do not indicate that he existed *prior* to his birth, just as the New Testament books that appear to presuppose his preexistence (cf. John 1:1–3, 18; Phil. 2:5–11) never mention his virgin birth."[50] Thus John was faced with two bi-polar options and made a choice between a physical human birth in history and a preexistent *Logos* outside the scope of human history. John's vote for preexistence resulted in a Hellenistic Jesus who was far less human and far more other-worldly

---

is that John knew Jewish law but falsified it purposely. Standing between these two choices places one in the position of Buridan's ass, forced to choose between two equally unacceptable options.

47. This attitude of "them" as the enemy continued once Jews were no longer a significant part of the Johannine community membership, and as will become apparent in Essay VI, the way in which the new enemies were treated sets the treatment of "the Jews" by John in wider perspective.

48. See Matthew 6:9 ("Our Father") and Luke 11:2 ("Father").

49. The issue in John 8:58 is part of the discussion of John's "I AM" passages in Essay XI.

50. Ehrman, *Lost Christianities*, 100–1.

than the Jewish Jesus of the Synoptic Gospels. "But when all these books came to be included in the New Testament, both notions came to be affirmed simultaneously, so that Jesus was widely thought of as having been with God in eternity past (John, Paul) who became flesh (John) by being born of the Virgin Mary (Matthew and Luke)."[51]

Be that as it may, it is difficult to see how Jesus would have been indicted as a law breaker deserving of death based only upon such an unusual claim (pre-existence). People hearing an ordinary-looking man claiming to be more than 1,800 years old very well might have deemed him mentally unbalanced, demon-possessed (John 8:48, 52), or otherwise peculiar, and some in his audience did perceive him to be quite out of the ordinary. But it does not follow that such a reaction would lead "the Jews" or their legal authorities to determine that Jesus should pay for his peculiarity with his life.

Final Thoughts on False Charges

In the process of examining the various charges that John accused "the Jews" of bringing against Jesus, the reaction of a typical modern Jewish reader of John is surely "Why?" Why claim that "the Jews" tried to indict Jesus with actions that are not violations of Jewish law, that are not acts Jesus became the first or only Jew in history to perform, and that the Gospel of John itself undermines when its complete text assesses each charge in turn?

Reading the text honestly as one reads any written document, it is difficult to escape the impression that the author of the gospel harbored a deep hatred for and fear of "the Jews." When all these meaningless accusations are coupled with the assertion that in them one finds the reason why Jews longed for the *death* of Jesus, the incredibility level of the text rises to its highest point. Apparently, the author or his intended audience (or both) must have known little or nothing about Jewish law, legal procedures, and social norms. Otherwise, it is difficult to see how a knowledgeable Jew would write, or a knowledgeable Jewish readership would swallow as credible, a litany of indictments that failed to indicate any culpability on the part of Jesus. Nothing described by John as a "sin" was/is perceived as such in Jewish law. And nowhere can one discover a death penalty provision in Jewish law for anything John reports Jesus to have done or said. This was a point that even pagan Pilate was able to grasp.

In the end, the "WHY?" is unanswerable.

---

51. Ehrman, *Lost Christianities*, 101.

V. "Expulsion"

Preliminary Remarks

ONE OF THE MOST intriguing claims in the Gospel of John involves the concept of "expulsion," by which John meant the Jewish practice of expelling from synagogue worship anyone who professed the messiahship of Jesus. According to John chapter 9, this practice originated in the Jerusalem Temple when a blind man whose sight Jesus had restored was lured into an argument with the Pharisees (John's term for all Jews) about the character of Jesus. The Pharisees viewed Jesus in a completely negative light and when the former blind man refused to agree with them, they kicked him out of the Temple.

John also argued that this initial incident in the Jerusalem *Temple* became the pattern for a standard policy involving multiple *synagogues*. Following this pattern in synagogue after synagogue, the Jews ultimately succeeded in expelling so many followers of Jesus that a complete rupture between Jews and Christians resulted. This Johannine concept of unbelieving Jews expelling righteous Jewish Christians places the blame for the breakup completely on the shoulders of the Jews.

This essay examines the portrait of the break drawn by John and the way in which John's portrait has been interpreted by most Christian NT scholars. In the following essay, Jewish sources that paint a very different picture of this Jewish practice and this historical period are then compared with John and his interpreters.

John's Introduction of the Theory

According to John 9:34, a man whom Jesus had healed of blindness is expelled from the Temple in Jerusalem. In a "glittering generality," John 12:42 asserts that this action subsequently became a standard practice in the *synagogue* while Jesus was still alive. In an apparent admission that the practice of expulsion did not begin as early as the lifetime of Jesus, John 16:2 appends a prediction by Jesus himself that this disastrous policy would be extended at some unspecified *future* date from the Temple to include the network of multiple synagogues. Although scant attention has been given to this outward movement from the Jerusalem Temple to the surrounding territories and their numerous synagogues, many NT scholars assume these gospel accusations to be true in the later Johannine community, although not during the lifetime of Jesus. But the story told by John is that this expulsion began with an incident in which Jesus was heavily involved. Regardless of which period individual scholars choose, "A central concern of the Johannine community was the fact that its members had been or were being expelled from the Jewish synagogue."[1]

The most widely followed theory about the development of a traumatic expulsion policy from synagogues is grounded in the seminal work of J. Louis Martyn, whose presentation of "The Expulsion Theory" is offered in detail in his *History and Theology in the Fourth Gospel*.[2] Since 1968, almost all NT scholars who have examined the accusations of "expulsion" found in John have followed the line of argument set forth by Martyn. His theory also has been adapted and expanded by many other scholars, including most notably Martyn's colleague, Raymond Brown. But partially because the Gospel of John erroneously (or purposefully) links the action of expulsion directly to the time of Jesus in the first third of the first century, and partially due to the difficulty of dating the Jewish sources on which Martyn relied, his theoretical reconstruction has faced numerous challenges.

Aposynagōgos in John

Martyn begins by explaining that John uses a hybrid or made-up word to describe what Martyn has chosen to call "expulsion." That word is *aposynagōgos*, a combination of "out of" [*apo*] and "synagogue." Using the hybrid word of John, Martyn spends little time examining the single foundational incident in the Temple but turns quickly to his belief that this initial event grew into multiple incidents that occurred in various local synagogues outside Jerusalem. Thus, Martyn apparently presumes that John's report of the initial incident in the Jerusalem Temple was accurate despite its impossible claim of direct involvement by Jesus personally.

---

1. Burkett, *Introduction*, 224.

2. Reinhartz, *Cast Out of the Covenant*, p. 125 n. 3 notes that there were two earlier editions of Martyn's book in 1968 and 1979. I have been unable to consult either of these two.

Martyn also accepts John's misrepresentation of a single event in the Temple morphing into a widespread official Jewish *policy* of expulsion in multiple synagogues throughout the land.

Martyn's presuppositions face difficulties at the outset. John's hybrid word offers no clue either about *how* a person came to be out of the synagogue or whether any specific *procedure* was developed to enforce the policy. But as Martyn saw it, there must have been some formal process that resulted in certain Jews ending up outside the synagogue, no longer worshiping as Jews. Martyn's presuppositions about such a hypothetical process were crucial, continuing throughout to blur the line between John's Temple incident and multiple synagogues elsewhere. Ultimately, he settled upon three assumptions.

First, formal "expulsion" would have to have been triggered by a clearly defined breach of synagogue custom or procedure. According to John 9:22, which Martyn accepted as factual, that trigger was a simple expression of belief in the *messiahship* of Jesus.

Second, formal "expulsion" from the synagogue would have required action on the part of a recognized group of Jewish *authorities*. Following John again, Martyn nominated "the Pharisees," the group John mistakenly believed had the authority to identify and expel offenders of synagogue custom already in the time of Jesus (John 9:13–34).

Third, although Martyn could not explain in detail the way in which the hybrid word *aposynagōgos* functioned in John as the *method* by which punishment of a *synagogue* transgression would occur, he based his argument on the presumption that *aposynagōgos* should be retained as the most important reference to what he perceived as a widespread *policy* of exclusion from synagogues. But Martyn chose to ignore the fact that the foundational incident with the blind man described by John had occurred in the Jerusalem *Temple* (not a *synagogue*). This makes the phrase "out of the synagogue" a faulty foundation on which to base an elaborate theory.[3]

Jewish Expulsion of Believers According to John

Here are the two episodes from the Gospel of John which Martyn attempted to interpret and that he linked to his reliance on several pertinent Jewish documents of the period he believed supported his theory.

In the first episode, set in the Jerusalem Temple, Jesus and his disciples spied a man who had been blind since his birth (John 9:1) and Jesus assured his disciples that neither the blind man nor his parents were responsible

3. See further below on *aposynagōgos* and *ekballō*.

for his blindness, but "this happened so that the works of God might be displayed in him" (9:3). Reminding the disciples that he "must perform the works of him who sent me" (9:4), Jesus "spat on the ground, made mud out of his spittle, anointed the man's eyes with the mud," (9:6) and dispatched him to rinse his eyes in the pool of Siloam (9:7a). From there, the man returned to the Temple able to see (9:7b).

Other worshipers in the Temple were divided about the identity of the man returning from his visit to Siloam (9:8–9), but when he insisted that he was the former blind man, his fellow worshipers asked how his eyes had been opened (9:10). He offered them a terse account, including his specific identification of his healer as "the man they call Jesus" (9:11). In John's account, Jesus had no additional dialogue with other worshipers following his treatment of the man's eyes, and readers learn at this point that Jesus has exited the Temple (9:12).

Then the man was brought to "the Pharisees," and they were given a shortened version of the incident (9:15). Mention of "the Pharisees" in this context leaves the impression that they were the party in control of the Temple and thus the proper authorities from whom to seek an opinion about a technical matter of Jewish law. And since the story is set on the Jewish Sabbath (Shabbat), in support of his thesis, John needed to include a Jewish authority group that would serve as the ultimate symbol of opposition to the work of Jesus. John's story, accepted by Martyn, nominates "the Pharisees," some of whom issued the ruling that Jesus could not be an authentic healer because, "he does not keep Shabbat" (9:16a). This is John's depiction of the Pharisees both acting as the authoritative group in charge of the Temple and offering their binding legal opinion about healing on Shabbat. But John either did not know that the Pharisees were not the party in power at the time of Jesus, or he did not wish to have his narrative bogged down over an inconvenient historical fact.

Martyn fails to account for the fact that the description in "John" is historically inaccurate and misleading. He also ignores the confusion woven into the narrative itself. When a second group of Pharisees opined that a sinner could not have performed such a miracle (9:16b), the narrative appears to argue that the first group of Pharisees had issued a false ruling simply because they wished to oppose Jesus. Authoritative Pharisees issuing a patently false ruling simply to oppose Jesus fit perfectly into the narrative John wished to write. Finally, the narrative notes rather lamely that the healed man preferred the opinion of the second group of Pharisees because he thought Jesus must have been "a prophet" (9:17).

Then a third position developed. Because "the Jews [now not just the Pharisees] did not believe [the man] had been blind," they summoned the man's parents to settle the issue. The parental answer: "We know that this is our son. He was born blind. But how he sees now, we do not know, nor do we know who opened his eyes. Ask him. He is of age. He will speak for himself" (9:18b–21). The author of John then explained in detail why the parents answered in this fashion. "They feared the Jews, because the Jews had *already agreed* that if anyone should confess [Jesus] to be the messiah, he was to find himself put outside the synagogue" (9:22).[4] Now it is startling, and not a little troubling for Martyn's theory, that neither the parents nor their son had identified Jesus as the *messiah*. In other words, no triggering action of acknowledging Jesus as messiah had taken place to justify such a disturbing expulsion story. This is an important detail that Martyn failed to acknowledge, and both John and Martyn omit any explanation about why the healed man was expelled for no reason except gratitude, and even without having named Jesus as messiah.

Then the man was summoned again, not merely to be questioned but to respond to the accusation that his benefactor was "a sinner" (9:24). After explaining that he did not know anything about the qualifications of Jesus, his refreshingly simple conclusion was, "I *was* blind, but I see *now*" (9:25). Pressed to repeat the details of his experience, the frustrated man asked whether the Pharisees wanted to hear his account a second time because they might be interested in becoming disciples of Jesus (9:26–27). After an angry exchange and repeated insults hurled at the healed man, the Jews denounced the man as "born in utter sin" (and thus incapable of teaching *them*) and "they *expelled* him" (9:34).

"Out of the Synagogue" and Violently "Expelled"

The word used by John both in 9:34 and the following verse is *ekballō*, a much stronger term than John's earlier hybrid term *aposynagōgos* on which Martyn based his theory. While *aposynagōgos* has the sense of a person who is no longer part of a synagogue, it offers no hint of how or why this had occurred. In sharp contrast, *ekballō* signifies an action using physical force or violence. But even in the context of the claim that the once blind man had been violently expelled, John's narrative still includes no mention of "messiah," the specific charge stipulated in John 9:22 and demanded by Martyn's theory to trigger the policy of expulsion.

The second incident involving expulsion is chronicled in John chapter 12. The occasion was the entry of Jesus into Jerusalem which drew large numbers of Jews at a feast where Jesus was present, people hoping to

---

4. The expression here is *aposynagōgos genytai*, not *ekballō* discussed below.

see not only Jesus but also his recently resurrected friend Lazarus (12:9). Although the Pharisees and the "chief priests" had issued orders that Jesus should be arrested on sight (11:57) and killed (11:53), these orders were complicated by the fact that the crowd grew large quickly. Then the report that Jesus was visiting Lazarus presented a roadblock to the would-be killers of Jesus. As John explains it, "the Pharisees" seemed almost in total despair over what to do about Jesus because of his extreme popularity: "the whole world has started following him" (12:19).

But if the Pharisees were at a loss, "the chief priests" had a simple answer: "[they] planned to kill Lazarus as well" (12:10). By such action, not only would the troublesome Jesus be out of the picture, but anyone inclined to believe in him would be warned by the example of the murdered Lazarus. Indeed, although one of his sisters had affirmed Jesus as messiah (11:27), "the Jews" could not even accuse the hapless Lazarus of having done so.[5] He would have to pay with his life for his friendship with Jesus, not his false Christology.

Finally, the end of the narrative shows the full extent of the problem Jesus posed: "even some of the authorities (*archontes*) believed in [Jesus]" (12:42). But since John's argument in 9:34 had been that siding with Jesus had triggered the violent expulsion of the blind man, he notes that even these high-ranking Jews had declined to voice their belief in Jesus, "because of the Pharisees . . . lest they should be put out of the synagogue" (12:42).[6] John apparently failed to realize that he had already portrayed the Pharisees as the high-ranking Jews in charge of legal opinions and expulsion from the Temple, leaving the reader wondering who John's *believing* authorities were if not Pharisees.

Yet again, even at this point in the narrative, these unidentified authorities are said only to have believed in Jesus, but there is still no mention of the possible *messiahship* of Jesus. Thus, the trigger promised by John and presumed by Martyn is still absent from the narrative. All that is really asserted in the passage is that Jesus was a popular healer, a worker of miracles able to attract large crowds. But John is so certain of the power wielded by the Pharisees that he portrays even Jewish "leaders" (whom he

---

5. Despite his fame as a person resurrected by Jesus, there is no NT citation of anything Lazarus might have said to or about Jesus. Luke (16:19–31) had earlier used the name Lazarus as one of the characters in his parable about two men, one rich and the other poor. Luke's Lazarus was a beggar who never met Jesus. John's Lazarus was the brother of sisters who were wealthy enough to offer expensive gifts to Jesus (John 11:2); Lazarus himself was known well enough to be beloved by Jesus (John 11:3 and especially 11:35–36).

6. Here using *aposynagōgos* rather than *ekballō*.

has given every reason to believe *were* Pharisees), as frightened of them. Frightened of themselves?

Although John links both "expulsion" reports to Jesus living in the first one-third of the first century CE, these two incidents are apparently referencing the final break between Jews and Christians that occurred sixty or seventy years after the crucifixion. Surprisingly, John appears to have been at least dimly aware that the actual separation of Christians from Judaism did not occur during the lifetime of Jesus. To accommodate this inconvenient fact, John inserts a prediction by Jesus to be fulfilled at some future date when, "they will put you out of the synagogues" (16:2).[7]

Violent Expulsion and Historical Reality

Three points are important in comparing John's portrait of "expulsion" with historical reality. First, the jumbled Johannine references in various narratives to the Pharisees, the "chief priests," the Sadducees, and "the authorities" clearly stem from an author who has no clear idea of the various sects and/or parties that comprised "the Jews" during the lifetime of Jesus. Nor did John acknowledge any awareness that the Pharisees had not yet developed into an organized party during the lifetime of Jesus. At the earliest, they gained political and liturgical control over the Temple only four or five decades after the crucifixion. Until that time, the Sadducees had been the party in power.

Second, John's choice of the verb *ekballō* is an egregiously inaccurate way to describe what happened, even years later, at the time of the split between Jews and Christians. As noted above, *ekballō* ("to expel," "drive out by force") describes a harsh and often violent act. For example, it is the way in which Mark 9:47 advises ridding oneself of an eye that causes one to sin (*skandalidzein*). Its most frequent function in the Synoptic Gospels is to describe the expulsion of demons, although it is not used in this context by John because the Fourth Gospel does not include any exorcisms.[8]

---

7. John does not cite Jesus as having used *ekballō* in 16:2. The expression is, "they will make you [be] out of the synagogues" (*aposynagōgous poiēsosin hymas*), again including no clue about the method by which this might be done. *Aposynagōgous poiēsosin hymas* in 16:2 should be compared to *aposynagōgoi genōntai* in 12:42 and *aposynagōgos genetai* in 9:22, idiomatic expressions meaning "banned from," but lacking the inference of force or violence carried by *ekballō*. The use of different terms for the same action often indicates that an author or editor is citing two different original sources.

8. See Hauck, "*ekballo*," *TDNT* I 527–528 for citations and additional examples of the word as a description of violent action.

A broader context in which to understand the Greek term *ekballō* is offered by the LXX. Its use of *ekballō* to translate the equally harsh Hebrew term *legaresh* ("to expel, drive out") leaves no doubt about the meaning of the word. Thus, Adam was "driven out" from Eden (Gen 3:24); Cain lamented that "You [YHWH] have driven me" from the soil, forcing him to live under a curse that could bring about his death at any moment (Gen 4:14); and most remarkably, YHWH promises, "I will drive out" the inhabitants of Canaan to make room for the Israelites (Exod 33:2). Each of these incidents describes forceful or violent action, and each time Hebrew *legaresh* is rendered by *ekballō* in the LXX.[9]

When it is remembered that John used *ekballō* to describe the action of Jesus "expelling" moneychangers from the Temple *using a whip* (2:15), it is readily apparent that he understood the Greek term correctly. Even though John offers no details about the exact kind of violence he believed the Pharisees used on the healed former blind man when they had expelled him from the Temple, his description of the expulsion as a violent act was made *deliberately*.

Third, a complete breakaway of Christianity from Judaism certainly did occur seventy or more years after the death of Jesus. However, the stories narrated in John do not fulfill Martyn's requirement of an explanation about *why* or *how* one became an excommunicate. The important point is that although the schism between Christians and Jews came to a head several decades after the death of Jesus, John described it as having occurred while Jesus was still living, and he traced it to a specific moment when Jesus had been physically present in the Temple.

This attempt to backdate the breakup by more than seven decades has the effect of assigning complete responsibility for the separation of Christianity from Judaism to the Jews, beginning with those who had interacted with Jesus during his lifetime. Beyond that, John's decision to accuse Jews of physical violence as their method of separating Jews and early Jewish-Christians is not verified by the evidence.

The Mission of Paul and the Split from Judaism

In fact, the historical reality concerning the "expulsion" of Jewish Christians from synagogues is radically different from John's version. In the sixty to seventy years between the death of Jesus and the writing of the Gospel of John, tensions between the followers of the crucified Jesus and practicing

9. See a complete list of comparable references in Ringgren, "Garash," *TDOT* III 68–69.

Jews had increased. During the early years of this period, one major factor exacerbating the tension was the determination of Paul to force his way into synagogues with the avowed purpose of attempting to convert Jews away from Judaism and into Christianity.[10] A brief survey of Paul's actions uncovers valuable evidence about what happened.

Taken at face value, some NT accounts of Paul's activity indicate that there was never any reason for disagreement between Paul and fellow Jews. In his earliest NT letter, Paul stated flatly that his Damascus Road experience of conversion to Christianity and his subsequent commission as an Apostle had been for one purpose only: "so that I might preach [Jesus] among the Gentiles" (Gal 1:16). He further asserted that his "*immediate response*" (*eutheōs*) had been to take steps leading to the fulfillment of that commission. By this account directly from Paul, his "conversion" *en route* to Damascus had occurred as a prelude to his work as a *Christian* missionary only. Since Paul would have been preaching only in Gentile meetings, it is plausible to presume that no Jews would have been impacted by his views.

In support of this hypothesis, the Book of Acts offers three versions of Saul's Damascus-road experience, all linking Paul's visionary experience with his sense of mission to Gentiles.[11] These accounts, added to the testimony of Paul himself, had nothing to do with Jews and synagogues; they led to his designation in church tradition as "the Apostle to the Gentiles." If this picture had been true, and if Paul always had been evangelizing among Gentiles only, it is difficult to imagine that he would have numerous disagreeable arguments with his fellow Jews.

But there is another side to the story, an alternate series of NT accounts related to the period almost fifty years before the Gospel of John was written. In these narratives, Paul's repeated failures in multiple *synagogues* provoked him to charge bitterly that, the Jews "killed the Lord Jesus and the prophets" and "the Jews . . . also *persecuted us severely*" (1 Thess 2:15).[12] Here it is necessary to recall that Paul was the man who testified without apology that he pretended to be "a Jew in order to win Jews," feigned *torah*-observance to one audience and celebrated being *torah*-free to another crowd, and even pretended to be "weak" to appeal to others who were "weak."[13] He then

---

10. Isbell, "Paul and Judaism" and "Saul the Sadducee."

11. Acts 9:1–18; 22:1–16; 26:1–18.

12. The word he uses is *ekdiôkein*. Contrary to the way it is translated in various versions like *The New International Version* and *The New Revised Standard Version*, *ekdiôkein* does not mean "to drive out." *The New Jerusalem Bible* has it correct: "the Jews . . . persecuted us also." It is used elsewhere in the NT only by Luke 11:49.

13. It is difficult to determine the identity of "the weak" to whom Paul was referring. One possibility is that he had in mind people who thought they should be Jewishly

announced proudly that he willingly became whatever was necessary for the success of his mission: "I have become all things to all people in order that by any means I might win someone" (1 Cor 9:20–22).

In line with this confession of his ethical flexibility, it must be recalled that despite the series of reports claiming that Paul's designation as the Apostle to the Gentiles was earned by his evangelization among non-Jews, other NT reports of his Damascus vision and subsequent career reveal a flatly contradictory version. In Acts chapter 9, the story is that after he had regained his sight in Damascus, "immediately (*eutheōs*) he began to proclaim Jesus in the synagogues" (9:20). Then the version offered in Acts chapter 26 includes Paul's first-person description of his evangelical method: "I was not disobedient to the heavenly vision. I preached first to those in Damascus, then in Jerusalem, and throughout the countryside of Judea," but *only then* "also to the Gentiles" (26:19–20).

Elsewhere in Acts there is additional evidence of this second, far different picture. When the church in Antioch was commanded by the "Holy Spirit" to "set apart Barnabas and Saul for the work to which I have called them" (Acts 13:1), the two men traveled to the island of Salamis and "proclaimed the word of God in the synagogues of the Jews" (Acts 13:5). Nothing is said about preaching to Gentiles until the notation that the Roman proconsul at the far end of the island in Paphos "believed" because of his astonishment at the skill of Paul in a contest with a local Jewish prophet who was famous as a magician (Acts 13:6–12). At this point in the narrative, Luke begins to refer to *Paul* (the Greek name reflecting his Roman citizenship) instead of his Hebrew name *Saul*.

The ensuing mission of Barnabas and Paul to Antioch in Pisidia also began in synagogues (Acts 13:14). But then their second Shabbat sermons there attracted such large crowds that "the Jews . . . were filled with jealousy, blasphemed,[14] and contradicted what was spoken by Paul" (Acts 13:46). In

---

observant but found it difficult to do so. Paul appears to be assuring them that they need not worry about their inability to do things like observing *kashrut*, circumcision, or even Shabbat because their faith alone is sufficient. Since Paul had just said that he sometimes became "*torah*-observant" when he clearly was not, it is plausible to presume that he meant to say that he "pretended to be weak" to make things easier for others who were having trouble abandoning Judaism. This aligns with his intention to make his message palatable to people from a wide range of backgrounds and customs. Surprisingly, despite his admitted dishonesty about his true beliefs, Paul sees himself as a victim of "the Jews."

14. As essay XI explains, some NT scholars argue that John portrays Jesus as taking for himself the sacred name of God, the very essence of blasphemy (as explained and illustrated in essay IV). Here, Luke accuses "the Jews" of blasphemy, a classic case of transference.

response, Paul and Barnabas announced the following: "It was necessary that the word of God should be spoken first to you [Jews]. But because you reject it . . . we are now turning to the Gentiles" (13:46). Yet even that experience did not bring about a change in pattern. At Iconium, "Paul and Barnabas went into the Jewish synagogue as usual" (Acts 14:1), then to Lystra, and Derbe (14:6). Likewise, Romans 11:11–24 repeatedly underscores Paul's feeling that only because Jews ["Israel"] had rejected the gospel was it possible for Gentiles to be offered the chance at salvation.

In other words, the simplistic explanation that he received his calling to the Gentiles at the same time he experienced a vision of Jesus just outside Damascus is contradicted by the fact that in city after city, Paul began his missionary activities in synagogues. These multiple NT accounts must be taken seriously and linked with Paul's own words cited above from First Corinthians. In synagogues, Paul was presenting himself as a *torah*-observant Jew who was seeking to convert other *torah*-observant Jews to his new conception of appropriate *torah* observance. In city after city, these initial activities failed, so he turned to the Gentiles to whom he blatantly presented himself as free from *torah*-obligations of any sort, or even "weak" with respect to Jewish laws and customs that might become burdensome to those who were contemplating conversion.

Goaded forward perhaps by his belief that the resurrected Jesus was soon to return to assemble all members of his flock, Paul became willing to morph into whatever theological shape might resonate with his audience of the moment, becoming the preacher to whom each audience might be expected to respond best. He granted this flexibility to himself, as he explains, "in order that by any means I might win someone" (1 Cor 9:22). It is not difficult to guess what an average hearer might have thought if, after sitting in a *synagogue* and hearing Saul tout his *torah*-observant life as a Jew, the same person might visit a *church* and hear Paul bragging about his total freedom from the burdensome regulations and restrictions of *torah*.

It is astounding that Paul's Machiavellian morality and callous proclivity to deceive his audience by pretending to be someone other than his true self for the sole purpose of gaining a hearing should be applauded as "a fundamental and exemplary accommodation to people as and where he finds them" or a "principle of accommodation . . . so fundamental to life lived in the gospel."[15] What Paul did and bragged about doing fifty years before the composition of John was not gracious accommodation, but raw deceit.

15. Sampley, *First Letter to the Corinthians, New Interpreter's Bible* X 907–908. It is not difficult to imagine what might happen if a local rabbi were invited to address a Christian church congregation and seized the occasion as an opportunity to trash Christianity in the process of explaining how Judaism was far superior, perhaps by

It should not be surprising that Jews in different places found multiple reasons to want Paul excluded from appointing himself as the official Jewish service leader speaking publicly in a synagogue, along with any of his followers who aped his methods. Bart Ehrman notes correctly that "First-century Jews by and large rejected any idea that Jesus could be the messiah."[16] And then Ehrman attempts to tie this rejection to an established policy, speculating with no basis that once Christian Jews proved incapable of keeping "a low profile" in the synagogue, they were "no doubt rejected by the majority of the Jews and probably mocked and marginalized."[17] But there is no evidence that excluding Paul from speaking in a synagogue was part of an established policy.

As Ehrman sees it, the resulting tension caused Jews to become more antagonistic and Christians to heighten their efforts at evangelization. In his words, "these believers in Jesus became something more than a headache. Perhaps because of their persistent badgering[18] of the skeptical and their refusal to keep their views to themselves, or perhaps for some other unknown reason, this group of believers in Jesus was forced to leave the Jewish community."[19] Here Ehrman is making the mistake of failing to realize that refusing to allow someone to take over and dominate a service of worship and prayer is not the same thing as forcing them "to leave the Jewish community." His mistake demands a clear and fact-based response.

If the only thing that happened was that Christian Jews badgered believing Jews and were mocked in exchange, Ehrman's view would be a plausible description of a spat between two fourth-grade children. But the truth about the split between Jews and Christians is quite different from his simplistic and factually incorrect explanation.

---

explaining how circumcision or keeping kosher would make one a superior Christian. On the other hand, maybe Paul was saying only that one might well be both an observant Jew and a Christian, but that it is not necessary for Gentiles to become Jews first to be faithful followers of Jesus. It may not be fair to be dogmatic about either option. But he is specific in noting that he claimed his Jewishness only to Jews, and his Gentile-ness to other Gentiles. Professor Stephen Gunter opines in private correspondence that a less harsh judgement is possible if Paul is heard to say, "I am free to be observant or not to be observant, and still be a Jesus-follower. And so are you. The one does not entail the other."

16. Ehrman, *New Testament*, 150.

17. Ehrman, *New Testament*, 150.

18. "Persistent badgering" is not a bad description of the evangelization methods forced on Jews by Christians over the past 2,000 years. Ehrman should be applauded for recognizing it for what it always was/is.

19. Ehrman, *New Testament*, 150.

The missionary activities of Paul and other Christian missionaries were a major contributing factor to the gradually widening chasm between Jews and Christians in the interval between the death of Jesus and the composition of the Gospel of John. Because these activities must be understood in the context of first century Jewish customs of worship, a survey of these customs related to the split between Judaism and Christianity forms the basis for the next essay.

VI. Jewish and Christian Responses to Dissidents

The *Shemoneh 'Esreh*

As NOTED IN ESSAY V, it is impossible to understand the argument about Jews expelling believers from their synagogues without understanding the way in which synagogue services of worship were conducted.

Well before the time of Jesus, one of the important rituals celebrated during the ancient Shabbat-morning prayer service was the recitation of eighteen benedictions,[1] known by the Hebrew title *Shemoneh 'Esreh* ("Eighteen"). The significance of these eighteen as a series grew to such an extent that they ultimately constituted the central prayer in the liturgy of the synagogue and came to be called *Tefillah*, "Prayer." At the appropriate moment in the Shabbat morning service, congregations stood while the leader of the service, acting as the representative of the people, recited all eighteen benedictions.[2] After each benediction, the congregation responded with "Amen," signifying their approval and acceptance of all eighteen sentiments being expressed. Because worshipers stood throughout the recitation of all eighteen, the benedictions also came to be known as the *'Amidah*, the "standing" [prayer].

Partly because they derive from different historical periods, there is no way to know the original order of the Eighteen from their inception. The best reading of the available evidence has led most scholars to

---

1. The translation "benediction" for Hebrew *berakhah* (the lexical form of *birkat*) is only partially correct. The broader referential field of a *berakhah* is the intention to call to the attention of God a matter of importance to a worshiping congregation or individual. In most cases, divine attention results in a "blessing," while in other cases, an opposite divine response may be implied. The word "benediction" is the term that has come to be used among virtually all scholars.

2. In many modern congregations, the worshipers read the Eighteen silently first and then join the leader in a second recital aloud. It is difficult to know which tradition is earlier in origin.

conclude that the 'Amidah was set in its present order late in the first or early in the second century. The recital by the leader was given in three sections, grouped together as blessings numbered 1–3, 4–15, and 16–18.[3] In section one, worshipers paid homage to God, offering praise and thanksgiving for His mercy. Section two originally contained twelve petitions or requests underscoring the acknowledgement of the worshipers that all human needs were dependent on the beneficence of God alone. Section three returned once again to the theme of thanksgiving and the confidence of the worshipers that their petitions had been heard.

The *Birkat ha-Mînîm*

Politics also came into play in the way in which the *Shemoneh 'Esreh* was used in synagogue services. A nineteenth benediction not originally included in the 'Amidah played a separate role in Jewish worship as well. Its title was *birkat ha-mînîm* ("benediction against heretics"). Long *before* it was introduced into the 'Amidah, several groups viewed as heretical were named by this benediction. The list included the Samaritans, Gnostics, Boethusians,[4] and Sadducees.[5] The most noteworthy group in the list of heretics, the Sadducees, had been dominant in Jewish life when Jesus was alive, but they had begun losing political influence to the Pharisees gradually during the fifth, sixth, and seventh decades of the century. Ultimately, they lost all political power and influence in the wake of the Roman destruction of the Temple in the year 70 CE. Shortly afterward, at least twenty or more years before the insertion of the *birkat ha-mînîm* into the 'Amidah, the Pharisees made a new political deal with their Roman overlords, replacing the earlier pact that had given the Sadducees authority over the Temple that Rome had now destroyed along with its treasury.

Thus, well *after* the lifetime of Jesus but well *before* the writing of the Gospel of John, the Pharisees became the most influential and dominant Jewish party for the first time.[6]

By virtue of their enhanced political stature, the Pharisees also seized control of Temple worship. One way in which they celebrated their victory

3. See Appendix A.

4. A Jewish sect that shared multiple tenets with the Sadducees, including rejection of the doctrine of resurrection.

5. Christians were not on the list for the first several decades of its use in synagogue services.

6. The Pharisees did not become a "party" until the mid-first century at the earliest. Before that time, the term "Pharisee" identified a *method* of study, personal conduct including an emphasis on laws of cultic purity, and the interpretation of Scripture.

over their old political and theological opponents was by including multiple references in the *'Amidah* to the resurrection of the dead, a major doctrine denied by the Sadducees and not a part of official Temple worship as long as they had held power. With the Pharisees firmly in control, denial of the resurrection was deemed to be a "*mîn*," a heresy. "The Hebrew word *mîn* [singular of *mînîm*] has the basic meaning of 'species' and can denote any special or exceptional group—hence, all those who separate themselves from the way of the Torah, heretics."[7]

When the *'Amidah* was re-edited late in the first or early in the second century, several decades after the takeover by the Pharisees, an additional major change was introduced into the liturgy when the *birkat ha-mînîm* was inserted into the middle of the *'Amidah* as number twelve.[8]

Soon after its inclusion in the *'Amidah*, the *birkat ha-mînîm* became an important component of Jewish synagogue worship. It is impossible to reconstruct its original wording. Initially, the opening words were apparently the generic designation "Concerning the sectarians and the apostates" (*la-mînîm u-la-meshumadîm*) was changed at some unknown point to "and concerning the slanderers"[9] (*ve-la-malshinîm*). Among the various surviving versions of the remainder of the prayer, the wording of an unpublished copy from fourth or fifth century Palestine is the most blatant: "May there be no hope for apostates, may the arrogant kingdom be uprooted speedily in our era, and may the Christians and the sectarians perish instantly."[10]

To soften this harsh wording, some versions added, "Unless they return to Your covenant." Other versions removed the names of these specific enemies of Judaism (Sadducees, Samaritans, Gnostics, Christians, etc.) and inserted the generic phrase "all our enemies." Because of the number of possible variations, it is not surprising that David Abudarham, the fourteenth-century Spanish rabbi and authority on Jewish liturgy, could remark that even in his day no two congregations in the world recited the *'Amidah* with the same exact wording.[11]

As noted, for the Pharisees, holding the winning hand theologically was not the only issue involved. Their struggles for the right to both (a)

7. Elbogen, *Jewish Liturgy*, 31.

8. Although this additional *berakhah* brought the total number of benedictions to nineteen, the names *Shemoneh 'Esreh* ("Eighteen"), and the *'Amidah* ("standing") remained.

9. Or "speakers of evil."

10. Langer, *Cursing the Christians?* includes a comprehensive accounting of the hundreds of manuscripts that include part or all the prayer.

11. On the final page of his 14th century liturgy commentary, *Sefer Abudarham*. Cited in EJ under "Abudarham."

political leadership in Jewish life and (b) congregational leadership of *worship* in the Temple had been equally important. The Temple privileges disappeared in 70 CE when the Romans destroyed the Jerusalem Temple. At that time, Pharisaical influence over the rituals of worship shifted to local synagogues that were appearing in increasing numbers. At this point, the importance of the *birkat ha-mînîm* became evident, especially in the task of choosing leaders for synagogue worship. Simply put, the *birkat ha-mînîm* proved useful to the ruling Pharisees in a practical manner.

One benefit derived from the recitation of the entire *'Amidah* was its value in identifying people who held heretical views (inimical to traditional Judaism) that would disqualify them for leadership. By requiring a service leader to articulate nineteen affirmations of Jewish worship and belief, the *'Amidah* served above all else as a test that would ensure that anyone proposing to serve as a worship leader believed in the resurrection, in accordance with the teachings of the ruling Pharisees. Its generic wording also served to discern whether he might hold any other beliefs not acceptable to the new ruling party.

Various Jewish sources, all well past the time of John, make it clear how this was done. During the recitation of all nineteen parts of the *'Amidah*, it was quite common for a short phrase to be omitted inadvertently or for a tiny pronunciation error or two to creep into the reading by a service leader. 2,000 years ago, as is still the case today, such errors "were passed over with indulgence and in silence."[12] There was one exception: the service *leader* was not allowed any latitude in reciting the *birkat ha-mînîm*. Two later sources explain.

> If someone has made an error in any of the benedictions, he is not removed [from leadership]. But if he did so during the *birkat ha-mînîm*, he is removed; they suspect him of being a heretic.[13]
>
> If one passes before the ark [containing the Torah scrolls] and makes a mistake in any of the benedictions, he is not made to repeat it; but in the *birkat ha-mînîm* he must be made to repeat it [correctly] against his will. The reason he must repeat it

12. Elbogen, *Jewish Liturgy*, 32. Note also his citation of the Midrash from *Tanhuma* B., Leviticus, 2a.

13. *T.B. Berakhot* 29A. "Remove" here is not *legaresh* signifying a violent driving out of someone. It is the simpler word *lehaser*. And it clearly refers to the removal of someone as leader of the worship-service, not to his permanent expulsion from the synagogue or from the Jewish community. A fair comparison might be the removal of a Christian pastor whose theological views shift away from the established doctrines of his denomination and leave his congregants uncomfortable with his leadership.

is that, if he has in him any element of heresy, he will be cursing himself and the congregation will respond "amen."[14]

This is a clear explanation of the reason why any service leader who failed to recite this one specific benediction precisely and correctly would be *replaced as service leader*.

Following the destruction of the Jerusalem Temple in 70 CE, the importance of the synagogues that arose as local centers of worship cannot be overstated. In addition to service as the spiritual center for Jewish life, sanctuaries where large numbers of Jews gathered for worship also "provided excellent opportunities for disseminating propaganda."[15] It is plausible to assume that other early Jewish-Christian missionaries followed the lead of Paul and attempted to use the synagogue as a forum for preaching their new religion. To his credit, eminent Christian scholar Raymond Brown recognized that such actions had consequences: "Local synagogues at different times in different places no longer tolerated the presence of Christians. Gradually (early 2d century?) a 'blessing' formula (the *birkat ha-mînîm*) denouncing heretics or deviants of various sorts was understood to include Christians and much later to be specifically aimed at them."[16]

In other words, although Christians were not included in the earliest forms of the *birkat ha-mînîm*, the definition of heretical beliefs ultimately came to include the question of "whether he was inclined to Jewish Christianity or not. A Jewish Christian could not recite this prayer if he did not want to curse himself."[17] In addition, all worshipers sitting in the sanctuary were expected to respond to each benediction with an approving "Amen," and any individual failing to respond would be noticeable to other congregants. Heretics in the audience other than Christians would also be revealed, but the *birkat ha-mînîm* became the primary method by which the rabbis targeted a Christian who was posing as a Jew, hoping to take over and dominate the service exactly as Paul had done much earlier.

"Thus, Benediction 12 [*birkat ha-mînîm*] became a touchstone for the presence of Jewish Christians in the synagogue and for their participation in prayer. Unwilling to listen to this prayer on a daily basis, they left the synagogue."[18] Obviously, the recitation of the 'Amidah made sectarian Jews, apostates, Christians and others who had abandoned the teachings of the Torah uncomfortable. *That was its purpose!* But making uncomfortable a

---

14. See the late eighth or early ninth century CE work, *Midrash Tanhuma* B, Lev, 2a.

15. Elbogen, *Jewish Liturgy*, 32.

16. Brown, *Introduction*, 82.

17. Elbogen, *Jewish Liturgy*, 33.

18. Elbogen, *Jewish Liturgy*, 33.

person who denies the core beliefs of others with whom he is worshiping and removing him from leadership is a far cry from the hysterical claim of John that "the Jews" *expelled* Christians forcefully or violently.

Based on the available evidence, the idea that Jewish Christians left voluntarily is more believable than the idea that they were violently expelled. One example that leads to this inference involves Paul and his missionary partner Barnabas. They both became uncomfortable with the teachings of Judaism, and they clearly felt at home in the company of non-Jews who would allow them to exercise leadership in their services. Acts 13:42–48 appears to describe such a situation.

Forty years ago, Reuven Kimelman, Professor of Classical Rabbinic Literature at Brandeis University whose academic specialty was Jewish history, made a compelling case that John could not have known about incidents involving Jewish Christians that took place after Christianity was added to the list of heresies condemned by the *birkat ha-mînîm*.[19] Rather, the version of the *birkat ha-mînîm* that included the Christians was not installed in the 'Amidah until well after the beginning of the second century, not in time for it to have influenced John at all.

But Professor Martyn and other Christian scholars declined to accept the evidence brought forward by Professor Kimelman. In his search for a method by which "expulsion" must have occurred, Martyn continued his attempt to establish a link between the *birkat ha-mînîm* and John's contention that a policy of violent expulsion had been inaugurated already in the time of Jesus. Numerous other Christian scholars, ignoring Kimelman to follow Martyn, have assumed that the *birkat ha-mînîm* was created specifically to target Christians. This stance relieves Christianity of all culpability and places total blame for the split between Judaism and Christianity squarely on the shoulders of unbelieving Jews. Worse still, its misleading title ("Expulsion") implies that violence was the regnant method by which evil Jews acted to force the split.[20]

19. Kimelman, "Birkat Ha-Minim."

20. To his credit, Raymond Brown (*Introduction*, 82), did not fall into this error, but he noted that "the idea that it was a universal Jewish decree against Christians is almost certainly wrong." Brown also understood that the *birkat ha-mînîm* had been in place for several years, originally referring to other so-called heretical groups before it was expanded to include Christians.

What Really Happened?

Observant Jews defended their right to worship in the manner they believed appropriate by resisting ex-Jews (like Paul and doubtless many others) who wanted to continue pretending to be Jews even after they no longer were willing to follow the teachings of Judaism, specifically the Jewish belief in the absolute oneness of God. However, once Christian believers had been targeted by the *birkat ha-mînîm*, the evidence cited above shows clearly that a person who purposefully misread the *birkat ha-mînîm* would be removed as a *leader* of the service, not that he would have been *expelled* violently from the synagogue and the Jewish *community* against his will. "As long as a person did not consider himself a *min* the benediction would be irrelevant and his participation in synagogue life would continue."[21]

Even the traditionalist Raymond Brown admitted that the *birkat ha-mînîm* simply made it clear that "they were no longer Jews."[22] In fact, if hearing this benediction prompted the realization that they were no longer Jews, their voluntary decision to abandon the Judaism they no longer were willing to practice would have been a natural and honorable response.

But once again, Brown took an additional and unwarranted step, insisting that the decision to leave *licit* Judaism "created legal problems" for Jewish Christians with Rome. He insisted further that this made Jews who had remained true to Judaism guilty of "indirect participation in executions through expulsion from synagogues."[23]

This ridiculous charge is repugnant, especially because Rome had a valid reason to be suspicious of Christianity. Jesus had been convicted of insurrection under Roman law. His "crime" in Roman eyes was his claim to be "the king of the Jews" (John 19:19) and Rome surely thought that putting him to death on a cross had ended any threat he might have posed. But despite his death, his followers began to organize a religion dedicated to worshiping him as a living deity. Ex-Jews who became vulnerable to persecution under Roman law because they had voluntarily chosen to create this new, *illicit* religion might be admired for the courage of their convictions. Conversely, they also could be faulted for their failure to respect Roman

---

21. Katz, "Issues in the Separation of Judaism and Christianity," 74. It is not unheard of for an agnostic or even an atheist Jew to participate in synagogue life without fearing excommunication (or violent expulsion!). In such a case as well, it would not be proper for the non-traditional member to be allowed to lead/co-opt a service for the purpose of espousing his or her view of God that does not respect the wording of a traditional liturgy practiced by the congregation.

22. Brown, *Community*, 43.

23. Brown, *Community*, 43.

law. But charging loyal Jews who wanted to protect their own sanctuaries with responsibility for the legal troubles faced by Jews who had abandoned Judaism to embrace Christianity is beneath contempt.

Not surprisingly, it soon became apparent that this impulse to protect one's sanctuary manifested itself within the nascent *Christian* community as well.

New Enemies of the Johannine Community

Once the Gospel of John was published, the idea that "the Jews" had killed Jesus was firmly established in the minds of those who would soon comprise the church. But the issue of what to believe about Jesus was not yet fully developed.

What ultimately became the standard Christian view began with three short works written in the opening decade of the second century—First, Second, and Third John. In them, the theological perspective of Jesus that the Gospel of John had portrayed in seminal form was enhanced. All three short letters were probably written by a single anonymous author. He does not identify himself in First John, while Second and Third John refer to him only by his title, "the elder" (*ho presbyteros*), rather than his name. All three epistles appear to be addressing what scholars have come to call the "Johannine Community."

But there is one major difference between the three epistles and the Gospel. The author of First John was clearly concerned with incidents that were occurring at the time of his writing as the second century dawned. By contrast, as has been shown repeatedly, the author of the Gospel of John retrojected to the time of Jesus in the first one-third of the first century incidents that illustrate his sense of conflict with "the Jews" of his day (ca. 90 to 100 CE). This means that "I John makes most sense if understood as written in a period following the appearance of the Gospel, when the struggle with the synagogue and 'the Jews' was no longer a major issue."[24] By the dawn of the second century CE, Jews had become a smaller minority within the young Christian community, and they posed a far less serious threat than that portrayed in John.

But if the troubles with Jews had ceased to be a significant factor within Christianity by the time of First John, if they were "no longer a major issue," as Brown alleged, it seems fair to ask why the gospel writer had gone to such lengths to assure the much later Johannine community that whatever troubles they faced were directly traceable to "the Pharisees"

24. Brown, *Introduction*, 383.

("the Jews") and their opposition to Jesus himself seventy years earlier. Other than the obvious anti-Jewish feelings of John, no answer to this question has been proffered.

Unlike "John" (the gospel author), the author of First John did not perceive "the Jews" to be a major problem for his Johannine Christian readers this long after the death of Jesus. But all was not well within the young Christian Church as the second century dawned. The largest of the three Johannine letters relates sorrowfully that the addressees of the epistles of John had suffered a theological controversy so severe that it had led to a split in the congregation: "They have left us" (1 John 2:19).

It is impossible to identify these secessionists with certainty, but the general nature of their religious views may be intuited by examining the way in which First John opposes them. By the beginning of the second century, two strains of thought had begun to appear in Christianity, either of which might plausibly represent the kinds of ideas being refuted by "the Elder" writing First John. *Gnosticism* is the term that came to signify a wide range of ideas, all holding in common the belief that secret knowledge (*gnōsis*) was available only to insiders or believers in a faith system.[25] All branches of Gnosticism viewed the world in dualistic terms in which spirit was pure or good, while physical matter was evil.

A partial spinoff of Gnosticism was *Docetism*. Starting from the premise that God (pure spirit) could not have a human body and struggling with the possibility that Jesus might have been divine, some early Christians developed the view that Jesus could not in fact have been born as a normal person who inhabited a physical (and therefore evil) body. To explain the apparent physical presence of the human Jesus in the evil world of matter, Docetists argued that Jesus had only "appeared" to have a flesh and blood body as an accommodation to humanity, i.e., as a way for God to communicate with humans.[26]

The theory that the secessionists in First John were early or proto-Gnostics or Docetists helps explain why second century proto-orthodox church theologians like Ignatius of Antioch[27] (died 110 CE), Polycarp (died ca. 156 CE),[28] and Bishop Serapion of Antioch (died 203 CE) became so alarmed

---

25. The "knowledge" being referenced was not inferential or intellectual, but some form of direct experience or intuition.

26. Cf. the Greek word *dokein*, "to seem," "to appear."

27. Ignatius was believed in Church tradition to have been a disciple of the Apostle John who, also according to early church tradition, authored the gospel and the three epistles.

28. Perhaps the strongest hint that the secessionists in I John might have been proto-docetic comes from Polycarp's "Letter to the Philippians" (7:1), where Polycarp, attacks

in the years following the publication of the Synoptic Gospels and John. All three of these early church fathers placed great emphasis on the very real physical atoning death of Jesus and none of them could accept the idea that the life and death of Jesus had merely *appeared* to be real. To the contrary, they championed the theological position that was destined to triumph in early (second century) Christianity and beyond: Jesus *was* real, had a real body, shed real blood that provided real atonement, died an actual death, and experienced an actual bodily resurrection.

When the author of First John accused the secessionists of having refused to acknowledge that Jesus had come "in the flesh," i.e., not merely in human *form* but fully human in every aspect (4:2), he was illustrating why he believed that "they were not part of us" (2:19b). The final phrase of this statement is virtually the same thing John the son of Zebedee ("Son of Thunder") had said decades earlier about the unfortunate non-member of the apostles who was attempting to cast out demons in the name of Jesus: "he was not one of us" (Mark 9:38).[29]

In Mark it had been the apostles ("good guys") who refused to accept the participation of the man who was not part of their group ("bad guy").[30] In First John, it was the separatists ("bad guys") who voluntarily made the decision to leave the Johannine group of those who were dedicated to the preservation of what they believed to be the true faith ("good guys").

Before leaving this concept of separation over a theological dispute, it should be recalled that in the Fourth Gospel, the persons held responsible by John for the rift with Christianity are easily recognized: "the Jews!" That John deemed "the Jews" to be bad is illustrated by his specious claim that they violently expelled (*ekballō*) the believers, the obvious good guys. Thus, clearly the perception of who was "good" and who was "bad," as well as who should leave and who should remain, changed as the ideology being propagated shifted. The fact that early Christendom was never without a perceived enemy is the one thing that remained unchanged

It is understandable that the author of First John appeared to be saddened by the theological rupture that had split his congregation. About theological splits and their consequences, Ehrman writes that the experience of leaving Judaism, which he persists in describing as being "expelled," was an emotionally wrenching experience separating believers in Jesus "from the Jewish community, the community, presumably, of their families

as an "antichrist" any person who "does not confess that Jesus Christ has come in the flesh," a close parallel to 1 John 4:2–3. His letter is enough later than 1 John to have allowed the idea of Docetism to produce a more structured and highly developed form.

29. Luke (9:49) is the only other gospel that records this incident.

30. Although Jesus rebukes John for his intolerance.

and friends and neighbors, in which they had worshipped God and had fellowship with one another."[31]

Obviously, Ehrman cannot free himself from the erroneous premise of a violent expulsion (*ekballō*) that is to be blamed completely on "the Jews." And he refuses to admit the wisdom of removing from leadership an individual who no longer believes in the validity of the prayers he is leading in worship. Worse still is Ehrman's inability to grasp the fact that relieving someone of his role as *service leader* is not the same thing as expelling him from the Jewish *community*. Ehrman also declines to consider the idea that once a dissident no longer believes in the values of the group, fellowship with other worshipers in that group is no longer possible.

Ehrman concludes that the experience which John describes was so traumatic that it created among Johannine Christians a "fortress mentality."[32] But the whining historical revisionism of John is undermined by all available evidence and cannot be taken seriously. The "us against the world" mentality is apparent in both the Fourth Gospel and First John. In both books, the words and actions of persons whose views differ from those of the Johannine believers were being described by a Christian author who was their avowed enemy. And in each case the enemies were portrayed in the worst possible light.

It is impossible to know whether the Johannine Community secessionists were Gnostics, Docetists, or part of some other group that held similar views unacceptable to the author of First John.[33] But he had no hesitation in launching a blistering attack on those with whom he disagreed. Those who had left *his* group were "liars" and "antichrists" (1 John 2:18–22), they failed to love other Christians, and they broke the commandments of God in the process of engaging in a lifestyle of sinfulness (1 John 3:11–24). The author of First John (3:8) also tied the secessionists of his day to "the devil" (*diabolos*) in a manner closely akin to the way in

31. Ehrman, *New Testament*, 151. He refers to but does not cite sociologists who "studied a number of religious communities that have been expelled from larger social groups and forced to carry on their communal activities on their own." He offers no comment about the potential emotional and social impact of voluntarily abandoning a religious community in search of a better one.

32. Ehrman, *New Testament*, 159.

33. Technically, of course, the development of Gnosticism and Docetism can be documented only at some time later than the date of the Johannine epistles. But the description given in First John can be interpreted as the pre-cursor of what would shortly become a form of one of these two belief sets that the Roman Catholic Church labeled as heresy. Burkett (*Introduction*, 453) is confident enough to state that the three Johannine epistles "reflect a conflict between two groups within the church, one Proto-Orthodox and one docetic." There is no reason to doubt his judgment on the point.

which the Gospel of John 8:44 had tagged "the Jews" as children "from your father the devil" (*ek tou patros tou diabolou*).

All these charges are remarkably like the accusations leveled against "the Jews" who had been identified as the chief opponents of Jesus in the Gospel of John. Throughout John, the evil Jewish loyalists are accused of violence and perfidy, and the innocent separatists are the victims. In the short letter of First John, the Christian loyalists are the faithful and only authentic believers, and the separatists have become representatives of the devil.

"You can never rely on an enemy's reports for a fair and disinterested presentation."[34] Thus, in reading the indictments by the First John author, one learns more about him than about the Docetists or whatever other kind of heretics the author deemed the secessionists to be. It is also fair to note that the negative characterization of the secessionists in the epistles conveys as little about their true theology, culture, and customs as the Gospel of John does about the regnant legal system and customs of "the Jews" during the lifetime of Jesus. When the author of First John depicts his opponents in so similar a fashion as the characterization of "the Jews" found in the earlier Gospel of John—liars, unloving, enemies of God, wrong about the definition of Jesus, devils—it becomes clear that here was a man who shared a basic tenet that had guided the author of the gospel: brook no disagreement, and never back down from a knife fight. What is more, his characterizations of his opponents follow the pattern originally seen in the Gospel of John, including literary style, and even specific wording. Once "the Jews" were replaced in the epistle by a different enemy group, the kind of negativity aimed against Jews by John was aimed at the new foes in First John.

First John and the Christian Response to "Heretics"

Although the similarity between the responses to theological differences of the two communities is remarkable, modern NT scholars seldom bother to compare the *expulsion* claims of the Gospel of John with the attitude toward the internal schism that developed in the Johannine community. Thus, virtually no attention has been focused on the illogicality of the radically different interpretation of two similar incidents, one reported in "John" and the other lamented in First John by "The Elder." Instead, the standard Christian view about the rights of worshippers effortlessly made a 180-degree turn when the congregation involved was Christian rather than Jewish. Jews were concerned about those whose ideas about monotheism and other norms of acceptable Jewish behavior were incompatible with Judaism. When Johannine

34. Ehrman, *Lost Christianities*, 104. This admission is telling.

Christians became worried about those whose Christology was not high enough for their standards, they insisted on public wording that was designed to function very much like the *birkat ha-mînîm*.

In his comments about the use of the word "confession" in First and Second John, Raymond Brown wholeheartedly approved the decision of the Johannine community to demand a *public* confession from worshippers, and to insist that such a demand was necessary because only the position of Johannine Christianity regarding the incarnation of Jesus was correct (1 John 4:2; 2 John 7).[35] This is nothing less than a Christian *birkat ha-mînîm*. The author of First John deemed a docetic view of Jesus so unacceptable that he flung out wild accusations that contributed to, if they did not cause, a rupture of the congregation. Not satisfied with challenging the Christology of those with whom he disagreed, he could not resist the temptation to label them liars, diabolic, lacking collegiality, and disobedient to church law, etc.

As noted above, Brown had no hesitation in accusing *Jews* of having violently expelled Jesus followers from synagogues and thereby contributing to the murder of those with whom they disagreed theologically. But the *Christian* actions of the Johannine community warranted not a single word of disapproval. To the contrary, Brown argued that First John simply indicates that "the author is trying to weed out his opponents."[36] Indeed! The Christian author was surely motivated by his "presiding concern for Christian integrity,"[37] in much the same manner that Torah-observant Jews were concerned for Jewish integrity. But for the authors of the Fourth Gospel and of First John, as well as for modern Christian scholars like Martyn, Brown, Ehrman, and others, concern for theological "integrity" is acceptable only when Christian integrity is involved. This same concern is considered violent *expulsion* only when Jews employ it.

Final Thoughts About Expulsion

One perplexing aspect of this inner-Christian controversy is that Docetists might have been taking at least one aspect of Johannine theology quite seriously. The proto-orthodox demand that the Docetists accept the *physical* reality of the humanity of Jesus was quite at odds with one aspect of the nature of the Logos introduced in the opening verses of John. According to John 4:24, "God is a spirit." If God is a spirit, and if "the Logos became flesh" (John 1:14),

---

35. Brown, *Epistles of John*, 504.

36. Brown, *Community*, 123.

37. This is the felicitous phrase of Black, *The First, Second, and Third Letters of John*, NIB XII: 386.

one might well wonder how "the Logos was God" (John 1:1–2). In short, here the Docetists were confronted with two absolute statements of "John" that contradict each other, and it is easy to imagine that Docetists might have found it difficult to meld these two Johannine tenets of belief about Jesus into a single unified doctrine. When they could not do so to the satisfaction of First John, their variation from the accepted Johannine version of Jesus-ology drew the wrath of the community leader.

Significantly, there is no hint that proto-orthodox Johannine Christians used violence to expel those who argued against what they believed to be *the* correct expression of faith in Jesus. First John 2:19 simply notes that, "they have gone out from us because they were not part of us." To the contrary, the whining of "John" about Jewish attempts "to weed out *their* opponents," was retrojected back some sixty to seventy years to create the impression that the root of the persistent problem between Jews and Christians had begun as opposition aimed directly at Jesus himself. And John assures his audience that the nature of that early opposition was violent expulsion.

Modern readers of the Fourth Gospel must recognize the fact that John offered no credible evidence to sustain the idea that violent expulsion was the method chosen by Jews against proto-Christians either during the lifetime of Jesus or any other time after his death. In fact, the prime example of "expulsion" using the violent term *ekballō* offered in John 9:34 lacks credibility altogether, and all the Johannine uses of the hybrid word "out-of-the-synagogue" in John chapters 9, 12, and 14 are equally bereft of any hint of violence. It is far more plausible to assert that Jews who decided to become Christians abandoned their Jewish faith because the sanctuaries in which they worshiped were led by Jews whose standards of Jewish belief surpassed theirs. Because these loyal Jewish members decried as heresy the radical belief in a divine Jesus that was inimical with their fealty to the one who alone is God, their services included affirmations of faith that the dissidents could no longer affirm.

In truth, evidence of violence against theological opponents perpetrated by either "the Jews" or the Johannine Christians is non-existent. And it is plausible to believe that the two cases were quite similar. Ex-Jews who became Christian were no longer at ease with basic Jewish teachings, so they sought to form their own religious community elsewhere. Docetic Christians who could not affirm Johannine Christology forsook the Johannine community. And these two controversies were occurring in the same general era.[38] It is not difficult to imagine why the dissidents in both cases felt uncomfortable in an environment that held fast to beliefs they no longer shared. Abandoning the

---

38. Late in the first century CE — early in the second.

old religion for the freedom to affirm publicly their beliefs about a new and different religion was the only honorable response.

Modern Christian scholars are correct to understand and interpret as reasonable the impulse to defend the right of an early Christian community to worship in peace without being verbally and emotionally assaulted in their own sanctuary by people who had come to deny the basic doctrine of their faith. Surely the same level of understanding for which these scholars plead in the case of the Johannine community should be accorded to followers of all faiths. That such an understanding is routinely withheld in the case of *Jewish* worshipers is to be lamented. By their inability to recognize the inconsistencies and prejudice in their sources, and by their failure to acknowledge the pain thus inflicted on Jews, multiple modern interpreters of John continue in the twenty-first century to propagate the same prejudice against Judaism that the late first century "John" promoted among his contemporaries.

VII. John and the Recent History of Anti-Semitism

Introduction

THE EMINENT CATHOLIC SCHOLAR Raymond Brown (1928–1998), whose work has been cited frequently in earlier essays, was "the most influential American New Testament scholar of the twentieth century."[1] His interpretations and theoretical reconstructions of John's gospel have influenced two entire generations of NT scholars, including those whose current works on John are the best known and most widely shared. It is not surprising that some of Father Brown's views shifted over the period of almost fifty years during which he wrote about John. These shifts involved eight crucial issues that are still being debated by current NT scholars. Brown's answers to these crucial eight and their continuing influence on current scholars are the focus of this essay.

To begin, it is necessary to trace what one scholar has called Brown's changing views about the anti-Judaism in John from "apologia[2] to apology," or what might be called more broadly, "The Metamorphosis of Raymond Brown." This lengthy metamorphosis may be illustrated by the way in which Brown's views changed regarding the following issues:

Who are "the Jews" in John?

Who does John believe killed Jesus?

"What Crucified Jesus?"

Are modern liberal scholars guilty of crucifixion revisionism?

Did Jews murder not only Jesus, but multitudes of his followers?

1. See the extended discussion of Brown's influence by R. Alan Culpepper, "Preaching," 49–50.

2. "Apologia" is the Greek word describing a formal defense of an academic or philosophical position.

What does "God so Loved the World" mean?

Brown's Brand of anti-Judaism

The Metamorphosis of Raymond Brown

Who are "the Jews" in John?

Assigning multiple meanings to a single phrase like "the Jews" yields a theo-ry that is difficult to follow for anyone approaching the Gospel of John with the intention of taking its words at face value. Raymond Brown became the foremost proponent of assigning multiple meanings to "the Jews" depend-ing upon real or perceived contextual shifts in the gospel narratives. Under the influence of Brown, current NT scholars remain determined to interpret the phrase "the Jews" in the Fourth Gospel by carving it into four or five (or seven!) different specific references. This assignment of multiple specific meanings to "the Jews" depending upon contextual shifts in the narrative has become the best example of overkill expended in efforts to combat the obviously anti-Jewish attitudes in John.

Sonya Cronin has argued that Brown's treatment of "the Jews" in John involved a slow and lengthy metamorphosis "from apologia to apology."[3] But although Cronin's masterful study is helpful in tracing Brown's move-ment over the decades from explaining away John's anti-Judaism to apolo-gizing for it, and even though his laudable growth over almost fifty years involving multiple publications is explained precisely and accurately, an analysis of Cronin's survey reveals the fact that Brown's metamorphosis was never completed.[4]

In his earliest (1960) book on the Fourth Gospel,[5] Brown showed no awareness of any anti-Jewish bias in John, and he explained the obviously negative uses of "the Jews" as applicable only to "hostile Jerusalem authori-ties." In the first volume of his 1966 *Anchor Bible* commentary on John, Brown rolled out his thesis of *multiple* meanings of "the Jews." He also acknowledged that the gospel opinion of "the Jews" reflected John's own late first century era rather than furnishing an accurate portrayal of the lifetime of Jesus. Professor Alan Culpepper correctly notes Cronin's obser-vation that in a further step, the second volume of Brown's commentary in

---

3. Cronin, *Raymond Brown.*

4. The following paragraphs follow closely Alan Culpepper's treatment of Cronin's survey in "Preaching," 49–50.

5. *The Gospel of John and the Johannine Epistles.*

1970 exhibits "subtle" shifts in Brown's thinking moving closer to an honest appraisal of the anti-Judaism of John.[6]

By 1979, in *The Community of the Beloved Disciple*, Brown, "speculated that the use of the term 'the Jews' . . . originated with Samaritan converts."[7] This view was designed to show that "the Jews" simply did not mean *all* Jews. In this same work, Brown once again acknowledged that John reflects a late first century situation, but he returned to his insistence that by reading John on multiple layers, he was not disabused of his determination to demonstrate that the Fourth Gospel includes "limited [but not absent] means for reconstructing the ministry and message of the historical Jesus."[8]

If true, this insistence also must mean that John's Gospel was deemed to be at least partially accurate in blaming "the Jews" as the originators of obstinate resistance to Jesus, beginning in Jesus' own lifetime. Anxious to support the modern Catholic view of Jesus, Brown began to lobby for the kind of Christology he was certain "John" himself advocated. But he did not acknowledge that the Catholic Christology he championed included patently post-Johannine development that was more ecclesiastical than biblical. Although Cronin does not connect the dots at this juncture, accepting as even partially true the idea that "the Jews" accused Jesus of blasphemy, and a god complex, etc., all the while plotting his murder, was surely a step backwards by Brown.

Who Killed Jesus?

Another step backwards was Brown's stubborn insistence that "the Jews" were heavily involved in the death of Jesus, a view espoused both in his massive 1994 *Death of the Messiah* and his 1997 *Introduction to the New Testament*. Surprisingly, he found compelling the statement of Paul in First Thessalonians 2:13–16 that it was "the Jews who killed the Lord Jesus," and saw this statement, which he did not doubt was genuinely Pauline, as "a very early, major refutation of the revisionist theory that the Romans were almost exclusively responsible for Jesus' death."[9] This stance alerts the reader that even late in his career, only one year before his death, Brown continued to accept selected (but not all) NT passages as reliable and historically factual. Accordingly, his stance regarding the death of Jesus relied heavily on a single Pauline verse that

6. Culpepper, "Preaching," 50.

7. Culpepper, "Preaching," 50. Here Culpepper is summarizing his review of Cronin in *RBL*, 2016.

8. Brown, *Community*, 17.

9. Brown, *Introduction*, 463.

supported his theories. This practice of selective literalism seriously weakened Brown's treatment of John, "the Jews," and anti-Judaism.

Although John is at pains to nominate the Pharisees as the quintessential opponents of Jesus, they are not mentioned at all in the Passion narratives of Mark and Luke, and only once in that of Matthew.[10] And given the dominance of the Sanhedrin by the Sadducees in the first third of the first century CE, Professor Brown was partially correct to note that it was, "quite likely that Jewish Temple and Sanhedrin authorities were seriously involved in the death of Jesus and handed him over to the Romans who executed him."[11] This statement contradicts both Paul's Thessalonian assertion that indicts "the Jews" for the death of Jesus and makes no mention of Rome. It also undermines Brown's attempt to define Roman involvement in the crucifixion as historical "revision."

Handing Jesus over to Pilate is one thing, but it is remarkable to see that to approve the Pauline accusation cited above, Brown simply ignored the blunt statement that John himself attributed to "the Jews" who had remanded Jesus to the Roman authority for trial: "It is not legal for us to put anyone to death." This statement from John (18:31), the author whom Brown was attempting to interpret, is an admission that the Jews did not kill Jesus if for no reason other than that they could not. Thus, Roman legal responsibility is a simple historical fact that is evident from a reading of John standing alone. But even the meaningless phrase "seriously involved" with respect to the Jews does not indicate that Brown was backing away from his endorsement of Paul on the point.

Apart from Paul, John was also desperate to pin the death of Jesus on "the Jews." Rather than narrating a straightforward account of a popular Jewish teacher being put to death by Rome because Rome feared his popularity might bubble over into rebellion, John takes a different tack. On the one hand, he goes to great lengths to portray Pilate as reasonable. According to John, Pilate pled repeatedly with the Jews to show mercy to Jesus, assuring them three times that, "I find no basis for a charge against him" (John 18:38; 19:4, 19:6). On the other hand, "the Jews" are depicted by John as screaming the word "crucify" three times (19:6, 6, 15), choosing the brigand Barabbas over Jesus (18:40), and threatening to tattle to Caesar unless Pilate caved to their demands (19:12). This hand-over of Barabbas is linked by John to a Roman custom of releasing a Jewish prisoner at Passover (John 18:39), for which there is no evidence in any Roman historical source.

10. Cook, *New Testament*, 45–46, has argued that since "Scribes" and "Pharisees" are equivalent terms, and since scribes *are* present in the Passion narrative of Mark, the omission of the specific term "Pharisees" means very little.

11. Brown, *Introduction*, 166.

But Brown was not discouraged: "we think that the evidence points, at least, to the historicity of the release of a guerrilla warrior named Barabbas at the time when Jesus was condemned." But because he was unable to offer any credible evidence of such a custom, Brown was forced to admit his real reason: "Otherwise it is too difficult to explain why the story was invented and how it found its way independently into diverse pre-Gospel traditions"[12] To the contrary, (a) insistence on a multi-year plot by "the Jews" determined to kill Jesus with no basis in fact or in Jewish law, (b) patently false claims of a policy of "expulsion" launched against "the Jews" in the lifetime of Jesus, and (c) the jumbling together of snippets of ideas from disparate sources all reveal that John was an author who did not hesitate to create his own set of "alternative facts" with no supporting evidence.

The gospel record is also clear that because Pilate found the Jewish charges against Jesus unconvincing, he did not base his decision on anything remotely theological or distinctively Jewish. In other words, the Jews may have tried to get Jesus killed, but their accusations failed to convince Pilate, who was flummoxed by the whole incident. It is almost amusing to hear Pilate, asked to settle a theological spat between Jews, respond in total frustration, "Am I a Jew?" (John 18:35). Apparently, the cacophonous accusations against Jesus of which John accuses "the Jews" either failed to reach Pilate's ears, or they made no sense even to a non-Jewish pagan.

"What Crucified Jesus?"

Almost twenty-five years ago, Professor Ellis Rivkin proposed a theory that is far more plausible than the special pleadings of Brown.[13] To maintain *pax Romana*, the Romans regularly demanded the crucifixion of public figures popular enough to hint at the *potential* for making trouble. Pilate must have realized that a popular teacher like Jesus, who had been drawing large crowds, might prove to be a danger. Professor Rivkin viewed Jesus as a magnetic man of eloquence and miracles, and he argued that such a person potentially posed an enormous threat to the Roman authorities. Indeed, Rivkin was convinced that the fate of Jesus had become inevitable from the moment that his popularity as a teacher and healer began to spread. This Roman policy fits well with the idea that what a few Jewish eggheads happened to think of Jesus' theology played no role in the mind of the Roman Procurator. Pilate simply ignored the hysterical claim that Jesus should be killed for standing

---

12. Brown, *Gospel According to John XIII-XXI*, 871–2.
13. Rivkin, *What Crucified Jesus?*

on the wrong side of an inner-Jewish theological debate and had him killed to protect Roman sovereignty.

In other words, Pilate easily found a cause for crucifying Jesus that had nothing to do with the way in which a few Jewish scholars might have viewed his theology. In his Roman eyes, the crime of Jesus was the seditious act of drawing on his popularity to set himself up as a *king* in opposition to the Caesar. This is the significance of John 19:19 and Pilate's order to append to the cross the inscription, "THE KING OF THE JEWS."

Although John first asserts that Jesus was handed over to the Jews after Pilate had sentenced him, he corrects himself almost at once to note that, "The soldiers took charge of Jesus" (John 19:16). In sum, a Roman procurator trumped up a fake *criminal* charge against Jesus, that same Roman sentenced him to be crucified, Roman soldiers carried out the dirty deed, and at the end, it was a Roman soldier who pierced his side to verify his actual death (John 19:34). Based on these Johannine texts alone, it is intellectually insulting for the world's foremost John specialist to have labelled the idea of Roman responsibility for the death of Jesus "the revisionist theory."

Crucifixion Revisionism

The true "revisionist" theory of the crucifixion is an integral part of the little known "Gospel of Peter." In the mid-second century, this non-canonical gospel presented a distinctly docetic point of view via a narrative that described Herod Antipas delivering Jesus over to the Jews, who did the actual crucifixion. As Professor Delbert Burkett notes, "the Gospel [of Peter] thus represents a growing tendency in early Christianity to shift the responsibility for Jesus' death away from the Romans onto the Jews."[14] In other words, Brown had the historical revisionism backwards.

The sad fact is that generations of Christians have bought into the claim of the Jewish crucifixion of Jesus. Among early Christian sermons based on John, Jews who were not yet born when Jesus was crucified still were being blamed for his death.[15] Pontius Pilate is the person who alone issued the legal order of crucifixion. Yet even he is not a candidate to replace "the Jews" as the murderer of Jesus. Nor have "the Romans" ever been vilified for their role. For the past 2,000 years, few Christians have known or cared that what the church has taught them to believe about the death of Jesus is contradicted in the beloved *canonical* Gospel of John (as just seen

---

14. Burkett, *Introduction*, 239.

15. See Appendix D.

above), but wholeheartedly supported by a book (*Gospel of Peter*) that the Church *refused to canonize* and left out of its official Bible.

It is certainly plausible to believe that the small and élite Jewish party of the Sadducees, fearful of losing their privileged status as trustees of the Temple, *backed* the idea of doing away with Jesus. Josephus noted that Pilate condemned Jesus to the cross "upon indictment of the first ranking men among us,"[16] and he clearly was referring to the Sadducees. Yet when Paul indicts "the Jews" for having murdered Jesus, it is not possible to explain away the plain meaning of his words by assuming that he too, like Brown and his followers, imagined multiple meanings of the simple phrase, "the Jews." Thus, in First Thessalonians 2:13–16 cited above, Paul did not say that *only* the Sadducees were responsible for murdering Jesus. And even if the argument is made that Paul meant to indict only one small group of Jews, such an understanding of "the Jews" is certainly not all that the early Church Fathers believed.

To the contrary, at the dawn of the second century CE, blaming the Jews directly for the killing of God (sic!) became a prominent feature of post NT preaching and writing. These sermons and letters were not carefully nuanced to speak about only the "first ranking men." Instead, they were blazing indictments of every Jew alive during the life of Jesus, and most of these early post-NT sermons expanded their indictments to include all Jews alive in their own day as well.[17] Nor is it possible to overlook evidence of the personal theological convictions of numerous NT scholars in the matter when their treatment of the issue in the Fourth Gospel is examined. So, it is not surprising that Brown plainly relied on his twentieth century Roman Catholic ideology, a single Pauline phrase, and the latest and most anti-Jewish of all four gospels (John) to inform his position. In the final analysis, Brown never atoned for fifty years not only of denial and avoidance but also his blatant espousal of the anti-Jewish rhetoric in John's Gospel.

Three points are important about Jewish involvement in the crucifixion of Jesus.

First, the opposition to Jesus by the Sadducees was grounded in politics and money, rather than in theology. Their fear was that if Jesus continued to gain popularity and followers, "the Romans will come and destroy both our holy place and our nation" (John 11:48). That "place" was the Temple,

---

16. *Antiquities of the Jews* 18.3.3; # 64). This citation is part of a longer section that has been considered spurious by virtually all scholars for more than a century. See Schürer, *History of the Jewish People*, 143–149.

17. Appendix D includes only a tiny sampling of early Church anti-Jewish sermons and writings. They originate in the period during which the stage was set for centuries of anti-Jewish rhetoric to follow.

control over which the Romans had granted to the Sadducees as the élite party in Judea because the Sadducees had confidently assured Rome of their ability to keep the masses under control. Management of the Temple also included control of the annual Temple tax sent to Jerusalem by Jews around the world. And the deal between Rome and the Sadducees also included the ability to choose the "high priest," a purely political choice often made in favor of the man who paid the largest bribe to Rome. This provision resulted in numerous high priests who did not meet the Jewish legal qualifications for the position. These "authorities," or "first ranking men," had a lot to lose if the crowds following Jesus swelled to a size large enough to become unruly, or if worse, they might demand to make him their king.[18]

A second point is equally important. The Sadducees were not "the Jews," any more than the College of Cardinals and "the Christians" are one and the same. Jewish literature does not refer to the Sadducees as the "the Jews" in the way that John used "the Pharisees" to refer to all Jews. During the lifetime of Jesus, the Sadducees were at best the élite 1 percent. And by the time of John's writing, the Sadducees had disappeared from the political landscape.

Third, the melodramatic portrayals of the Synoptic Passion narratives blur the lines of precision about a Jewish trial, accusations brought by the political partners of Rome (Sadducees), a Roman trial, and Roman execution by crucifixion on a charge of sedition. The persistent insistence that all Jews were (and remain) complicit in, fully comfortable with, and ultimately responsible for the death of Jesus has resulted in horrific damage done to successive generations of Jews by Christian readers of the gospels.

It was this viewpoint that has allowed conspiracy theories like the desecration of the host[19] or the "Blood Libel"[20] to flourish among medieval European Christian congregations. The idea that Jews killed God (Jesus!) is the charge most often repeated to fuel a process of discrimination and death for Jews that has thus far continued for two millennia. Brown's refusal to condemn outright those passages in John describing even the Jews in John who "believed" as nonetheless part of the intent-to-murder crowd

18. A possibility that John 6:15 raises candidly.

19. The charge that Jews would break into churches, steal Eucharistic wafers, stab them, and torture them, to satisfy their urge to witness Jesus suffer. Catholic Christians, who partook of the communion wafer ("Host") believed that, although their external physical characteristics did not morph into human flesh, yet a miraculous transformation occurred, turning them into the body of Jesus. No one seemed to notice that Jews never believed in the possibility of transubstantiation and would have considered stabbing an innocent wafer to be a meaningless action and a complete waste of time.

20. The claim that just before Passover, Jews kidnapped and killed a young child to use his blood in making *matzah*.

was irresponsible. This refusal was due to Brown's assumption that since their Jewish belief did not represent a high enough Christology to satisfy his twentieth century Roman Catholic ideology, they would not have been dissuaded from their desire to commit murder.

Jews and the Murder of Christians

In describing his breakdown of the multiple meanings of "the Jews" in John, Brown was convinced that in addition to Jesus, Jews murdered numerous other Christians, specifically Christian Jews, in the process of defending their version of the faith. The evidence he presented is not compelling. It came mostly from NT sources like John 16:3, which Brown knew well is not historically reliable,[21] and Acts, which portrays major incidents like the conversion of the Samaritans in a manner radically different from the process posited by Brown. And as has been noted often, Acts also disputes the testimony of Paul about his own career on more than one occasion. Still, the fact that the most highly regarded Catholic scholar of the twentieth century returned repeatedly to the idea that "the Jews" routinely killed Jesus as well as other Christians is shocking. His argument calls for examination.[22]

Brown's first point was that, although modern readers dare not affirm the Johannine contention that "the Jews" are children of the devil, it is not helpful to deny that that attitude existed in John. This grudging admission was as close as Brown came to acknowledging that any anti-Judaism existed in the Gospel of John (so much for complete metamorphosis). Second, he quickly "surmised"[23] that the synagogue authorities must have responded to harsh words of Jesus about Judaism by speaking about Christians equally rudely. But he cites no evidence to back this claim. Third, citing Acts and Josephus, Brown recalled three first century Christians put to death by Jews: Stephen, James the son of Zebedee (and brother of John), and James the brother of Jesus. But he failed to note the lack of confidence among modern scholars in the historical accuracy of Acts, as well as the scholarly consensus that the report of the death of James the brother of Jesus also appears in a Josephus passage that is almost surely spurious.[24]

Brown's fourth point is a citation of Mishnah *Sanhedrin* 9:6, which he erroneously presumed "acknowledges certain instances where zealots may

---

21. See again Brown, *Community*, 17.
22. The following quotations and citations are from Brown, *Community*, 40–43.
23. This is the term he uses, but for which he offers no evidence.
24. Mason, *Josephus and the New Testament*, 9.

slay people for religious offenses."[25] Sanhedrin 9:6 does list various liturgical or cultic offenses that permit "zealots" (*qanna'îm*, like Phineas) to "fall upon" (*pôg'îm*) heretics. But the primary meaning of the Hebrew verb *paga'* is not "to slay," as Brown supposed. It can have a hostile sense, but it often means "to encounter" someone, not necessarily in a hostile fashion. In post-biblical literature, *paga'* often means "to entreat" or "to plead with" someone. It can also describe praying to or pleading with God.[26]

In the discussion among the *Tanna'im*[27] cited by Brown, the only clear reference to *execution* at the hands of zealots is about the case of a non-priest attempting to serve a sacerdotal function; the opinion cited was derived from second century Rabbi Akiva. But Brown failed to note that that very passage concludes when the "sages" (*hakhamîm*) disputed the eminent Akiva and issued a majority opinion that the punishment of even a heretic should be left in the control of God alone (lit., "the hands of heaven").

Brown's citation of a rabbinic sermon in *Midrash Rabbah* xxi 3 on Numbers 25:13 is likewise meaningless. The comment he cited[28] is about Phineas, the descendant of Aaron who killed an Israelite male (Zimri) and his Baal-worshipping Moabite sexual partner (Cozbi) upon catching them *in flagrante delicto*. Because his quick action was judged to have protected all Israel from divine wrath (Num 25:11), Phineas was promised a perpetual priesthood for himself and his descendants; and he was said to have "made atonement for the people of Israel" (Num 25:13). The midrashic homily wonders why Phineas is credited with "atonement," without having offered an appropriate sacrifice in the Temple, which of course did not yet exist when Phineas was alive. The answer given is that in this specific instance, by "shedding the blood of the wicked, it is the same as if he had offered a sacrifice" (the sentence cited by Brown). The statement is not about a wicked Jew killing a believing Christian (long before the lifetime of Jesus), but about a zealous Israelite offing both a foreign Baal devotee *and* her Israelite sexual partner whom she was attempting to lure into Baal worship.[29] Further, this half sentence was not formulated into a custom (*minhag*) or a rule (*halakhah*) in Judaism. And Brown failed to note the numerous rabbinic passages that castigate Phineas for his impulsive act, a clear sign that such a

25. Brown, *Community*, 42.

26. Jastrow, *Dictionary*, 1135.

27. Authors of the Mishnaic discussion on which the later debate among the *'Amoraim* cited by Brown is based.

28. "If a man sheds the blood of the wicked, it is as though he had offered a sacrifice." See Brown, *Community*, 42, note 69.

29. Number 25:3 describes the incident as more about *religious* apostasy than sex: "Israel *yoked itself* to Baal-Peor."

deed was *not* acceptable in normative Judaism, amid the fear that it might become a model for similar actions by the overly zealous.[30]

At any rate, a third century CE *midrash* about twelfth century BCE wandering Israelites in Numbers is hardly historically reliable evidence about first century Jewish-Christian relations.

What is particularly disturbing is that Brown saw the post-NT centuries of Christian anti-Semitism as the natural response to the first century killing of Christians by Jews. His implied explanation would fit well on a grade school playground: "they ["the Jews"] started it." After quoting approvingly second-century Justin's accusation cited in *Dialogue with Trypho*, that Jews hate and murder Christians "as often as you get authority," Brown added a lengthy fifth point to his argument:

> Judaism was a tolerated religion, and in principle the Jews were not forced to take part in public worship. As long as Christians were considered Jews, there was no specific legal reason for the Romans to bother them. But once the synagogues expelled them and it was made clear that they were no longer Jews, their failure to adhere to pagan customs and to participate in emperor worship created legal problems. Second-century Christians accused Jews of betraying them to Roman inquisitors. The *Martyrdom of Polycarp* 13:1 says that "the Jews were extremely zealous, *as is their wont*" (sic!) in preparing material for burning the saint, a burning that was carried out by a Roman pro-consul ca. A.D. 155. Indirect participation in executions through expulsions from synagogues [could] have been a part of the background for John's charges against 'the Jews.'"[31]

Central to the point made by Brown was his erroneous assumption that the Jews "expelled" Christians from their synagogues. He then compounded his error by presuming that "the expulsion from the synagogues had already taken place by the time the Gospel was written, and so presumably had the killing."[32] Clearly, Brown did not understand his Jewish sources and he employed his second century patristic sources uncritically. Nonetheless, his conclusion was disappointing. If nothing else, it seems fair to wonder how *second*-century *Roman* action against Christians could have provided the grounds for a charge leveled against *Jews* early in the *first* century.

---

30. See *inter alia Sifre Num.* ¶131; *Sanhedrin* 27b, 29–34; *Sanhedrin* 82b.

31. Brown, *Community*, 42–43.

32. Brown, *Community*, 42, note 67. Essay VI explains his error about "expulsion" in detail.

"God so Loved the World?"

At this point, Brown's assertion that the author of John did not expect his audience to love anyone except fellow members of their own small Johannine sect must be brought into sharper focus. Maybe the life of Jesus demonstrated that *God* loved the whole world, but John's readers and presumably the Johannine community were under no obligation to do so. If Brown was correct that the Fourth Gospel "articulates no demand to love all human beings or to love one's enemies,"[33] the implication for modern readers is terrifying. Such a view is at least partly responsible for the continuance of the 2,000-year tradition founded on the way "John" has been used to give readers *carte blanche* to think in the narrowest of terms about "others." In the hands of zealous interpreters of John and his community, the original list grew quickly from "the Jews" in the gospel to include the separatists in the Johannine Epistles discussed in essay VI. Given Brown's characterization, perhaps it is not surprising that the list of those eligible for excoriation, discrimination, and demeaning treatment (rising at times to murder), has continued to expand as history has advanced.

In fact, a modern reader may be excused for interpreting this Johannine emphasis as implying that God Himself (Jesus?) exacts no penalty for the way all "others" are treated. Defining "others" as broadly as anyone who is not "a member of our group"[34] is a horrifying prospect that continues to be played out in modern life with devastating frequency.[35]

Brown's Brand of anti-Judaism

A final issue became problematic when Brown discarded his scholar's mortar board and donned his priestly garb to discuss late twentieth century relationships between Christians and Jews. In his mind, the Johannine situation pitting Jews against Christians had changed for the better, "partly out of revulsion for the holocaust."[36] Given Brown's conviction that the Jews were responsible for the troubles between the two faiths, this is a startling explanation. How could Christian revulsion for the holocaust solve the problem of Jewish persecution of Christians? Still, Brown lamented, "I have an uneasy

33. A longer citation of this assertion by Brown is noted in essay I, note 22.

34. Recall yet again the dismissive statement of John the Son of Thunder about the would-be Jesus missionary whom he dismissed because, "he was not one of us!"

35. And it is especially repugnant when membership in "our group" is delimited by definitions of color, theology, sexual orientation, or any other criterion from a long list of additional qualifiers.

36. Brown, *Community*, 69.

feeling that the basic Johannine difficulty still faces us."[37] At this point, Brown's sensitivity sounded praiseworthy, and his metamorphosis seemed to be nearing completion. But then he articulated his understanding of "the basic Johannine difficulty" and offered his shocking idea of a "final solution" to this difficulty that has now lasted for two millennia: "Both parties, today as then, need to wrestle with the question of *believing in Jesus and remaining a practicing Jew*—a question that ultimately reflects upon the compatibility of Christianity and Judaism."[38] It would be stunning to read such an opinion from any modern scholar. It is heart-breaking to read such words from the most influential John scholar of his generation.

In the context of this explanation and the possible compatibility between Jews and Christians as envisioned by Brown, two questions arise. First, do current followers of Brown's interpretation think that if Jews would believe in Jesus to the point of the High Christology deemed satisfactory by the church, Christianity and Judaism would become compatible and modern Jews would then be eligible to be loved by John and his followers? Second, do current Christian interpreters of John not understand that an honorable "practicing Jew" cannot recite both the *shǝma'* (God is One) and the Nicene Creed (God is three)?

Both questions evoke the same response. A "practicing Jew" cannot affirm that "Yahweh is One," and at the same time accept the definition of a Jesus who is also God.

It should be recalled that Brown was furious at the idea that first century Jews had refused to allow apostates to remain in the synagogue and continue assaulting the faith of their Jewish brothers who remained faithful to Judaism. In this, his final published opinion about Jews before his death, it was perfectly clear that Brown believed Jewish apostates should be accepted and allowed to remain in the synagogue *still today*.

One can only hope that Brown's followers will realize that this brand of Christianity and Judaism are *not* compatible.

Final Thoughts on the Compatibility of John's Christianity and Judaism

The most recent attempt to salvage the text of John in a way that commends itself to modern Jews is that of Christopher M. Blumhofer.[39] Blumhofer is a careful and thorough researcher, and his work synthesizes the status of

37. Brown, *Community*, 69.

38. Brown, *Community*, 69, emphasis added.

39. Blumhofer, *The Gospel of John*, 226-233.

Johannine studies by surveying an impressive number of modern authors and their theories. He begins with the thesis that "the Gospel of John ought to be read as a narrative argument about how Israel might embrace its future."[40] For this position to have merit, it is necessary to presume the Jewishness of John, arguably because a Christian John would lack the authority to speak for Judaism about the Jewish future.

There are detailed reasons to doubt the Jewishness of John (offered in Essay II). But Professor Stephen Gunter offers credible support for Blumhofer's view. "As a historian, I find it believable that [John] was previously a Jew in formal and confessional ways." But Gunter also recognizes that "from his narrative apologetic for the veracity of Christianity, it is now apparent that he is no longer confessionally a Jew."[41] And Gunter argues further that John wrote in the only way possible for a "confessional Christian" living in the context of emergent late first century Christianity: "This is the only Gospel he could have written because its design was to be an apologetic for the veracity of Christianity."

But regardless of how or when John became a Christian, at the time of his writing he was a *Christian* author arrogating to himself the authority to dictate to *Jews* what they should believe. In so doing, he crossed the line from apology to polemic, a step Gunter believes unnecessary.[42] "What I do not believe is that it was necessary existentially to assert the 'inadequacy of Judaism' and the 'complicity' of Jews in Jesus's crucifixion. The former is exegetically unnecessary, and the latter is historically unwarranted."

In contrast to this balanced view of the matter, Blumhofer envisions a unification of Johannine Judaism with Johannine Christology that ultimately makes sense to Jews because of the crucifixion. When the crucifixion is factored into the equation, Jews can ignore the stinging polemic, embrace the veracity of the Johannine apologetic, and understand finally how "Jesus offers an innovative continuity to a tradition facing a (perceived) epistemological crisis."[43]

But is it Jesus or "John" who offers this authority to the church? The long gap between the death of Jesus and the writing of John was not devoted to a continuing discussion of the relevance of Jesus and his crucifixion for Jews. It was devoted to the ruminations of an increasingly non-Jewish proto church seeking to secure its place outside of Judaism. From the dispute in which

---

40. Blumhofer, 1.

41. This and the following citations of Gunter are from private correspondence, January 8, 2022.

42. The apologetic function of John is discussed further in Essay VIII.

43. Blumhofer, 232.

John's Jesus taunts "the Jews" about "their law"—not his—until the moment that blame for the death of Jesus is placed squarely on the shoulders of "the Jews," the author of John speaks *only* polemically about "the Jews."[44]

Further, long before John described a Jesus who is far more Christian than Jewish, Paul had noted that the crucified Jesus was "a scandal" to Jews (1 Cor 1:23), using a Greek word (*skandalon*) that implies revulsion or anger, thus pushing *away from* rather than drawing *toward* something—in this case, the crucifixion.[45] It is unrealistic to argue that the very people John fingered as having used false charges to engineer the crucifixion would see crucifixion as "an act that might reverse unbelief."[46] And it is naïve to take literally John's idea that the crucifixion destroys the devil posited by John's Jesus as the father of all Jews. But to Blumhofer, "the devil whose power once expressed itself through the violent rejection[47] of Jesus no longer operates in the same way after the crucifixion."[48] Thus, "it is the crucifixion that makes accessible the identity of Jesus and the eschatological promise of life that he offers."[49]

This remarkable result can be possible only if Jews read John and accept the promise of his Jesus and the victory over sin won by his crucifixion. Then John's Jesus can become acknowledged as both continuity with Israel's past and link to its future. But in this scenario, there is no future of an Israel without Jesus squarely at its center. Jewish-Christian conflict can be solved only after Jews abandon the God of Abraham to embrace the Jesus of John, who is "*the* way."

But acknowledging the soteriological necessity of Jesus' crucifixion is the act of persons seeking to secure their future in the Christian faith. It is not a legitimate component of Judaism, but an anachronistic definition of modern redemption theology about which first century Jewish believers and followers of Jesus would have been unaware.[50]

---

44. Specifically, by defining the claim to be a messiah or a child of God as breaking Jewish law and so egregious as to warrant the death penalty. This idea is examined in Essay IV.

45. See *AG*, 753.

46. Blumhofer, 229.

47. Like Ehrman, Brown, and numerous other Christian scholars, Blumhofer assumes that the Jews treated Jesus and his followers with violence.

48. Blumhofer, 229.

49. Blumhofer, 229-30.

50. Gunter suggests in private correspondence that it should have been possible for John to interpret Jesus as the long expected one without devolving into denigration of Jews and Judaism.

VIII. Preaching John: Homiletical Accommodation

The Gospel of John as "Sermon"

THE PLETHORA OF THEORIES and contortions of logic employed by innumerable scholars of John over the centuries reflect the textual difficulties presented by what appears to be a Greek narrative composed in plain, simple, language—the Fourth Gospel.

But John is anything but simple. Two of the more influential modern scholars and their complex theories about the interpretation of John have been highlighted in earlier essays. J. Louis Martyn reacted to John by dividing his work into two levels that represented eras separated by seven or eight decades. Raymond Brown responded by parsing words, phrases, and even entire narratives into ever more minute components, ultimately performing an exhaustive literary autopsy on the text. The followers of these two men are legion.

And yet, John was not written to serve as a case study for scholars. Whatever the definition of a "gospel" may be, John might be received better as a sermon, a passionate challenge that calls for readers to respond to its unique definition of Jesus of Nazareth. This fact may be illustrated from the sheer number of post-NT sermons that have been and continue to be based on John. And while the expository intentions of some modern NT preachers to turn away from the direct blasts of anti-Judaism in John are laudable, many of the most difficult texts in the Gospel continue to serve as the basis for sermons in both Catholic and Protestant worship.

Thus, the words of John continue to land with devastating impact. In sermon after sermon, "the Jews" still play the role of everything evil and they still are portrayed as angry and unyielding opponents of Jesus, narrow-minded and ungracious at best, murderous at worst. And because the Fourth Gospel has become "the dominant Christology of the church,"[1]

1. Brown, *Community*, 45.

sermons based on Johannine texts are still an integral part of the lectionary cycle in Catholic and mainline Protestant denominations.

Texts in John also are often the basis for a popular topical sermon[2] in more conservative Christian circles as well. Particularly because of the Holocaust, but also as a sign of growing mutual respect between the two different faiths, proclaiming gospel truth from John has become a challenge requiring Christian preachers to search for a way to tease from the text of John a positive Christian message while avoiding the negative implications of anti-Jewish rhetoric in the heart of that same text. Recent examples of concern about sermons from John are instructive.

George Smiga and the Catholic Lectionary

Catholic scholar George M. Smiga's book, *The Gospel of John Set Free*, is part of a series created by the 1982 Commission for Religious Relations with the Jews, titled "Notes on the Correct way to Present the Jews and Judaism in Preaching and Catechesis in the Roman Catholic Church."[3] The intention of Smiga to discover this correct way is signaled by his chosen subtitle: *Preaching Without Anti-Judaism*. A look at the treatment of three narratives in John illustrates Smiga's perception of his task.

First, commenting on John's repeated description of plots to murder Jesus, Smiga ends with a warning: "We must be careful not to conclude that these early plots against Jesus in John's narrative accurately reflect an opposition that was leveled against the historical Jesus."[4] This is an astonishing piece of advice. Accusing "the Jews" of the desire to murder the historical Jesus is exactly what John was attempting. Honest preachers are thus charged with the challenge of building a sermon that declares to their congregants the bi-polar opposite of what the Gospel of John repeats to his readers nine times, encompassing every section of the book.[5] In explaining his perception of the phrase "the Jews" found throughout John, Smiga borrows a favorite tactic of Brown: "although it can refer to all the Jewish people, in John's Gospel it does not seem to carry that connotation when used polemically."[6] What this means, apparently, is that when John uses

---

2. As opposed to expository sermons which derive topics from the issues treated in a specific biblical passage.

3. Smiga, *John*, 167–180. This is the title of an Appendix written by Johannes Cardinal Willebrands, Pierre Duprey, and Jorge Meija.

4. Smiga, *John*, 23.

5. Essay III treats this idea in detail.

6. Smiga, *John*, 20.

the phrase in an anti-Jewish way, "the Jews" does not mean "the Jews."
Given the fact that the phrase is used "polemically" in narrative after narrative throughout the entire gospel, Smiga's statement is as close as one can come to sheer nonsense.

Since John does not always use the phrase "the Jews" appropriately, Smiga's solution is to authorize the modern preacher to make correct distinctions for the gospel writer, turning the plain sense of the gospel text on its head in the process. To this end, Smiga appeals to the 1975 Conciliar Declaration, *Nostra Aetate* to affirm that sometimes the modern Catholic preacher can choose "terms which express better the thought of the Evangelist and avoid appearing to arraign the Jewish people as such."[7] Here the astonishment meter rises even higher. How can any preacher be expected to enter the pulpit charged with the responsibility of expressing the thoughts of John better than John expressed his own thoughts? Well, as Smiga would have it, when choosing a sermon from John, the proper method is not to read John and allow his words to guide the homily, but to turn to a Conciliar Declaration for permission to change ("express better," really!) what John *actually said* into what John *should have said*. The preacher who makes this decision is thus the ultimate authority, not the New Testament Gospel of John. Smiga never considers the idea that wholesale revision of an ancient author is not a legitimate method of interpretation.

Second, commenting on the story of the blind man whom Jesus healed (John chapter 9), Smiga simply affirms that as a modern scholar, he knows he is reading a narrative that is "not to be located in the time of the historical Jesus."[8] Yet in John, the historical Jesus is the hero of the entire narrative. Here again, Smiga is advising modern preachers that they must tell the truth to their congregations because John lied to his readers. How, it might be asked, does such an approach encourage confidence in the sacred text?

Third, turning to the episode of Jesus cleansing the Temple by expelling money changers and their paraphernalia (John 2:13–25), Smiga discards several ideas that he fears might be invoked erroneously to sound anti-Jewish if John's narrative is left unedited and unchecked. Yet again, the focus and clear intention of John must be stood on its head, and the way in which Smiga reasons is instructive. He does not think the historical Jesus was opposed to Temple worship or animal sacrifice or that he was against selling animals in the Temple as a service for worshipers traveling from outside Jerusalem to offer a legally mandated sacrifice. He also rejects the idea that Jesus was opposed to "the *way* in which these necessary

---

7. Smiga, *John*, 21.

8. Smiga, *John*, 81. Essay V discusses this episode in detail.

aspects of Temple worship were carried out," perhaps by unfair rates of money exchanges or the *way* priests performed their duties.[9] So, Smiga opts for a third alternative, appropriating the theory of E. P. Sanders that Jesus was acting in a way symbolic of the arrival of the messianic age. "This interpretation has the advantage of tying Jesus' action in the Temple to a theme that we are quite certain was central to his historical ministry: the announcement of the imminent reign of God."[10]

Trustworthy exegetes do not choose a particular interpretation merely because it sounds better for their personal theories. But in this particular case, that is exactly what Smiga does—"If Sanders is correct, it is possible to understand Jesus' action in stage one of the gospel tradition not as a criticism of the Jewish Temple or its functioning, but rather as a symbolic announcement that the reign of God was at hand."[11]

There is one gigantic fly in the ointment of this approach, and once again it is the words of John himself. John portrays the historical Jesus fashioning a whip with which to drive out from the outer precinct of the Temple (not the adjoining sanctuary where worship occurred) every Jewish official in charge of assisting individual worshipers who had traveled from their homes to Jerusalem and needed to procure animals appropriate for sacrifice. John's Jesus then dramatically overturns their tables and scatters their money on the floor, topping off his performance with a thunderous prophetic word.

But his pronouncement was not, "Behold the Kingdom of God is at hand" as Smiga imagined. It was: "Take these out of here and stop making my father's house a marketplace" (John 2:16). To be sure, Smiga has constructed a milder version of the incident to fit his own theory about what happened. But Smiga's theory requires him to ignore what John wrote in favor of a version of his own creation that works to the advantage of his opinion. This is not an advantage demanded by critical analysis of the biblical text. Instead, it is merely a homiletical accommodation necessary to support an imaginary theory.

A basic comprehension of the sacrificial system in force at the time of Jesus is essential to an understanding of the narrative. Professor Marianne Thompson offers a balanced view of the custom to which Jesus was portrayed as opposing: "Since pilgrims would have journeyed some distance to the temple, they would have needed to buy animals for their

9. Smiga, *John*, 100.

10. Smiga, *John*, 100.

11. Smiga, *John*, 100.

sacrifices."[12] It was legally mandated that an animal appropriate for sacrifice must be unblemished (Lev 5:15, 18). But there would be only a slight chance of a sacrificial animal arriving at the Jerusalem Temple without a single bruise or blemish sustained during the journey from home. Thus, furnishing animals on site that were physically acceptable and could serve as a qualified sacrifice was an important and necessary function, a fact that every Jew in the world would have known. But John's Jesus did not. He appears unaware of any legitimate reason for animals to be sold on the temple grounds. Accordingly, John has Jesus dramatically drive out the animals along with their human handlers.

John's portrait dovetails nicely with the observation of Luke that the Pharisees sneered at Jesus because they "loved money" instead of God (Luke 16:14). It also evokes the image of Judas, the greedy treasurer who betrayed Jesus for money (Matt 26:15) as well as duplicitous Jews who paid Roman soldiers to lie about the resurrection (Matt 28:12). And it underscores the observation of 1 Timothy 6:10: "the love of money [i.e., the quintessential characteristic of a Pharisee] is the root of every evil."

Obviously, John was not the only NT author to offer this negative "money-lovers" characterization of Jews that would stalk them for the next 2000 years, but he painted with a unique brush and his words graphically portray Jesus mocking an integral component of Jewish worship. According to John, the central sanctuary that supported Jewish worship around the world was viewed by Jesus as nothing more than a money-making scheme, a pitiful "marketplace." Once again, the moral chasm between "the Jews" and Jesus is emphasized, and the two are shown to be implacable enemies. Jesus and "the Jews" are not even viewed by John as members of the same family, for while the father of "the Jews" is the devil (John 8:44), the Father of Jesus is Almighty God.[13] Once again, a Christian Jesus opposes Judaism at its core.[14]

There are numerous other passages in John that are subjected by Smiga to the same kind of treatment depicted in these three examples. It is not necessary to cite and critique them all. But there is one broader issue in the book that deserves notice. Often throughout his text, Smiga has added "Rabbinic Notes" that he believes illustrate a Jewish custom underlying a Johannine narrative or reference. This is misleading. For the most part, isolated ideas mined haphazardly from a huge corpus of rabbinic texts

12. Thompson, *John*, 71.

13. "My Father" in John 2:16.

14. Smiga offers no comparable condemnation of the widespread practice of selling prayer candles, music recordings, or religious literature including Missals and Bibles in church vestibules.

have no connection to anything in John. Further, it is notoriously difficult to date rabbinic material, especially Talmudic passages. Matching a sixth century rabbinic opinion to a late first century Johannine story is fraught with peril. And the links that Smiga imagines are puzzling at times and frankly irrelevant at other times.

Rabbinic Judaism had no interest in John or his cacophony of hatred against Jews, and the opinions of the rabbis were not formed in the context of the Christian world in which they were neither respected nor welcome. In this context, it is tempting to recall the words of Samuel Sandmel regarding non-Jewish scholars combing through rabbinic literature looking for half sentences and phrases that sound like they might support a particular view of the New Testament: "more than one scholar who has never read a full page in a rabbinic text has been grossly misled."[15]

In sum, then, Smiga does not "read the anti-Judaism out of John" because it cannot be done. His advice to sermonizers is that Christian congregations need to be told that "John" must be heavily edited and rephrased because he wrote numerous things now known to be untrue. If Smiga is correct, "John" is an acceptable source from which to preach—except when it is historically inaccurate, misleading, or misguided. The modern preacher can still preach even from these flawed texts in John, but he must *fix* the biblical passage first. The spiritual value of sermons based upon texts re-constructed in such a wholesale manner is surely nil.

Of equal concern is the fact that this stance of Smiga ignores the results of virtually an entire 2000-year history of anti-Judaism based solidly on exegesis of the Gospel of John. These exegetes typically explained accurately what John says and seldom resorted to stating the opposite of what John says just to boost book sales. But Smiga's position implies that these early interpreters of the Gospel were wrong about "the Jews" because they did not know better, or because they could not parse gospel verses as carefully as modern scholars can do now. In his dogged determination to sanitize the Gospel on which Catholic sermons have been based for two millennia, Smiga simply announces that for the first time in 2000 years, Catholic preachers have discovered that John was not anti-Jewish. Nonetheless, his open admission that at least some texts in John require rewriting is irrefutable evidence that John is indeed troubling and unacceptable to modern sensibility. Otherwise, why would it be thought necessary to write a detailed book on how to sanitize an entire gospel?

Modern listeners to a Smiga-inspired sermon might be encouraged to hear the sanitized John in a Christian context. But after the sermon, they

15. Sandmel, "Bultmann on Judaism," 213.

would be disheartened to open the NT and find John still there, unchanged, and still bristling with anti-Jewish animus. These hearers might be forgiven for wondering why a modern preacher who is clearly determined not to sound anti-Jewish would consider John inspired and sacred. In fact, admitting that John got numerous important issues historically or factually wrong while at the same time insisting that John must continue to be preached in the Church is still the great unresolved conundrum.

Eileen Schuller and the Catholic Lectionary II

Three recent articles about "Preaching John" offer more serious and scholarly approaches than the instruction booklet by Smiga. Professor Eileen Schuller has also authored an attempt to define Catholic preaching of John in a positive way.[16] But she does a helpful job of examining the Catholic lectionary without the wooden links to Catholic ideology that characterize the work of Smiga. In her essay, Schuller treats some of the recent changes that have been made in the Catholic lectionary cycles, particularly in the passion narrative of John. Along the way, she also discovers how difficult it is to make permanent and meaningful changes in a canonical text. Her final hope is that the search for "different approaches to the reading of the Johannine passion narrative on Good Friday" will continue.[17]

Schuller begins her careful and nuanced approach to the problem by introducing the descriptive term "Sunday Catholic." A Sunday Catholic, apparently, will hear only certain vetted portions of John read from the Lectionary, all chosen because they are not overly lengthy, they lack hard-to-pronounce names, and/or they omit references that puzzle modern listeners unfamiliar with biblical geography. If Schuller is correct, these three factors are hardly a list of criteria calculated to inspire confidence in their selection.

In a doff of the cap to the methodology of Smiga, Schuller also notes that the "*Lectionary for Mass*" (section 76) defines a more telling criterion: "texts that present real difficulties are avoided for pastoral reasons."[18] Schuller offers no specific explanation of what these "pastoral reasons" might be, but it appears to be the case that Lectionary readings are selected to ensure that "many of the most negative and anti-Jewish passages in John's Gospel are not proclaimed on Sunday."[19] On the opposite side of the ledger, however, Schuller also admits that additional "passages that would help the listener

16. Schuller, "The Gospel of John in the Catholic Lectionary," 71–85.

17. Schuller, "The Gospel of John in the Catholic Lectionary," 81.

18. Schuller, "The Gospel of John in the Catholic Lectionary," 77.

19. Schuller, "The Gospel of John in the Catholic Lectionary," 79.

to understand Jesus as a Jew and as a member of the Jewish people, our Sunday Catholics will not hear."[20] Failing to refer to the Jewishness of Jesus may allow Sunday Catholics to remain comfortable, but Schuller appears reluctant to admit that this kind of selectivity does nothing to ameliorate the pain that anti-Jewish John continues to inflict upon its readers and hearers. Catholics who attend mass only on Sunday will probably never be forced to think about that pain or its 2000-year history in the church.

But Schuller is clearly concerned about the impact of the term "the Jews" on Jewish-Christian relations. Surveying the lectionary in Canada, she notes the confident assertion published in 1987 by the Canadian bishops' conference: "It would be well for us to recall that when the evangelist [John] refers to 'the Jews' we know he is not saying that all Jews, either of Jesus' time or our time, are responsible for his death."[21] As discussed above, this is the familiar stance spelled out by Smiga: "We moderns" know what those who came earlier did not know. This stance also doffs the cap to Brown and his followers: "the Jews" does not always mean "the Jews." Once again, the modern preacher must edit John before preaching him.

But when the 2009 edition appeared, certain changes were made to meet the Vatican requirements of a new document, "On the Use of Vernacular Languages in the Publication of the Books of the Roman Liturgy."[22] Among other things, these new instructions demand that "in every case *hoi Ioudaioi* must be translated 'literally,' that is, 'the Jews.'"[23] Schuller is bothered by the fact that this translation, which "had not been used for over twenty years,"[24] is reintroduced rather than retaining the Brown-inspired multi-level translations. But the 2009 rescension suggests an escape route: "shifting the focus from translation to homiletics." The way out of the morass for Schuller is clear: "While 'the Jews' is set out as a strict translation of the original text, it must always [*sic!*] be made clear that the term, especially in the Gospel of John, refers to religious leaders and authorities of the day. Homilists and catechists are encouraged to address this issue sensitively and clearly."[25]

The recommendations of Schuller appear to focus on the need to insist on moral honesty expressed specifically enough to make a substantive

20. Schuller, "The Gospel of John in the Catholic Lectionary," 79.

21. For citations, see Schuller, "The Gospel of John in the Catholic Lectionary," 80-81.

22. Available online by its title.

23. Schuller, "The Gospel of John in the Catholic Lectionary," 81.

24. Schuller, "The Gospel of John in the Catholic Lectionary," 81.

25. Schuller, "The Gospel of John in the Catholic Lectionary," 81.

difference. But the simplistic solution she has chosen is to explain that "the Jews" means what modern homilists now believe John *should have said*. This is very close to the approach taken by Smiga. Two key questions arise. First, what new level of sensitivity and clarity could possibly cleanse John from the stain of hostility and his historically unfounded, false, and misleading characterizations of "the Jews?" Second, once the anti-Judaism of John has been properly explained, what Christian messages of "good news" will remain?

After her survey of the ways in which John is included and preached in the Catholic Lectionary and her hope for the process of seeking other and "perhaps more satisfactory" approaches, Schuller's concluding sentence is wistful: "Hopefully such considerations as have been raised in this chapter can be part of the reflection of those who will be entrusted with further revision and development of the Sunday lectionary."[26] Her hope is laudable, but in this case, as is so often true, the devil will lurk in the details.

Alan Culpepper and a Protestant Lectionary

Professor Alan Culpepper works from a mainline Protestant perspective and adds his impressive knowledge of all things Johannine to offer a balanced point of view that includes current Johannine research, modern cultural difficulties, and the necessity of producing sermons in touch with reality as well as biblical honesty. For Culpepper, the biggest difficulty faced by interpreters of John is how often it "tells the story of the past in terms of the setting of its intended hearers or readers, as though Jesus were acting or speaking to their context."[27] The problem with this Johannine framework is that "a bridge was created over which the hostility with the Pharisees [or any other tag word for "the Jews"] in Jesus's day is conveyed into the present of each new generation of readers."[28]

Like Schuller, Culpepper is open to ideas that have the potential for meaningful progress. Once again, the first task is to define the Johannine phrase "the Jews" adequately. Here Culpepper outdoes Brown by creating seven categories into which Johannine references to Jews or Jewish groups might be classified: (1) hostile authorities; (2) skeptical authorities; (3) Jews who are not authorities, but skeptical; (4) "Johannine Jews," [Jews from the time of John sixty to seventy years after the lifetime of Jesus] probably not authorities, but intensely hostile; (5) references too brief to tell; (6) common people as hostile as authorities; and (7) "two texts that do not fit any of the

26. Schuller, "The Gospel of John in the Catholic Lectionary," 82.

27. Culpepper, "Preaching," 49-69.

28. Culpepper, "Preaching," 49.

above categories: 8:31; 10:19."[29] This kind of categorization, common in some form or another to almost all modern Christian NT scholars since Martyn and Brown, has the goal of culling the number of openly *hostile* references to a more manageable number. Even so, Culpepper runs into a roadblock when he arrives at his personal suggestions for sermons from the few hostile Johannine texts that remain. No matter how greatly their number has been reduced, the anti-Jewish bias of John refuses to go away.[30]

Here is the four-step approach that Culpepper commends, traced back through a prominent rabbi (Chaim Seidler-Feller) and a world-famous Christian theologian (Krister Stendahl):

1. Acknowledge the problem.

2. Set the texts in their historical context.

3. Reinterpret the texts.

4. Condemn the text on moral grounds.[31]

It is *hard* to imagine a more honest scholar than Culpepper or four more worthy goals for Johannine sermons. It is also *impossible* to imagine their successful implementation in the average Christian congregation.

First, acknowledging the problem can be done faithfully, as Smiga, Schuller, Culpepper, and numerous other Christian interpreters have shown.

Second, setting a difficult text into historical context is more suited to a three-hour graduate seminar than it is to a twenty-minute sermon. A title like "Seven translations of John's phrase 'The Jews'" would mean that even to establish for the congregation into which of seven possible Johannine categories "the Jews" of the morning service should be placed would leave the preacher with little time to proclaim the good news of the gospel. Further, such an exercise would surely imply to listeners that whatever English translation of John they were reading needed serious surgery.

Third, if "the Jews" could mean so many different things, what about other Johannine vocabulary? How many definitions of "the world" or "believe" or even "messiah" did John have in mind? Perhaps no one should be surprised to read from Raymond Brown that "For John *Messias* or *Christos* ("Anointed") is not a term with only one meaning. Sometimes messiah can be an adequate description of Jesus, but sometimes it is not."[32] The Greek original

---

29. Culpepper, "Preaching," 51-52.

30. Culpepper, "Preaching," 65-66.

31. Culpepper, "Preaching," 65.

32. Brown, *Community*, 43-44.

does not make this distinction, so once again, the final authority must be what the modern exegete thinks it means in each specific passage.

Fourth, but even with all the time in the world, to reinterpret a text that has a 2000-year history in the Church, the creativity of even the world's greatest preachers would be taxed.

These first four steps are essential components of the scientific task of exegesis, a well-defined process designed to lead scholars and students to an encounter with texts as proclamations that at some moment in the past *occurred*. In preaching, the tense of these proclamations must be shifted from the past to the present, i.e., as proclamation that occurs anew in the moment, the "now." It is in the transference of the text from past to present that a fifth step will present itself. How can the anti-Judaism of John written 2000 years ago translate into the present moment as anything other than recurring anti-Judaism in the now?

Additional questions arise. "Moral grounds?" Whose moral grounds? Is the twenty-first century preacher more enlightened morally than the first century author of a canonical text? Could it be the case that the inspired author of the sacred Gospel of John produced an *im*moral text? What induced the early Church to include such a text in its sacred canon? If a biblical text is read only to be condemned, why read it in the first place? Better still, if an offending text needs to be reinterpreted and *condemned*, perhaps the solution would be to add one more step and treat the anti-Judaism of John as Matthew 5:29 advised doing about an offending right eye: "Gouge it out and throw it away."

If such an action were taken, it is to be wondered what if anything would be left of John.

Amy-Jill Levine and "Jewish Ears"

An essay by Amy-Jill Levine addresses the issue of Christian preaching from a decidedly Jewish perspective.[33] Her opening sentence zeros in on the precise nature of the problem: "The critical exegeses regarding how to address 'the Jews' in John's Gospel provided by biblicists and historians generally fail to make the transition from classroom to pew."[34] Levine is an exceptionally skilled writer, and she expands the scope of her inquiry well beyond the parameters of Smiga, Schuller, and Culpepper to include social and even socio-political, racial, and gender considerations.

33. Levine, "Christian Privilege," 87–110.
34. Levine, "Christian Privilege," 87.

Beginning with the concept of "Christian privilege," Levine articulates her belief that the first problem of preaching from John is the fact that just as white people have difficulty in recognizing white privilege in themselves, so also Christian people often do not address anti-Judaism in John (or elsewhere) because they fail to recognize it in themselves. In short, the anti-Jewish rhetoric of John has found such a central place in the Christian ecclesiastical world that it sounds "normal" to Christian ears. Consequently, as Levine puts it, the "toxicity of hermeneutical language" is "often unrecognized."[35] This lack of recognition routinely produces resentment from Christian church members or students in university classes who are offended at the mere suggestion of anti-Jewish bias in their holy book.

But it is not only congregants and students who resist what they do not recognize: "Many Christian preachers [are] unaware of how John's Gospel is implicated in anti-Jewish thought and action or how John's Gospel may sound to Jewish ears."[36] Levine's point is clear—with respect to anti-Judaism, as also with all other forms of prejudice, few people are aware except the targeted victims. Levine graciously concedes the following: "People should be neither blamed nor shamed for not recognizing problems in their own tradition. We are all embedded in various structures of inequity. We do not hear the hate. We cannot see it. And when we are confronted with it, we usually go into defensive mode. That is a normal human reaction."[37] But she does not shrink from the consequences of this "normal human reaction" with respect to the preaching of John: "It is this defensiveness, born of privilege and fragility, that undermines the standard homiletic approaches to the hostile texts."[38]

With unerring aim, Levine attacks the issues that contribute to the failure of "the standard homiletic approaches." These include (a) our lack of knowledge about the author of John, whether he was a Jew, a Samarian, or a gentile;[39] (b) the inadequacy of narrowing "the Jews" to "Jewish authorities," "religious authorities," or "political authorities" only,[40] a tactic that Levine later labels "a mechanism of exculpating the text for its general presentation of Jews;"[41] (c) the explanation that John was only speaking as other classical authors did: "The mere fact that a type of polemic is conventional does not

35. Levine, "Christian Privilege," 88.
36. Levine, "Christian Privilege," 106.
37. Levine, "Christian Privilege," 92.
38. Levine, "Christian Privilege," 92.
39. Levine, "Christian Privilege," 93
40. Levine, "Christian Privilege," 94-95.
41. Levine, "Christian Privilege," 99.

thereby rob it of its capacity to do harm;"[42] (d) the idea that John represents only a "family squabble" (as discussed in Essay II). Levine has it right yet again: "John is a saint of the church talking to the Christian faithful."[43]

Because the kinds of suggestions offered by Smiga, Schuller, and Culpepper are "insufficient," Levine offers her own formula. Whereas the suggestions of well-intentioned Christian scholars are designed to inform sermons preached for *Christian* ears, Levine recommends that preachers ask "how John's Gospel may sound to Jewish ears."[44]

1. "Pretend there is a Jew in the congregation."

2. "Learn about how anti-Jewish preaching functions in places and times where anti-Jewish or anti-Semitic action also occurs."

3. "Recognize the intersectionality of racism and anti-Semitism."[45]

The practical nature of these suggestions extends beyond the scholar's study. All three are beamed to the preacher—pretend, learn, recognize. But having done these three things, the text of John still stands, and while a "woke" preacher may soften the blow of a particular passage or two, when the sermon ends, the congregants will still be left with the text of John intact.

Revising the New Testament

In the light of all the suggestions for defending John to be able to preach him, what really has been accomplished? A reasonable Christian preacher cannot simply say, "I will continue to read the hateful anti-Jewish passages in John, but you must understand that John did not mean them the way they sound, and I don't mean them that way either." Surely preachers who insist on reading regularly, aloud and in public, passages of hate that they now know must be condemned on moral grounds cannot escape the impression that at some level their choice of such passages continues to imply their personal approval of the gospel writer.

No! The first step to preaching from John must be to face squarely the central question posed by sermons from John: Why continue to preach what needs to be explained away or said better? Store it in a museum. Stack it in a part of the library devoted to ancient Etruscan grammar. But stop endorsing a Johannine sermon as the highlight of morning worship.

42. Levine, "Christian Privilege," 95.

43. Levine, "Christian Privilege," 97.

44. Levine, "Christian Privilege," 106.

45. Levine, "Christian Privilege," 106.

Of course, there are multiple plausible objections to the idea of a wholesale re-editing of a sacred text. First, of course, is the fact that such an attempt would encounter universal and stiff resistance. The appropriate response to this objection may be plainly stated: to shrink from the task because it is uncomfortable and difficult is merely to say that the problem will remain unresolved. It is also to concede that the chasm between Jews and Christians cannot be bridged.

The bold idea of re-programming an entire segment of sacred Scripture is far from unprecedented. Such re-programming is as old as Christianity itself. The original NT authors themselves introduced the first major change by citing the OT from Greek throughout. The Greek LXX and the Hebrew Masoretic text are often quite different, and the effects of this substitution of Greek for Hebrew cannot be emphasized enough. A single example will suffice. The Hebrew text of Genesis 15:5 envisions the future descendants of Abraham growing to a number as uncountable as the stars in the heavens. These innumerable offspring are the "seed" (Hebrew *zera‘*) of Abraham. Paul, working with the LXX, did not grasp the collective force of the word "seed," and so he noted that the promise made to Abraham had not been made to many future seeds of Abraham but to one person only, none other than Jesus (Gal 3:16).[46]

Even a cursory look at the later differences between the Roman Catholic Old Testament and the Protestant Hebrew Scriptures illustrates that post-NT Christian scholars began very early to modify and/or excise parts of their Greek Old Testament that did not work well with their proffered interpretation of the new faith. Along the way, Catholics made significant changes in the OT itself, the literature they insisted was their inheritance from Judaism. Not satisfied with a translation, they added supplemental extensions to books like Esther and Jeremiah. They also inserted complete books not found in the Hebrew Masoretic text at all.[47]

In addition, broad distinctions were routinely drawn between the "legal" and the "ethical" definitions of different parts of the Jewish Scriptures that the church proposed to adopt. To soften the impact of a literal interpretation in numerous passages, early Christians turned to typological, allegorical, tropological, metaphorical, anagogical, and parabolic schemes.[48]

---

46. Essay IX will explain that a comparable misunderstanding of the collective force of the word "servant" in Isaiah 53 led early Christian scholars who were dependent on the LXX to assume that *'eved* was a reference to one person only rather than the entire Israelite people. On this grammatical point, see Isbell, *Jews and Christians*, 190–95.

47. Tobit, Judith, I and II Maccabees, Wisdom, and Ecclesiasticus (ben Sira).

48. Isbell, *Jews and Christians*, 153-7.

In the sixteenth century, Martin Luther's wrestling match with Scripture at the dawning of *Protestant* Christianity began with his decision to return to the Hebrew Scriptures of Judaism rather than the LXX version that had become official Catholic canon. But he also offered his own startling expansion of the tendency to change the Bible. James A. Sanders has shown that after consulting all manuscripts available to him, Luther always selected the variant "that led most clearly to the Gospel of Jesus Christ (his understanding, of course)."[49] Luther also created virtually a canon within a canon by his strenuous objection to NT books like James, Jude, Hebrews, and the Apocalypse of John.

Most pastors and priests do something similar. Few indeed are the Christian congregants who can cite a stirring message from Jude or III John, to say nothing of Leviticus, Ecclesiastes, or Obadiah. In other words, radical transvaluation was exactly what Christianity has always known it must do if it wished to retain ownership of its "Old" Testament.

The Authority of the Church vs. The Responsibility of the Church

Finally, it would surely be objected in some quarters that because the Bible is the word of God, its *content* cannot be changed. Whatever one's view of Scripture may be, the fact is that the church, confident that it was guided by the wisdom and Spirit of God in the matter, arrogated to itself total authority to decide what it would sanctify into its sacred canon and what it would leave out. That authority still resides with the church, the same divine/human institution that chose its current sacred canon deliberately and carefully.

The earliest known complete list of the 27 books of the New Testament is found in a letter written by Athanasius, a fourth century bishop of Alexandria, dated to 367 CE. The current twenty-seven-book New Testament was first formally canonized during the councils of Hippo (393) and Carthage (397 at the earliest, or perhaps as late as 419) in North Africa. In other words, following the death of Jesus, the church had ample time to consider what literature it deemed essential long before it granted to itself complete authority to make the final decision about canonicity. When the moment of final judgment arrived, not a single gospel, epistle, or tractate was anointed to sacred canonical status by accident or without undergoing strict theological "vetting." To the contrary, because there were multiple literary candidates in every biblical genre from which to choose, this responsibility that the church arrogated to itself involved sifting, sorting, and debating its way through at

49. Sanders, "The Hermeneutics of Translation," 48.

least twenty-one gospels, countless other Christian-authored epistles (letters), and multiple sophisticated theological tractates. Withholding official approval meant the wholesale disuse and ultimate denial of canonicity for all but four of those gospels, while only a small percentage of other forms of Christian literature made the cut.[50]

And the scholars of the church did not take their responsibility lightly. Numerous works were hotly disputed. Some of these overcame the objections lodged against them and attained acceptance into the canon, while others ultimately failed.[51] The church that had originated as a small Jewish sect had become almost completely non-Jewish (Gentile) by the time it finalized its canon. Thus, Christianity in the late fourth century did not include former Jews who might have objected to John's raw anti-Jewish rhetoric. But it is also true that the Christian community of that era lacked non-Jewish scholars like Smiga, Schuller, Culpepper, and surely a multitude of others of like mind who now recognize and are offended by the worst passages in John. One consequence of this demographic shift was tragic—there is no evidence that any church father ever raised a single objection to the Gospel of John on grounds of its anti-Jewish rhetoric.

Unfortunately, the Gospel of John does more than *hint* at anti-Jewish rhetoric in a few places. Its position as the most prominent gospel elevates its anti-Jewish rhetoric to a level all out of proportion to its passages about a loving Jesus who was concerned for the physical and spiritual welfare of the entire world. In its present iteration, John is the favorite gospel of Christians, and perhaps the favorite book in the entire New Testament. It also happens to be the most anti-Jewish. Taken together, these two factors ensure that John's anti-Jewish rhetoric is read, heard, and preached more often than countless other themes that deserve to be proclaimed by a Christian faith that describes a Jesus who poured out compassion and healing on sick folk, kindly accommodation of wiggling small children, acceptance of social outcasts like lepers or an adulterous Samaritan woman, and infinite patience with dull students.

Jewish and Christian scholars and preachers can agree that John includes undeniably hateful and divisive language. They can agree on the

---

50. A helpful survey of this extra-biblical literature is available in Ehrman, *Lost Scriptures*.

51. The technical term for books that were disputed (i.e., not unanimous) while they were under consideration for canonicity is *antilegomena*. James, Jude, II Peter, II and III John, the Revelation, and the Book of Hebrews were among those that occasioned passionate debate. Although these seven eventually were approved and adopted into the NT, numerous other works did not survive the dispute about them. These include the Gospel of Hebrews, the Apocalypse of Peter, the Acts of Paul, the Shepherd of Hermas, the Epistle of Barnabas, and the Didache, all of which were considered "inspired" and read with approval in many unabashedly Christian locales. But they were kept out of the canon.

historical fact that the passages in which that language occurs spawned a negative Christian view of Jews that has proven ineradicable for two millennia. To continue reading these passages from John for the purpose of explaining them away cannot possibly change the minds of millions of Christians who know what they *read* in John and know what has come to sound normal to them when they hear John *preached*. In the Gospel of John, "the Jews" does not denote anyone in a positive light. Regardless of how complicated and multi-faceted modern interpreters and preachers imagine the referential field of "the Jews" to be, no one included in that category ever meets the approval of "John." In the end, the sad truth is that the church has always understood the Fourth Gospel to be defining *all* Jews as evil, not merely the authorities, not merely those with a "Low Christology," but all of them.

Two urgent but related questions still stand unanswered. [1] Can the Church that granted itself the authority to *create* "the Bible" now exercise its continuing authority to *amend* that Bible? [2] Will the Church that assumed the *authority* to create the Bible finally accept not only kudos for its message of love and hope but also *responsibility* for its vitriolic anti-Jewish teaching of hate and despair?

Final Thoughts on Preaching John

If nothing short of major surgery can save the patient and major surgery is ruled out as an option, the only conclusion to draw is that the Johannine virus of anti-Judaism will continue to rage unchecked. How many more Jews will be forced to live as Other? How many will suffer or be murdered in their own synagogues?[52] No one can say. Can the moment arrive when the moral grounds for a fifth step will finally overcome the fear of radical surgery, the necessity of repentance, and the pain of rehabilitation? That too no one can say.

Christians and Jews do share much in common. Ethical monotheism still offers to the world at large a solution of hope for a badly fractured human society. But the one thing that no Jew should ever be forced to "confess" is the divinity of the human Jesus so defined as to satisfy "John," the Johannine community, the Roman Catholic Church, or any other brand of Christianity.

---

52. As was the case in Pittsburgh on October 27, 2018, ironically in the "Tree of *Life*" synagogue.

IX. "Search the Scriptures"

Preliminary Remarks

JOHN 5:17-38 IS A detailed soliloquy in which John depicts Jesus making his claim to be recognized as the promised messiah. As he nears the central point of his argument, John's Jesus issues a challenge to his Jewish opponents in 5:39: "Search the Scriptures."[1] The implication is that once persons accept this challenge, they will discover that the sacred writings of Judaism confirm John's portrayal of Jesus as messiah. A few verses later (5:46), John has Jesus sharpen his challenge: "If you believed Moses,[2] you would believe me, because he wrote about me."

Among modern Christians, the term "Scriptures" has a specific meaning. The Bible of the Roman (Catholic) Church includes the "Old Testament" with the Apocrypha and several shorter additions to books like Esther and Jeremiah. The Protestant OT accepts the twenty-four books of the Hebrew Scriptures but turns them into thirty-nine books using a different order and numbering system. But for the Christian, the "Scriptures" do not include literature that the church did not accept into either of these canons. As the following examples show, this belief that the Jewish "Scriptures" describe (or even predict) the life and person of Jesus appears in the works of multiple authors throughout NT literature.

First, the Synoptic Gospels feature numerous citations, including most prominently a series of actions and teachings from Jesus that are perceived by NT authors as the "fulfillment" of a prediction found in their LXX version of the Hebrew "Scriptures."[3]

1. The form of the word "search" may be either a simple statement, "you [Jews] search," or the imperative as I have translated it here.

2. Here Jesus is basing his argument on the common perception of that era that Moses was the author of the Pentateuch ("Torah" in Hebrew), comprising the first five books of the Bible. Modern scholarship has shown conclusively that Mosaic authorship of the Pentateuch is not a defensible position.

3. Additional information is offered in Isbell, "Hermeneutics of the New Testament,

Second, in his first letter to Corinth, the Apostle Paul declared that both the death and the resurrection of Jesus were "in accordance with Scripture" (1 Cor 15:3, 4).

Third, in Acts 17:2, Paul is portrayed by Luke as debating with Jews in the Thessalonican synagogue by "reasoning from the Scriptures," and later debating in the same manner with Jews in the Athenian synagogue as well (17:11). Later still, upon his arrival in Achaia, Paul "powerfully refuted the Jews in public" with evidence from "the Scriptures" (18:28). In such synagogue appearances, the burden of Paul's preaching was to demonstrate the messiahship of Jesus, to prove that his death had been a necessity, and that his resurrection had been precisely what "the Scriptures" had described.

Fourth, the most prominent of the original twelve apostles announces that a well-known stone referenced in Isaiah was not the "cornerstone" of the rebuilt Temple as Jews thought,[4] but Jesus Christ, the foundation of all Christian belief (1 Peter 2:6).

In responding to these and numerous other instances, the words of the eminent Rudolph Bultmann come to life. Speaking especially about messianic "prophesies," Bultmann explained, "the New Testament authors do not gain new knowledge from the Old Testament texts but read out of them or into them things they already know."[5] In other words, these ideas were not gleaned *from* the Scriptures, they were brought *to* the Scriptures seeking confirmation of a prior commitment to Christian faith.

The original NT authors possessed at best an elementary understanding of Jewish history and literature and no NT author, including Paul,[6] had more than a rudimentary grasp of the Scriptures in Hebrew. Unable to read the Hebrew originals of the Jewish holy writings that were venerated by Jewish scholars and teachers of that day, NT authors including John believed that numerous references to Jesus were readily identifiable via studying a *Greek translation* (LXX) of the Hebrew original.

In contrast to the interpretations followed by the NT authors and early Christians, Jewish scholars of Scripture worked from the original Hebrew text rather than the Hellenized version used by Christians. This does not mean

---

the Early Church, and Beyond," in *Jews and Christians*, 102–44.

4. See *Leviticus Rabbah* 17:7 and *Deuteronomy Rabbah* 3:13, both citing Isaiah 28:16, as does First Peter 2:6.

5. Rudolph Bultmann, *Essays, Philosophical and Theological*, 187. This is not an endorsement of the Bultmann "School" of thought which has come under attack in recent NT scholarship. But criticism of Bultmann's historical methodology does not negate his insight here into the way in which OT texts were utilized in the service of NT ideas. In this instance, Bultmann's theological judgment was quite sound.

6. Isbell, "Saul the Sadducee?"

that no Jew ever read the LXX. The Jewish translators of the LXX obviously knew that for areas where Greek was the primary language, ordinary Jews who could not read Hebrew may have employed the LXX as a matter of necessity. But there is no evidence that Jewish *scholarly* exegesis of the Hebrew original was ever overturned by appeal to the LXX. For example, no Jewish scholar would have read Genesis 13:15 where the "seed" of Abraham is predicted to be more numerous than the dust of the earth and concluded what Paul the Christian did by interpreting the LXX without reference to the Hebrew original: "It does not say 'and to seeds' meaning many people, but 'to your seed' meaning one person who is the messiah" (Gal 3:16).

And although Judaism never established an official *council* to create a canon of Scripture by majority vote, already by the time of John, there was general acceptance among contemporary Jewish scholars and teachers concerning the sanctity and authority of three literary compilations (Torah/Pentateuch, Prophets, Writings) that would be accepted as a fixed written *Hebrew* Jewish canon centuries later.[7]

Thus, although Christians and Jews were interpreting the same literature, the differences between the LXX (Greek translation) and the MT (Hebrew original) canons were/are palpable.[8]

The "Suffering Servant" of Isaiah[9]

What became perhaps the most significant idea held by the NT writers about Jesus was their conviction that the Scriptures included the picture of a messiah who suffered and then died for the sins of the world before returning to resurrected life, i.e., the precise stages of the life of Jesus. The problem is that in almost every case, when Paul or Luke writing about Paul or John promises a citation from the Scriptures, it is impossible to identify the passage(s) to which they are referring. For example, Luke depicts Paul not only "debating"

7. This threefold division of literature was known by ben Sira early in the second century BCE. In a textbook authored for his students, ben Sira described three divisions of "Scripture" as "the Law, the Prophets, and Writings" (*Ben Sira* 1:1, 8, 26).

8. It is worthy of notice that ben Sira's grandson translated his grandfather's text into Greek for use by Egyptian students. Schniedewind, *How the Bible Became a Book*, is a valuable survey of this extensive and complicated process that resulted in the establishment of the Christian canon with a Greek OT text.

9. For a different view of the "Suffering Servant" in the broader context of Jewish rabbinic interpretation, see Levine and Brettler, *The Bible with and Without Jesus*, 287–312. It is doubtful that the author of John was aware of any of the alternative positions of the rabbis from a later era. John was trying to prove that his plain sense reading of the *Greek translation of Isaiah 53* offered canonical "Scriptural" backing for his singular view of Jesus in the late first century CE.

the Jews in Thessalonica but also "explaining and proving that it was necessary for the messiah to suffer" (Acts:17:2-3). But there simply are no passages
in the Hebrew Scriptures that support this claim. Nor are there any teachings
in contemporary Jewish tradition that include it.

The idea that the suffering unto death of Jesus was a necessary component and identifying marker of his messianic and soteriological mission
cannot be linked to the *Hebrew* Scriptures. But lacking specific passages to
which Paul or other early Christian missionaries might have been referring
in Hebrew, NT authors expanded the search for a way to prove the case
of the suffering messiah from the Greek rendition of the Hebrew original.
Their efforts led them to an unlikely saga.

Some of the most elegant poetry in the entire Hebrew Bible is found in
chapters 40–55 of the Book of Isaiah, written by an anonymous sixth century
BCE author in Babylon[10] who was probably a member of the international
"school" of the eighth century prophet, Isaiah of Jerusalem.[11] Scattered within
this larger corpus, sometimes placed seemingly awkwardly, are four poems
dealing with the "servant of the Lord" (*'eved YHWH*).[12] These four contain
many of the key words and phrases that were commandeered by various NT
authors to evoke the image of Jesus. Countless modern readers have assumed
that most of these references seem indeed to be describing Jesus of Nazareth.
This assumption is open to challenge.

The first servant poem (Isaiah 42:1–4) opens with reference to "My
[God's] servant whom I have chosen, the one I love, in whom I delight. I
[God] have placed my spirit upon him." The second poem (Isaiah 49:1–6)
describes the servant as predestined for service in much the same manner
that the prophet Jeremiah had been,[13] and adds that the servant's assignment
would include not only the task of restoring the survivors of Israel to God,
but also extending divine salvation to "the remotest parts of the world" (49:6).
Although the third servant poem (Isaiah 50:4-11) lacks the startling phrases
of the first two, it portrays a faithful servant who functions more as a wise
teacher than a prophet of national and international salvation.

The fourth servant song (Isaiah 52:13–53:12) became the star attraction in the NT because of the rich tapestry of phrases that came to

10. Referred to by scholars as "Second Isaiah" or "Isaiah of Babylon," distinguished
from the eighth century BCE prophet "Isaiah son of Amoz," who lived and prophesied
in Jerusalem.

11. This would explain why his writings were appended to the original Isaiah book.
On the concept of prophetic schools in general and the Isaiah school, see Isbell, "The
Limmûdîm in the Book of Isaiah."

12. 42:1–4; 49:1–6; 50:4–9; 52:13–53:12.

13. Cf. Isa. 49:1b with Jer. 1:5.

be associated with the crucifixion, death, and burial of Jesus: "a man of suffering,[14] acquainted with disease" (53:3); "wounded because of our sins, crushed because of our iniquities" (53:5); "YHWH visited on him the guilt of us all" (53:6); "his grave was set among the wicked and the rich at his death" (53:9); "YHWH chose to crush him with grief" (53:10); "he bore the guilt of the many" (53:12).[15] As the great German theologian Claus Westermann noted, so central was this NT linkage back to Isaiah chapter 53, that the *Apostles' Creed* was based upon it "point for point."[16]

This Christian linkage requires examination. In the first place, the NT authors who found references to Jesus in the servant poems paid no attention to the central theme of Second Isaiah's messages in chapters 40–55. These messages of the sixth century BCE prophet of the Exile were designed specifically to comfort the Judean exiles in Babylon with the *positive* reassurance that their punishment, their alienation/separation from God during their Babylonian exile, had been completed (40:1–2), and that the full price of Israel's punishment had been exacted.[17] To the contrary, the NT authors focused on the *negative* fact that the time of alienation and punishment had *not* ended and that payment for human sin had not been made, thus making the birth of Jesus a necessary prelude to human redemption. For them, the experiences of Jesus illustrated the necessarily painful journey along the pathway leading to atonement for the consequences of disobedience and the obligation of faithfulness to God as a covenantal partner.

This point may be phrased another way. The sixth century BCE author of Isaiah chapter 53 believed that atonement for the sins of his Judean audience already had been made at the time of his writing. For the NT writers, sin had remained an ever-present reality for which the antidote had not been found until Jesus arrived. This is not to say that Isaiah viewed the Exile as a once-for-all solution to the problem of "sin." But it does illustrate the idea that because sin warrants punishment, people may not expect forgiveness without accepting and paying the penalty for their own disobedience. Having paid for their transgressions via the Exile, the Judeans became eligible for forgiveness and restoration.

14. Whence the descriptive phrase "suffering servant."

15. See Mk. 10:45; Matt. 12:17–21; Lk. 22:19–20; perhaps Jn. 1:29; Acts 8:26–39.

16. Claus Westermann, *Isaiah 40–66*, 257. This fourth century Creed is considered a distillation of the most important doctrinal points in early Christianity. It is still used in Roman Catholic, Anglican (and Episcopalian), Lutheran, Methodist, Presbyterian, churches as well as in many other smaller denominations.

17. Note the phrase "her iniquity has been expiated" (*nirtzah 'avonah*), and especially "At the hand of Yahweh, she has received double for all her sins."

However, the Christian concept of propitiation by means of which guilty persons escape the consequence of their transgression because someone else (Jesus) has agreed to be punished for it is foreign to Judaism. It is not legitimate to quote Isaiah of Babylon offering encouragement to his sixth century audience in Exile as evidence that the prophet really was talking about substitutionary atonement yet to be accomplished through Jesus six centuries later.

A second major point is equally telling. The inextricable link between these encouraging messages of the exilic prophet and historical reality is to the policies of Cyrus of Persia, the ruler who came to power in 539 BCE via military victory over Babylonia and inaugurated the end to the humiliating Judahite Exile in Babylon. In an act that exerted his authority over the whole of the Babylonian Empire he had vanquished, Cyrus decreed that Judean exiles in Babylon could return to Jerusalem. He even permitted Judahite law to govern in their reborn society except in cases where Jewish law clashed with Persian Imperial statutes.[18] This initial decision of Cyrus to allow exiled Jews to return to their homeland prompted the poet/prophet Isaiah of Babylon to assert in the Hebrew original that YHWH Himself had granted to this foreign emperor the title of משיח ("messiah" in Isaiah 45.1).[19] Successors of Cyrus ratified his decision to allow exiles to return, and furnished Persian military protection and financial support for the rebuilding of the Temple. Years later, Artaxerxes I (465-424 BCE) granted a leave of absence to his personal "cupbearer" (Nehemiah), who led the administrative effort to restore the city of Jerusalem.[20]

Throughout the ensuing centuries, these twin *foci*—bringing foreign domination to an end via military victory and re-establishing a new society in Jerusalem and Judah—became the major emphases of Jewish longing for a messiah: a spiritually enlightened human leader who was militarily powerful enough to recreate these two accomplishments of Cyrus and his successors. Jesus was not interested in either of these goals, asserting to Pilate that his followers had not resisted his arrest because his kingdom was not a restored Judah or any other earthly realm: "My kingdom is not of this world" (John 18:36).

It is fair to say that when Jesus evinced no interest in either of the two major pillars underpinning Jewish longing for a messianic hero, his disinterest was a big part of the reason why Jews who were groaning under

18. Isbell, "Persia and Yehud," 529–56.

19. Fried, "Cyrus the Messiah?" 373–93.

20. Isbell, "Persia and Yehud," 551. The title "cupbearer" describes a high-ranking official rather than a low-level "steward" or "common "butler."

the cruelty of Roman occupation did not identify him as the messiah upon whom they had pinned their hope for deliverance.

The realization that Jesus disdained the military credentials needed to overthrow the Roman occupiers apparently created anxiety among his own disciples as well. As the resurrected Jesus was preparing to return to the heavens, to be replaced by the divine "Spirit," the last question his disciples ever asked him was: "Will you restore the kingdom to Israel now?" The answer of Jesus was stunning: "It is not for you to know times or dates that the Father has reserved for His own authority" (Acts 1:6–8). In other words, to accept Jesus as the promised messiah, it would become necessary to forego both components that Jews deemed essential in defining the role of a true messiah. The scriptural account of the militaristic Cyrus and his restoration of Judah had furnished clear evidence of a foreign emperor's claim to the title of messiah. The life of Jesus did not.

In the context of the elevation to power of Cyrus and his designation as the messiah of YHWH, it is also critical to note that nowhere in any of the four "servant" poems does the title *messiah* appear either in the Hebrew original or in the Greek translation used by the NT authors. Instead, the subject of the poems is the enigmatic Israelite/Judahite servant. In addition, the servant is pointedly identified by the prophet/poet, not as one person who was yet unborn, but as all the people of Israel who had *already* endured the suffering of the Exile in real time and actual history.

The NT assumption that the *'eved YHWH* ("servant of the LORD") in Isaiah was a single individual who was the pre-figurement of Jesus requires a literal interpretation of the Greek translation of the original idea that the prophet expressed in Hebrew. A *collective* Hebrew noun *'eved* ("servant") in the first "servant song" (Isaiah 42:1) is translated as a *singular* in the Greek language of the LXX. When Matthew 12:18 quotes the voice of God saying, "Here is my servant whom I have chosen," the Greek singular ("servant") appears to be designating a single individual. But Isaiah 41:8 refutes such an understanding: "You, Israel, are My servant, Jacob whom I have chosen, offspring of Abraham My friend." 43:10 reads similarly: "You [*'atem*] are My servant whom I have chosen." Here Isaiah chose the Hebrew plural *'atem* to mean "all of you."

Then Isaiah 53:10 expresses the glorious hope of the future for the servant of the Lord who had suffered (all Israel): "they will see offspring and have long life." It was this *communal* experience of punishment in Exile that brought about forgiveness to the *entire nation*. Contrary to the Hebraic plain sense of Isaiah, the NT authors read the entire LXX ("Greek") version of the poem as describing Jesus the *individual*.

Burkett's characterization of the linkage between Jesus and the suffering servant of Isaiah 53 is precisely on point. It was nothing short of "a new, specifically Christian conception of the Messiah."[21]

The Suffering Servant as a Sacrifice for Sin

While the Hebrew Scriptures employ the term "messiah" (*mašîaḥ*) with reference to high priests, prophets, and above all to kings, "messiah" does not refer to anyone offering himself as a *human sacrifice* that redeems other people and thereby relieves them of the consequences of their sinfulness. The Hebrew term *zevaḥ* ("sacrifice") can refer to sacrifices in multiple different categories, none involving a human victim. But three general types are important to the NT and the Johannine understanding of Jesus as a sacrifice for sin.[22]

The first general category includes the *shelamim*, offerings seeking "shalom" with God, i.e., offerings seeking "well-being." Symbolic of the communion between the human and the deity, this type of sacrificed animal "is shared between the offerer and God, with God receiving the choice parts."[23] The blood of the sacrificed animal plays no role in this ritual.

The second main category, the *'olah*, is commonly translated as "whole burnt offering." An *'olah* belongs exclusively to God, in each case being transformed by ritual fire into smoke that ascends upwards as "a pleasing aroma to the Lord."[24] But the *'olah* is not designed to atone for willful, purposeful sins. The Book of Job includes a fascinating example of the purpose for which the *'olah* is suited, illustrating the fact that the "whole burnt offering" is designed for unintentional transgressions only. Worried about the inclination of his children to party excessively,[25] following each round of "drinking,"[26]

---

21. Burkett, *Introduction*, 66.

22. For a more detailed explanation of these categories, see Isbell, *Jews and Christians*, 187–190.

23. Levine and Brettler, *The Bible with and Without Jesus*, 228.

24. See Leviticus 1:9, 13, and 17.

25. "Eating" and "drinking" are emphasized in Job 1:4.

26. The word *mishteh* is often rendered "party" or "feast" in translations. But the root meaning of the word is "drink," and it refers to a social gathering involving alcohol. This is illustrated vividly in the Book of Esther, where the Jewish Queen Esther hosts a *mishteh* to which only King Ahasuerus and Haman, the evil enemy of the Jews, are invited. In Esther 7:2, the description of Esther's party for the two men is described as *mishteh ha-yayin* ("wine-drinking").

Job would send word to them to purify themselves, and, rising early in the morning, he would make burnt offerings for each child. [Because] Job thought "my children may have sinned and blasphemed God in their thoughts" [or "hearts"]. This is what Job did customarily.[27]

As this citation of Job illustrates, the burnt offering ritual (*'olah*) demanded a process of purification first, and only after that would an animal sacrifice be accepted.

The third general category of sacrifices is the *hata't*, usually rendered as a "sin offering." In fact, the term may refer to either an act of sin or the sacrifice that is offered in response to a sin. But it is crucial to note that the *hata't*, like the *'olah*, is not intended as an atoning act for *intentional* sins.[28] Leviticus 4:27–28 specify that *only* sins that are committed "unwittingly" (*bishegagah*) are eligible to be "covered" or atoned. The offending person may realize his guilt after the fact, or it may be brought to his attention by another, whereupon a ritual of atonement will be required.[29] But since the "sin" has been inadvertent or "unwitting," it was assumed that such behavior would cease immediately upon being recognized. In other words, the *hata't* was not a provision to take care of willful sin or sinful action that *continues* even after being pointed out to the "sinner."

If the action now understood to be sinful has ended, the same two steps outlined for the *'olah* are required for a "sin offering" ritual, the *hata't*: repentance and/or purification first, followed by the physical act of sacrifice. Further, since the *hata't* was considered efficacious for either an act of sin or for a physical ailment, it was not to be offered by a sinful person hoping to achieve pardon without ceasing to sin or by a person who was still ritually "unclean." To be effective, the sin offering had to be offered by someone grateful to have received pardon already, i.e., after having repented and ended an act of sin in the aftermath of his transgression or after having been cleansed ritually. To offer a *hata't before* repentance and cleansing, i.e., to kill an animal hoping to avoid the consequences of one's sin or illness, would have been sacrilegious.

A "sin offering" (*hata't*) was not an acceptable *substitute* either for repentance followed by a changed lifestyle or for ritual cleansing after an

---

27. Job 1:5. Cf. also 1 Sam 15:22; Isa 1:11; Jer 7:22–23; Amos 5:21–24; and especially Psalm 50:12–15.

28. See the masterful treatment of biblical sacrifices by Levine, *Leviticus*, 3–47. See also Milgrom, *Leviticus 1–16*.

29. Leviticus chapter 5 adds additional examples of the way in which guilt may be incurred unwittingly, each one requiring a "sin" or "guilt offering."

illness. The sacrifice itself was an expression of gratitude for the efficacy of the prescribed rituals of repentance and cleansing.

The "Sin Offering" and the Function of Blood

In the ritual involving the *ḥaṭa't*, unlike the *shelamim* or the *'olah*, blood did play a significant role. Its use in the final step to atonement was considered necessary because it symbolized life.[30] Even though the Levitical system was not designed to cover intentional sins, an imperfect human in the presence of God risked becoming the object of divine wrath because absolute justice would demand the forfeiture of a life for *any* violation of a divine edict, regardless of how minor or unintentional. The blood of the sacrificed animal symbolized and substituted for the human life that could otherwise be lost. Here it is important to remember that a symbol is not the equivalent of reality.

This idea of offering blood on an altar appears to hark back to ancient times and the worship of deities of the netherworld.[31] It was perceived to be a way of acknowledging the power of God (the gods) over life and death. Even an accidental erroneous act is technically an offense against a deity for which an appropriate penalty is required. But it is noteworthy that even the anonymous author of the NT Book of Hebrews acknowledges that, "It is impossible for the blood of bulls and goats to take away sin (10:4)." This thought is central to an understanding of the OT sacrificial system. Repentance earns forgiveness and a mandated regimen of health results in cleansing. But only the person who has "clean hands and a pure heart" (Ps 24:4) merits the right to stand in the presence of God forgiven and unashamed even though no sacrifice has been offered. The author of Psalm 25:11 also notes that YHWH may pardon the guilt of a sinner for His own name's sake, again without a sacrifice.[32]

Likewise, Psalm 51, the quintessential biblical expression regarding repentance and forgiveness, outlines a distinctive pathway. The transgressions of a supplicant may be blotted out according to the "abundant mercy" of God, an action that results in cleansing, purging, washing, and

---

30. Creatures and humans alike cease to live when their blood is "spilled" in any fashion, criminal, accidental, etc. See Lev 17:14: "the life of all flesh is its blood."

31. Belief in underworld deities spanned a wide variety of societies and cultures, especially ancient Greece. A useful survey is Taaunon, *The Path of Shadows: Chthonic Deities, Oneiromancy, and Necromancy in Ancient Greece.*

32. One would assume that every person who was pardoned would offer a sacrifice out of gratitude.

restoration to God, all apart from an animal sacrifice and without the shedding of blood (Ps 51:3–18).

Isaiah's "Servant of the Lord" and Jesus

The NT assumption that the reference in Isaiah 53:10a depicts the relationship between the suffering servant of Isaiah in the time of the Exile and Jesus making of himself a substitutionary sin offering six centuries later creates two specific difficulties.

First, the concept of an innocent person (Jesus) receiving undeserved punishment while guilty persons avoid fully justified consequences for their actions is nothing short of a double miscarriage of justice. The prophet Isaiah did not argue that the people of Israel (the "servant" in the "*servant* songs") had suffered undeservedly as Jesus was later said to do, but that the penalty for their fully *justified* punishment for having sinned against YHWH had been completed.

Second, if, as a condition of allowing the punishment of his fellow Judeans to come to an end, an individual servant had offered his own life as reparation in exchange for *their* sins, it is impossible to explain how he could then look forward to his own future that included children and a long life. But when the Hebrew collective "he" is translated properly as an English plural, the meaning of the prophet becomes clear—because the entire Judean community have endured their punishment, "they (i.e., the collective community returned from Babylonian Exile) will see their offspring, they will prolong their days" (53:10b). The collective community was the servant that had "borne the guilt of the many and made intersession for transgressors" (53:12).

The generation of the Exile in fact did suffer horribly, many did die, and the prophet speaks of their multiple "sins" for which they had paid the justly deserved penalty of the Exile. Their decision to renounce their sin and embrace faithfulness to God even in exile made possible a return to Jerusalem and a promise for the following generations. The *zera'*, or offspring ("seed," the nation collectively) of this exilic generation have prolonged their days, to date, from the middle of the sixth century BCE to the twenty-first century CE. This is the unfolding inheritance or reward for the faithfulness of the servant, all Israel.

Although Isaiah does not do so, a few rabbinic homilies (*Midrashim*) and one early Targum (Aramaic translation of the Hebrew Scriptures) identified the servant as a messianic *figure*. But they do not proceed to identify a specific person as messiah. One Talmudic passage identifies the

Isaianic figure as Moses (b. Sot. 14a), but in another (*Berakhot* 5a), the servant of Isaiah 53 is understood to represent righteous people in every generation who are persecuted for their faith. One later Jewish authority (Saadia Ga'on in the tenth century CE) thought it might refer to Jeremiah.[33] But nowhere does Isaiah of Babylon equate the *servant* with an individual messiah. He designates as "messiah" only Cyrus, the military hero who restored freedom to Jewish exiles.

The identification of Jesus as the servant of the Lord in Isaiah was made most explicitly in the Book of Acts 8:26–39.[34] The author of the narrative was someone predisposed to discover Jesus in the Scriptures. And the search for the individual identity of the "servant" could have been successful only for someone unaware of the way in which a Hebrew collective noun functions, someone limited to reading the Greek translation of Isaiah.

In addition, the passage in Acts shows no awareness of the context, original meaning, or theological function of the servant poems in Second Isaiah. As Luke explains the story, an Ethiopian high court official (national treasurer?) traveling along the desert road leading from Jerusalem to Gaza, happened to be reading from the fifty-third chapter of Isaiah when he was approached by Philip and asked whether he understood what he was reading. Admitting that he could not grasp the text without a guide, the Ethiopian invited Philip into his chariot, where the two of them examined Isaiah 53:7–8 together.[35] When the Ethiopian official inquired of Philip about the meaning of the text, his question was framed with the assumption that Isaiah was describing one specific person. "Of whom is the prophet saying this, of himself or of someone else?" But by responding to the question thus framed (to which *individual* the text referred), Philip's answer that the servant was Jesus ignored the clear implication of the Hebrew text with its *collective* reference to the people of Israel as a group.[36]

---

33. Saadia arrived at this opinion by comparing the Isaiah text with Jeremiah 10:18–24 and 11:19, while the overall allusive nature of the text calls forth comparison with Isaiah (1:5–6; 2:12–14; 11:1–10) and Psalm 91:15–16. Innumerable medieval Jewish authorities went to great lengths to refute the NT connection with Jesus of Nazareth.

34. See also Luke 2:49; 24:7, 26, 46; Acts 1:16; 3:18; 9:16.

35. "He was led as a sheep to slaughter, and as a lamb before his shearer is silent, so he did not open his mouth; he was taken away by oppressive judgment. Who [i.e., no one] can describe his descendants, because his life is taken up from the earth?"

36. As shown above. And see also Isaiah 42:1 and 49:3, where clearly the "servant" is all Israel.

The "Suffering Servant" and "the Lamb of God"

Another way in which the Gospel of John appropriates the scriptural depiction of the "suffering servant" is also instructive. "John" radically redesigns the meetings between Jesus and John the Baptizer by citing John the Baptizer referring twice to Jesus as "the lamb of God [who takes away the sin of the world]" (John 1:29, 36). In her discussion of this designation, Professor Marianne Thompson argues that, "the servant of Isa 53 is compared to a lamb that 'bears the sins of many' . . . even as Jesus takes away 'the sin of the world.'"[37] In her broader discussion of lambs in Scripture, Dr. Thompson notes the following: "the description of Jesus as the 'Lamb of God' who 'takes away' sin may allude more generally to the various sacrifices of lambs that atone or cleanse."[38]

This is an ideological Christian leap well past the function and symbolism of the lamb in the biblical system of sacrifices. As noted above, a dead lamb does not "atone or cleanse:" a lamb could be offered only by a person whose sin had *already* been forgiven via repentance or whose body had *already* been cleansed via ritual cleansing. A person who purposefully continued a life of sin by refusing to repent or remained ritually impure was not eligible to offer a sacrificial lamb. Should such a person kill a lamb, the result would be only a dead lamb, nothing more.

Final Thoughts about "Searching the Scriptures"

All through the era of Jewish history that included the career of Jesus and the writing of the New Testament (100 BCE–550 CE), Jewish rabbis/ scholars labored intensively to "search the Scriptures." During this time, they succeeded in rescuing biblical or Israelite religion from literalism by means of updating and modernizing classical sacred narratives, seeking assiduously to understand the new world in which they were forced to reside. Their reality was a world without an independent Israelite nation, no king, no army, no Temple, and a system of sacrificial liturgy that the Roman destruction of the Temple had ended. Their treatment of canonical "Scripture" functioned via the use of "*transvaluation*," an attempt to retain the core values of authoritative sacred texts that had arisen in and were bound to specific times and situations. Their method was to extrapolate from older texts *principles* that were still relevant to current faith and praxis. They then clothed those principles in modern dress. In other

37. Thompson, *John*, 47.
38. Thompson, *John*, 47.

words, they sought to express their understanding of Scripture by linking back to and reformulating their ancient narratives into a system that could function in modernity as they were experiencing it.

The results of their seven centuries of labor are published as the three parts of the Talmud (Mishnah, Tosefta, Gemara) in addition to thousands of pages of *Midrashim* (sermons), *Haggadot* (stories), and rabbinic exegeses. Each literary genre speaks to specific areas of Jewish social and spiritual life. Some writings provide serious scholarly debates about the interpretation of Scripture; some include stories of the life experiences of great Jews of the past that served as examples to later generations; some offer sermonic exploration of sacred texts; and so forth. But it would be factually wrong to presume that the early rabbis failed to search the Scriptures thoroughly, humbly, and reverently.

The problem faced by the authors of the NT was not that these Jewish scholars did not search the Scriptures as assiduously as Christian scholars did. The problem was that because the Jews did not share the ideological presuppositions of Christianity, they did not reach Christian conclusions. The rabbis strove mightily to formulate theological instruction *out of* the text (exegesis), and their interpretations began with the analysis of the text as it had been written, always honoring the plain meaning of a biblical narrative. But because what was plain to the Jewish interpreters did not satisfy the ideological needs of the early (or current) Christians, they sought (seek) for different ways to shore up their faith.

First and second century CE Christianity cannot be described as a single, coherent tradition. But no stratum within its ideological boundaries failed to realize early on that it could not define itself as it desired simply by reading out from and then reformulating or reparsing the old narratives of Judaism's sacred writings. Instead, the extensive use of "typology" and "allegory"[39] to interpret the Old Testament was necessary precisely because the old stories as they stood did *not* provide an adequate foundation for the system early Christian authors were determined to erect.

The way in which Christianity developed is instructive. Faith in the person of Jesus came first ideologically, above and beyond all else. In support of this belief, other basic tenets of faith were routinely set forth in advance of textual analysis. Interpretive work came later, done to support both faith in Jesus and the distinctive reading of the Greek Scriptures that supported that faith. The conclusions reached in this manner are more accurately described as *eisegesis* instead of *exegesis*. That is, the method was that of reading *into*

---

39. Beginning with Paul himself, as he notes in Gal 4:24. See Isbell, *Jews and Christians*, 128–35.

the text what early interpreters wanted, needed, and presumed to be there rather than the dogged reading *out of* the text the building blocks that could be forged into objective conclusions founded on the text.

Given the subjective nature of this enterprise, it is not surprising that NT authors often disagreed on significant matters even among themselves. Matthew and Luke offered different dates for the birth of Jesus. Paul specifically denied the virgin birth, and Mark ignored it. John switched the location of the place where Jesus originated (or was born) and radically altered the chronology of his life that the Synoptic Gospels had delineated. Some thought the resurrected Jesus a spirit that could materialize through locked doors, others described a very physical body with nail prints from his crucifixion clearly visible. Facts like these prompted Professor Bart Ehrman to note the following about the NT authors: "They had their own perspectives, their own beliefs, their own views, their own needs, their own desires, their own understandings, their own theologies; and these perspectives, beliefs, views, needs, desires, understandings, and theologies *informed everything they said.*"[40] Including, it must be acknowledged, the way in which they chose to re-interpret the text of their Old Testament to bring it into conformity with their own perspective of Jesus.

Clearly, early Christianity took seriously the Pauline concept that "the law of the spirit of life in Christ Jesus has set you free from the law of sin and of death" (Romans 8:2). Basking in their understanding of that freedom, they undertook the task of creating a people who had been "discharged from the law" (Romans 7:6).

An honest search of the Scriptures makes it clear that in the hands of early Christian apologists, the sacred Scriptures of Judaism were turned on their head. In one of numerous modern examples that might be cited, Professor Marianne Thompson argues forcefully that only those who believe *in advance* that "Jesus is the Messiah, the Son of God," can make sense of the way in which the NT radically departs from the teachings of the Bible Jesus himself read and loved.[41] This method of interpretation must be governed by pre-conceived ideology or it does not yield the pre-determined desired result. One does not search the Scriptures and there find Jesus. One commits to a distinctive form of belief in Jesus first, and then begins the search to find a plausible portrait of him that was envisioned before the search began.

---

40. Ehrman, *Misquoting Jesus*, 11–12, emphasis added.

41. Thompson, *John*, 281. Her argument is cited more fully in Essay X with respect to the Psalms and the Passion Narratives.

Still, the attempt to advance the idea that in Jesus we meet the person about whom "the Jewish Scriptures" speak refuses to die. It would not be offensive for a NT believer to say something like, "The Jews and their Scriptures got it wrong. Jesus is the real deal, and we have decided to follow him." But it is utterly mystifying to consider why NT interpreters have been so persistently intent on trying to make the case that only the NT authors, almost none of whom met or heard Jesus in person, correctly understood "the Jewish Scriptures" read in Greek when the people who wrote, studied, copied, and preserved their Bible all misunderstood them.

Herein lies a key to the perception of Jews fostered by NT authors and nurtured for 2000 years by their followers. Christians have found it difficult to explain the ideological differences between the two faiths, to accept the radically different ways in which Jews and Christians perceive basic matters of theology like God, humankind, sin, repentance, forgiveness, etc. The Christian explanation, beginning with the NT authors themselves, has been framed in the most radical way imaginable—in the Christian mind, the Jews do not see Jesus in the "Scriptures" because they are willfully blind, hard of heart, evil. This is not a difference of opinion, a matter of custom and training, or even a level of intelligence. No! It is not the *inability* of Jews to see and understand the truth, it is their *refusal* to see what is patently obvious to the Christian.

At times, an obscure reference from intertestamental literature can be cited as evidence that some Jews might have expected a suffering messiah. But such a reference does not result from a search of the Jewish Scriptures. Noting that an individual Jew writing a non-canonical text made a claim about messianic expectations that sounds good to Christians is not the same thing as the citation of evidence mined from within the Hebrew "Scriptures" that Judaism sanctified and canonized. Instead, such a reference must be identified as coming from literature that Judaism never canonized. It is fair to label it "Jewish" if it was authored by a Jew. But if that author stood outside the norm of the sacred Jewish canon with respect to the issue being treated or cited, his work was not accorded the title of Scripture.

In a similar fashion, multiple non-canonical, or what came to be viewed as "heretical" writings by authors who deemed themselves Christians lay claim to theological positions that proto-orthodox Christians ultimately rejected and suppressed, sometimes harshly. Claims from Marcionites, Ebionites, Gnostics, Docetists, Adoptionists, Montanists, and a host of others were advanced vigorously by people who thought themselves fully Christian. But their writings were rejected by mainstream Christians and not accepted into the canon of Christianity, placed in position to exercise authority over the church.

Who does the misunderstanding here? Only the Scripturally un-learned would have been convinced by the Pauline, Synoptic, and Johan-nine "proofs" of the messiahship of Jesus supposedly founded upon pillars of Jewish Scripture that many honest Christian scholars freely admit do not exist.[42] No canonical Jewish Scripture defines a messiah as someone who was destined to suffer and die for the sins of the entire world. No canonical Jewish prophet predicts a divine messiah, a virgin birth, or a propitiating/atoning death. No first century Jew longed for the appearance of a person who would be executed as a common criminal for the crime of sedition against the Roman Empire. No Jewish Scripture even hints at the death of God, who would then need to be raised from the grave by, well—God! Appeals to these yawning *lacunae* in the "Jewish Scriptures" have meaning only to those who had no familiarity with, or worse, no respect for the sacred texts of Judaism.

Not only are some appeals made to teachings that do not exist in "the Jewish Scriptures," but other teachings that do exist are simply ignored. For example, one thing Jewish Scripture did assert was that a future messiah would be a Davidide, and that he would come from Bethlehem in Judea (Micah 5:2). Luke, the author whose account of the birth of Jesus has be-come the primary version celebrated each Christmas, even has Joseph and Mary undertake an arduous journey from their Galilean home to Bethle-hem so their little boy could be born there (Luke 2:4).

The genealogy of Matthew makes a mess out of this Davidic concept, tracing the lineage of Joseph back all the way to David (1:16) before insist-ing that Joseph had nothing to do with the paternity of Jesus (1:18). Luke, who assumes the link with David and whose birth narrative clearly regards Mary as a virgin at conception, later refers to Joseph as the father of Jesus three times (Luke 2:33, 41, 48). This retains the Davidic connection via Jo-seph, but it destroys the idea of paternity via the Holy Spirit.

But "John" could not be bothered with such trivia. When "the Jews" overheard Jesus claiming to be the bread that has come down from heaven, they were puzzled (6:42). They knew what his own disciples knew. Jesus was not from heaven or from Bethlehem in Judea, he was a Galilean (1:46; 7:41, 52).[43] Rather than address this problem with a felicitous narrative

---

42. As do Burkett, Perkins, and Ehrman, *inter alios,* cited frequently in earlier essays.

43. According to Matthew 26:73, the accent of Peter gives away his identity as a Galilean. Notable here is the problem the early rabbis had with the strange accent of a Galilean native, whom they regularly *referred to as a gelili shoteh, a "stupid Galilean" (Eruvin 53b). Galilean rabbis were mocked because of their inability to distinguish con-sonants that were similar. For do*cumentation and a discussion of the Galilean language peculiarity, see Moore, *Jesus, An Emerging Jewish Mosaic.* Note Moore's comment on

that brings Jesus to Bethlehem to be born, John simply ignores this messianic credential and asserts that Jesus had *no* worldly place of origin. Clearly on this point, John's Jesus does not comport with Jewish Scripture. And John appears to be unbothered by the fact. Only a non-Jewish author, someone who had little loyalty to Jewish Scripture, would so easily dismiss a central point of the Bible in presenting his Jesus. Such a dismissal surely originates in the assumption that "the Jews," who wrote the Scriptures, had no idea what any of it meant.

Perhaps the main reason that Christians felt so strongly about their search for Jesus in the Jewish Scriptures was that they needed an ancient lineage to impress Rome 2000 years ago. Presented with a new religion, the Romans dismissed Christianity out of hand as lacking the *gravitas* necessary to be taken seriously.

But although Christianity is now one of the most dominant and powerful religious systems in the world, modern interpreters persist in presuming that a *Christian* spin on the *Jewish* Bible is still not only necessary but correct. In the second century, Christians were a tiny minority, and virtually all new non-Jewish Christians were converted from the lower classes of Roman society. Few of them were educated at all, and even fewer were educated well enough to write strong defenses of their faith. Not only that, but as Ehrman has shown, Christianity was "scattered and poorly financed, with little public presence and less public credence . . . in stark contrast to Judaism, which not only had far greater numbers but also had visible public structures, wide public recognition, and prominent public representatives, some of whom had the ear of the highest officials in the empire, on occasion even of the emperor himself."[44] So Ehrman pleads: "How was Christianity to justify its own existence in this world?" "What recourse was left to the Christian church?"[45]

Sadly, the recourse chosen was to act in the most *un*-Christian manner imaginable—to vilify, to reshape history, to attack "the Jews"—all in the guise of trying "to claim the promises of Israel for the followers of Jesus."[46]

---

page 247 that "even the Galileans who learned Hebrew [in addition to their native Aramaic] were reported to have not been allowed to read the Torah in other synagogues for fear that they might offend God by mispronouncing something."

44. Ehrman, *New Testament*, 363.

45. Ehrman, *New Testament*, 363.

46. Ehrman, *New Testament*, 363. These last three citations are from Ehrman's discussion of "The Rise of Christian anti-Semitism" in *New Testament*, 362–5.

X. The Psalms and the Passion Narratives

Why the Book of Psalms?

CURRENT NT SCHOLARS HAVE not abandoned the attempt to prove that the early Christians "searched the Scriptures" (the Greek version of "the Jewish Scriptures") and discovered there the direct linkage between normative Judaism and the new faith system they had already initiated. Despite their efforts, the evidence surveyed in Essay IX indicates that the links remain largely illusory. This essay concentrates on the Book of Psalms in its role as the contributor of the highest number of OT citations by the authors of the NT.

The NT authors selected the Psalms because they were so highly venerated and widely read in Jewish worship that mere mention of them bespoke the highest level of spiritual depth and authority. Because these NT writers assumed that David was the author of the entire book, some of their Psalm citations invite comparison between David and Jesus, at times to build upon the ancestry of Jesus as a Davidide.[1]

At the outset, it is important to note that these citations consist largely of multiplied half-verses, isolated phrases, or single words rather than contextually nuanced scriptural teachings. No attention was given to the fact that these NT choices were prayers that originally had addressed the most ordinary and frequently experienced crises of human life. And they were venerated and chosen to be prayed in worship precisely because they fit so many different circumstances, they comforted so many different troubled worshipers, and they expressed a depth of faith virtually unknown in any other source. When the NT authors linked these words to Jesus as if he

---

1. But while David is cited as the author (or sponsor) of numerous Psalms, the Psalter itself also lists several other authors who contributed one or more psalms to the canonical Book, including Moses, Solomon, Qorah, Asaph, Heman, and Ethan the Ezrahite.

were the only human in history to have suffered betrayal, false accusations, embarrassment, and even physical trauma, these original functions of the Psalms were ignored.

What Is a Psalm?

In addition to David and the other authors mentioned within the Book of Psalms, several additional individuals are cited as having authored a prayer from the heart that has been preserved outside the Psalter. These were psalms born out of a wide variety of life experiences: Miriam responded to the crossing of the Sea of Reeds ("Red Sea") out of Egypt with music, song, dancing (timbrel in hand), and celebrating the glorious victory of YHWH (Exod 15:20–21); the Song of Moses (Deut 32) celebrates the faithfulness of God; the prophetess Deborah exults at a military victory over King Jabin of Canaan that ushered in forty years of peace (Judg 5); Hannah expressed poetically first the grief of her childlessness (1 Sam 1:3–11) and then her exultation at the joy of motherhood (1 Sam 2:1–10); and Jonah renewed his vows to YHWH and gave thanks for deliverance from the belly of a huge fish (Jon 2:2–9).

In addition to psalms like these that reflect the life experiences of numerous "ordinary" people, great leaders throughout Israelite history (often a king or one of his representatives) sometimes experienced triumphs that prompted them to create songs of praise and thanksgiving. This is reflected in the Hebrew name of the Book of Psalms, *Tehillim* ("Praises").[2]

But song writers and poets ("psalmists"), famous and ordinary alike, also faced vexing crises. In a memorable description, prominent Protestant Old Testament specialist, Walter Brueggemann, notes that "Israel unflinchingly saw and affirmed that *life as it comes, along with joys, is beset by hurt*, betrayal, loneliness, disease, threat, anxiety, bewilderment, anger, hatred, and anguish."[3] As Israelites responded to moments of joy and victory with psalms of praise and thanksgiving, they also created psalms or poetic responses to these more negative or sorrowful experiences. Psalms occasioned by such moments have been titled "Lament" Psalms by scholars. They are notable for giving "authentic expression to *the real*

---

2. Many Jews are aware of the "Hallel" ("Praise") psalms that abound in the *Siddur* [Prayer Book], and most people will recognize the word "Hallelujah," literally "Praise the Lord" found often in the Psalter.

3. Brueggemann, "From Hurt to Joy," 4, emphasis in the original.

experiences of life,[4] as they bear witness to the negative and frightening aspects of human existence.

Ultimately, the "Lament" became the most common literary "type" of biblical psalm found in the Psalter itself. But the biblical editors also allowed a number of these laments to remain situated within the narrative context of their original creation instead of importing them into the Book of Psalms. For example, Job cried out heart-rending laments at the loss of his wealth, his children, his health, and the support of his wife (Job 3:3–12) and the Book of Lamentations contains a series of communal laments about the destruction of the Temple in 587 BCE at the hands of godless pagans.

Before examining the lament psalms in more detail, a brief review of the general nature and purpose of biblical psalms is necessary.

The Psalms in the Worship of Israel

In the worship of biblical Israel, three things were important. First, members of the worshiping community expressed their identity in terms of a shared relationship (covenant) with each other and with their own special deity named YHWH (Yahweh).[5]

Second, YHWH was portrayed as the deity who repeatedly interrupted history for the purpose of creating history, specifically the history of ancient Israel. Above all, this involvement included his intrusion into human affairs for the purpose of creating a people for himself: "They will be My people and I will be their God."[6]

Third, accordingly, an integral component of Israelite worship was "remembrance" of the actions of God in history, especially his actions on behalf of Israel. But to "remember" was not simply a mental exercise or a casual stroll down memory lane. To remember the past was to capture the *élan vital* of that past by recreating or reenacting it liturgically, and in this manner to appropriate the redemptive and sanctifying power of an ancient event for a present moment. This explains why the first *Siddur* (Prayer Book) of Judaism, the *Book of Psalms*, includes so much material that recounts the redemptive moments of Israel's past, requiring by the retelling of those moments not only a celebration, but also a re-experiencing that allowed members of the worshiping community to identify themselves as partners in the grand narrative of redemption that had begun long before their lifetimes.

---

4. Brueggemann, "From Hurt to Joy," 3.

5. Note the expression in Psalm 33:12: "Happy is the nation whose deity is Yahweh."

6. A formula found in Jeremiah 32:38 and over forty other verses.

Although the original situations that prompted most of the 150 canonical psalms have been lost, the presence of most psalms that have remained embedded in biblical narratives *outside* the Psalter are a reminder that most if not all the psalms had been created out of a specific moment in time, a unique life occurrence, or an unusual confluence of events. A moment involving the entire nation often produced a psalm that allowed the worshiping *community* to access its relationship with God in history. But the experiences of individual members of the community often prompted very *personal* responses to a critical moment in time that held specific meaning. In this manner, different individuals worshiping at a time later than that of the original author of the psalm, discovered the commonality of their own experiences with those of individuals who had preceded them. And they also learned that these earlier common experiences had often concluded with a moment of redemptive triumph or victory over the sorrow, the hurt, the grief.

Numerous canonical psalms include "superscriptions" that seek to identify the original composers and their original situation. It is unclear how such superscriptions were selected or why they were deemed necessary, and modern explanations of many of them are based on assumptions that cannot be proven.[7] But whether the worshiping community of Israel knew the correct identity of an original author and his situation or not, the treatment of history exemplified in the written psalms allowed these individuals from earlier eras to speak to later worshiping individuals and communities.

Psalm 51 is only one example of the attempt to match a psalm with history. It opens as follows: "A song from David when Nathan the prophet came to him because he had gone to Bat-Sheva." Yet a careful reading reveals not a single reference to 2 Samuel 11–12, the narration of the well-known incident that supposedly precipitated the composition of the psalm in question. Absent are the woman with whom David committed adultery (Bat-Sheva'), her murdered husband (Uriah), the faithful army commander (Joab) forced by David into complicity in the murder of Uriah, and even the prophet Nathan who played a central role in the story. What is more, verse 20b is a prayer for the walls of Jerusalem to be rebuilt, walls that were not breached until centuries after the death of David. No modern scholar would link Psalm 51 with the narrative of the incident involving Bat-Sheva'.

On the other hand, although David could not have composed Psalm 51 in its entirety following his great sin, and although there are no clues to the identity of the actual author, the prayer/poem still represents perhaps the most powerful expression in world literature of the emotional duress that accompanies moral failure, the sense of lost self-respect that

---

7. Isbell, "The Musical Notations in the Book of Psalms."

all individuals have experienced in their own lives, and the deep longing for forgiveness and wholeness. And had anyone been there to hear, Psalm 51 has the feeling of what David might well have cried out to God[8] lying alone in his palace in the dark of night, wearing sackcloth, and thinking about his moral breakdown.[9]

Regardless of its true author or the personal situation that prompted this cry from the depths of the soul, anyone who reads the psalm can recognize its power to express bluntly how it feels to have failed to keep faith with God, to have abdicated responsibility to other members of the community, to have broken one's personal moral code, to have abused one's power, to have harmed an innocent "other," to have "sinned."

The unique contribution made by the editors of the Book of Psalms, then, was their ability to take poems that had been originally *time-bound* and release them into the sphere of the *timeless*; to take words that were intensely *personal* and event-specific and release them into the timeless stream of *communal* liturgy and worship; to forge the experiences of *earlier* worshipers in the community of faith into expressions of reassurance and transformation for *current* worshipers. This condensation, transvaluation, and re-forging of Israelite history found in the Psalms was not merely an updating from one specific moment in the past to another equally specific current moment, but a recognition of the eternal and universal relevance of deeply spiritual and emotionally powerful songs and prayers. The "Lament" played a crucial role in this process.

The "Lament"

Some lament psalms are personal while others are communal. They may be recognized by the inclusion of expressions like "Why?" or "How long?" Some psalmists, like the author of Psalm 13 insisted that they had always "trusted" God, yet they complain of feeling personally forgotten by God while enemies rejoice over their distress. But psalms of lament or sorrow were never merely complaints.

Surprisingly, it was precisely in the moments of greatest anguish that the authors of the lament psalms found new and creative ways to express their trust in God. First, of course, they needed to express their sorrow plainly and honestly. And "the faith expressed in the lament is nervy, that honest facing of distress that can only be done effectively in dialogue with

---

8. "I know my transgressions and my sin is ever present with me" (Ps 51:3).

9. See 2 Samuel 12:16.

God who acts in transforming ways."[10] As a corollary to their honesty, these authors refused to remain mired in sorrow, wallowing in self-pity and despair. They needed to re-commit themselves to obedience, trust, and faithfulness to YHWH. In this process involving numerous authors and several centuries, great spiritual giants and ordinary people alike learned via prayer and worship to move from a *cri de coeur* to a *cri de joie*.

The community of Israel knew that not only spiritual giants, but also ordinary folk faced crisis moments exactly like those that earlier and greater Israelites had experienced. Throughout human history, virtually every individual has experienced fear so overwhelming that it is difficult even to breathe a tiny prayer silently; illness so frightful that it is almost impossible to think clearly; moments of despair that drive one to the bosom of his/her spiritual family in search of solace if not understanding. That is why, in addition to providing a litany of praise and thanksgiving to God for the goodness of life, a second major function of the lament psalms was to provide meaningful articulation in a time of unspeakable sorrow.

It is not surprising that later worshipers found resonance with these expressions of grief or fear, or failure or despair that were wrenched from the soul of an earlier worshiper. The biblical psalms are prayers from the heart, or better, from the depths of the human soul. They doubtless spoke to a multitude of later supplicants. No psalm would have been preserved on the list of elite canonical prayers unless it had resonated with people of later generations. That was the purpose! A broken-hearted supplicant, at times too burdened to give expression to his/her own sorrow, could lean on the wording of an earlier fellow traveler who had faced a similar crisis. To shrink this inter-generational connection to a single human person facing trauma is to misunderstand and limit the purpose and scope of the psalms.

Job lost everything. David's own son fomented a rebellion against him that almost cost David his kingdom and placed his very life in grave danger. An anonymous poet in Babylonian Exile expressed the depths of his grief at having lost his beloved national capital city; his poem became Psalm 137. Later Jews would also lose their homeland and would turn in their moments of loss to this magnificent expression that is both utterly sorrowful and tinged with hope.[11]

---

10. Brueggemann, "From Hurt to Joy," 5.

11. The scholarly literature on Lament psalms is enormous. In addition to the article cited above, Walter Brueggemann added a definitive treatment of lament psalms in "The Formfulness of Grief," 263–75. The eminent German theologian Claus Westermann offered a helpful treatment of the literary and form-critical elements characteristic of lament psalms in *The Praise of God in the Psalms*.

It is to these psalms of lament that the NT gospel authors turned most often.[12] But they seemed unaware of the fact that Jesus was not the first person, nor would he be the last, to feel fear, betrayal, grief, and even abandonment. In his hour of crisis, according to the NT gospels, Jesus did what countless Jewish worshipers before and after him have done—he sought help from someone whose mastery of language spoke for him, said it better than he could in his moment of stress, linked him to a profound tradition of trust in almighty God.

The idea of finding compelling evidence, not just of a messianic *figure* to arrive at some time in the future, but evidence pointing specifically to *Jesus of Nazareth*, is far too small a box in which to enclose the prayers of the Book of Psalms. The modern reader can indeed comprehend a link between Psalms and the terrifying moments that brought Jesus to the end of his life. But latching on to this crisis as if Jesus were the first and still the only person to endure a solitary Gethsemane experience ignores a fundamental reality of biblical faith: even the most ordinary persons may turn to the Psalms and discover that they are not alone in experiencing despair, sorrow, and suffering. For centuries, both before and after Jesus, the description of Bernard W. Anderson has been true: *"Out of the Depths, the Psalms Speak for Us Today."*[13] And they speak *for* us precisely because of our inability to understand fully and clearly express the meaning of our own moments of deepest woe.

If the Christian believes that a psalmic expression from the past connects Jesus to innumerable others who have sorrowed or suffered, that is a natural vote of appreciation for the power of the psalms to translate a time-bound moment into the timeless cycle of continuing worship. This was the method by which ancient Israel appropriated for the community of faith a uniquely event-specific experience, expanding its reach to include countless others whose own experiences of grief had also seemed to them to be unique. Words of an earlier psalmist reassured them not only that other people had endured what they now experienced, but also that those earlier worshipers had found a way to move from grief to joy. Through this process of communal worship, seemingly unique personal experiences acquired lasting meaning in the hour of tribulation.

Understood in this way, the links between the Psalms and Jesus show him as fully human, drawing strength for his crisis from the faith of earlier sufferers whom he would never meet, but who had lived through their

12. Their method of linking the Psalms and Jesus is illustrated by Norman Perrin, whose treatment is examined in detail later in this essay.

13. This is the title of a book by Bernard W. Anderson.

own crises and survived to offer others the wisdom of their experience. These references to the Psalms do not depict Jesus as the only and divine child of God, utterly unique from every other fearful, sorrowing Israelite (or modern worshiper), and it would be unjust to confine the psalms to Jesus exclusively while overlooking their power to offer support for every person of faith. Such a narrow confinement betrays the purpose of Psalms and undermines their history of sustaining the community of faith (Jewish and Christian). It also negates the strength and comfort provided by the heritage they embody.

But John was not reading the Psalms to search for their meaning in prayer and worship. He approached them determined to verify what he already had decided to be true about Jesus. And this action was not unique to John.

The Lament Psalms and The NT Passion Narratives

Modern Christian scholars have joined in the search for references from Psalms to the passion narratives of the New Testament. Norman Perrin, an eminent twentieth century scholar of the gospels, offered one of the most influential treatments of the issue by focusing on three important lament psalms (22, 31, and 69) that he believed allowed early Jerusalem-based Jewish Christians to "explain how it came about that Jesus, whom they claimed to be the Messiah of God, had suffered an ignominious death at the hands of the Romans."[14] Here it is important to note Perrin's acknowledgement that the designation of Jesus as "the Messiah of God" is a preliminary step that prompts early Christians to turn to the Psalms for an explanation of what they had already decided. This is akin to what has been termed "prophecy historicized" rather than "history remembered."[15]

1. Psalm 22

Perrin's first example is canonical Psalm 22, and the most noteworthy feature about it is its function as a personal lament, composed by someone who felt that God had abandoned him. It features all five of the standard components that are common to every lament psalm:[16]

I. *The Address to God*: "My God, my God" (22:2a).

14. Perrin, *The New Testament: An Introduction*, 45.

15. Crossan, *Who Killed Jesus?*

16. In "The Formfulness of Grief," Brueggemann compared the five components of a lament psalm to the five stages of grief articulated by Elizabeth Kübler Ross in her seminal book, *On Death and Dying*.

II. *The Lament Proper*: "Why have you abandoned me" (22:2b–19).

III. *The Petition Proper* (expressed in the imperative): "Be not far away, O my strength. Hasten to my assistance. Save my life from the sword, my precious life from the clutches of a dog. Deliver me from a lion's mouth, rescue me from the horns of wild oxen" (22:20–22).

IV. *Vow of Praise*: Once deliverance has been accomplished, the petitioner promises to offer praise to God, to pay his vows, etc. (22:23–26).

V. *Confession of Trust*: "[Future] generations will worship Him; [the fame of] the Lord will be told for generations; they will recount His righteousness to people yet to be born, because He has acted" (22:31–32).

As the following chart shows, numerous phrases from Psalm 22 are indeed tightly woven into the NT Passion Narratives.

22:2 "My God, my God, why have you forsaken me?" ['azavtani]	Cited in Aramaic by both Mark 15:34 and Matthew 27:46.
22:7: "All who see me mock me."[17]	Paraphrased in Mark 15:29 ("they derided him"); Matthew 27:29, 43 ("they mocked him"); and Luke 23:35 ("[the rulers] scoffed at him")
22:8: "Let him commit himself to YHWH; let Him rescue him, let Him save him, for He is pleased with him."	Matt 27:43: "he trusts in God; let Him deliver him, if He desires him."
22:18: "They divide my clothes among themselves, and they cast lots for my garments."	Matt 27:35–"they divided his garments among them by casting lots." Mark 15:24–"[they] divided his garments among them, casting lots for them." Luke 23:34–"they cast lots to divide his garments" John 19:24–"This was to fulfill the Scripture: 'they parted my garments among them, and they cast lots for my clothing.'"

17. The theme of feeling mocked by others while enduring trouble, suffering, or loss is repeated often in the psalms. See for example 1:1; 5:6; 10:7; 12:3; 17:10; 27:2; 31:11, 18; 35:11, 16, etc.

It is not difficult to imagine that Christian readers of the New Testament perceive a close connection between Psalm 22 and the suffering and death of Jesus as depicted in the Passion Narratives. But before it is concluded that the author of Psalm 22 was predicting or describing the death of Jesus, it is crucial to bear in mind several facts.

First, Psalm 22 has no reference to "messiah."

Second, the author of Psalm 22 does not die, but in fact lives to offer glorious praise to his deity (YHWH) who has "acted" (*'asah*) in his behalf (22:32).[18]

Third, these final words of Jesus on the cross have often been misinterpreted to imply the opposite of their true function.

In the study of the Psalter, Jewish rabbinical scholars learn to identify each psalm by its opening words. Then, having identified the psalm under consideration, they are expected to know the message of the entire psalm. Because a lament psalm could not end on a question ("Why?" or "How long?"), students are taught to keep reading until the text arrives at its answer(s) to each such question. And they must remember that each lament psalm represents a complete liturgical act of transformation whereby worshipers entered the sanctuary in grief, expressed themselves frankly to God, reconsidered their own lives of faithfulness, vowed to recommit to God, and through that process were brought to restate their faith in the goodness and power of God.

As a knowledgeable Jew who doubtlessly knew the Psalms very well, when Jesus chose to recite the opening words of Psalm 22 on the cross ("My God, my God, why have You forsaken Me?"), he was not succumbing to despair. He was making an affirmation of faith because he knew how the psalm ends: "[God] has acted."[19]

A Christian interpreter may certainly take this understanding of a lament psalm and conclude that in choosing Psalm 22, Jesus was exhibiting confidence in his coming resurrection by the power of God. But the point is that the original author of Psalm 22, perhaps an ordinary person facing ordinary though grievous troubles, prayed through his grief to joy in his faith and his God. He did not experience death and the need for resurrection. And he did not view himself, nor did the community view him, as a special "messiah" on whose shoulders the fate of the entire nation rested.

---

18. And see Psalm 37:5. "Commit your way to YHWH; trust in Him and He will act" (*ya'aseh*).

19. In his discussion of the Passion narrative as *midrash*, Wylen (*The Jews in the Time of Jesus*, 131-2), has drawn the same inference from Jesus' citation of Psalm 22:1.

2. Psalm 31

The second psalm to which Perrin alludes is number 31, in which the lamenting author cried to God: "Into Your hand I entrust my spirit" (31:6 in Hebrew, 31:5 in English), quoted by Jesus on the cross. Again, the context of the two statements is different. As Luke makes clear, this is the final statement made by Jesus immediately before "he breathed his last" (Luke 23:46). But the person speaking to God in Psalm 31 was not about to take his final breath and die. He was thanking God for having delivered him, and he was speaking to God optimistically about how he looked forward to the opportunity to "exult and rejoice in Your faithfulness" precisely because "You do *not* hand me over to my enemy" (31:8).

As is the case with the citations of Psalm 22, the early (or current) Christians could decide that the wonder of Jesus was that he could say at the very moment of death what the earlier psalmist could muster only in the context of being delivered from enemies and being granted additional life. And from his words, Christians may decide that the example of Jesus incorporates in one moment on the cross all the troubles of life which he overcame as he died. But that is a far cry from the idea that Psalm 31 identified Jesus and described him as a suffering and dying messiah whose death redeems all humanity.

3. Psalm 69

Example number three for Perrin is found in Psalm 69. Here too a lamenting author decries the fact that those who hate him are "more numerous than the hairs of my head" (69:5 in Hebrew, 69:4 in English). Those who hate the psalmist have acted terribly to him.[20] They have tried to destroy him by attacking him with lies, they have insulted him, drunks have made up songs about him, they have given him gall for food, and "vinegar to quench my thirst" (69:22 in Hebrew, 69:21 in English). But once again, the individual on whose lips these words were formed did not die.

The Passion narrative written in John 19:28–30 is shorter than those in the Synoptic Gospels and there is no evidence that John was relying on the earlier gospel accounts in composing his version of the actual death of Jesus. There is only one detail where John offers his variant of a theme that had been treated in Mark. A fragment of one statement from Psalm 69:21 appears in Mark when the crucifiers of Jesus gave him "wine mixed with

---

20. Called his "enemies" in 69:14; note that "hate" and "enemy" are from the same root in Hebrew.

myrrh" which he did not accept (Mark 15:23), but then "vinegar" a few moments later (Mark 15:36). In the case of Jesus, quite unlike the situation of the psalmist, this offering of vinegar is interspersed between his cry of "My God, my God" (Mark 15:34) and his final breath thereafter (Mark 15:38). John's depiction is more compact: "When he had received the drink [of vinegar], Jesus said, 'It is finished.' With that, he bowed his head and gave up his spirit" (John 19:30). The psalmist lived to offer praise to God for having overcome his enemies and their multiple attacks.[21] The victim of crucifixion in the gospels did not survive.

Final Thoughts about the Psalms and Jesus

Can one find Jesus in the Book of Psalms? Certainly, the gospel writers thought they had done so. But one can also find the image of countless ordinary worshipers whose lives faced the sorrowful wreckage that reality so often visits upon everyone. And herein lies an important caveat. To find Jesus in the Psalms, a clear method of eisegesis is required.

Professor Marianne Thompson, who authored a detailed and cogent analysis of John's use of the Psalms in his version of the Passion Narrative,"[22] pointedly notes that a *prior commitment* to Christian belief in Jesus has always been necessary to make sense of the way John uses the Psalms. Here is the extended statement of Thompson offering her own opinion of the argument to be made from Jesus to Psalms and back:

> The implied readers of the Gospel have adopted the stance of faith to which Jesus calls disciples and have undergone the "birth from above" of which he spoke to Nicodemus. They participate in those very same realities that are spoken of in the text: they have been born anew by the Spirit of God, who brings Jesus' word to remembrance (14:26), bears witness to Jesus (15:26), and guides into all truth (16:13). The Spirit thus works to grant fuller understanding of the truth of Jesus' identity (cf. e.g., 1 John 4:1–2, where appeals to Spirit-inspired prophecies ground divergent testimonies to the person of Jesus). Those who live out the realities of faith promised by Jesus in the Gospel, who believe that "Jesus is the Messiah, the Son of God," read the Scriptures as pointing to him as the King of Israel. Given their

---

21. See especially verses 19–30.

22. Thompson, "The Psalms in the Passion Narrative of the Gospel of John," 267–83.

faith in Jesus as Messiah, King of Israel, it is hard to imagine how any other reading of these psalms could make sense.[23]

The procedure Thompson describes is astonishing, as is her frank acknowledgement that only the born again, spirit-filled Christian can hope to understand the biblical psalms, but surely not the faithful Jew whose spiritual ancestors wrote, copied, treasured, prayed, and lived by them for centuries before there was a Jesus. Armed with an adequate measure of faith in "Jesus as Messiah," readers of the Psalms can even recognize "Spirit-inspired prophecies" that enhance the faith in Jesus with which their journey began.

But whereas Thompson and her followers look for and find confirmation of what they already believed about Jesus before they began to read, worshipers who serve the God of Abraham, Isaac, and Jacob hear the precious words of earlier brothers or sisters in the family of faith uttering words of praise and hope. At other times, they hear earlier burdened hearts pouring out their anguish to God as they face an awful moment of sorrow in their own lives. Hearing the ancient words, reciting them in the attempt to absorb their truth for themselves, later (and current) worshipers find the One deity whose action on behalf of ancient Israel ended Egyptian slavery, gave them the "tree of Life" (the sacred Torah), ended Babylonian Exile, and restored the kingdom to Israel under the Maccabees. Armed with this precious heritage, later and current worshipers gain the courage to forge ahead with lives that are triumphant.

Thompson was correct. No one finds Jesus in the Scriptures *except* a person who brings Jesus with him/her at the beginning of the search.

These words of Thompson underscore the many differences between Jewish ideology and the variegated needs of nascent Christianity. To be accepted and used by Christianity, the basic thrust of the "Scriptures" had to be altered radically. The Exodus could not serve as the center of New Testament theology. Jewish law was considered so outdated that it needed to be set aside *in toto*. The Temple could play no role even symbolically. A human political, military Davidic messiah needed to be upgraded to a divine/spiritual model who had no interest in "this world." Historical Israel needed to be phased out and replaced.

Before the first gospel was written, and well before systematic early Christian exegetical spadework began, a Christ of faith (*not* the Jesus of history) was believed necessary to stand in the place of the Exodus as the paradigmatic narrative of redemption.[24] A once-for-all-time sacrifice of

---

23. Thompson, "Psalms in the Passion Narrative of the Gospel of John," 281.

24. This required different theological "centers" for the Old Testament and the New, a problem that continuously bedevils scholars who wish to write a Christian "biblical"

the divine Christ replaced the repetitive animal sacrificial system of the Temple. A messiah heading a kingdom "not of this world" took the place of a human messiah who would go into battle to liberate Judah. And a new non-Jewish Israel was called into existence to replace the children of Abraham, Isaac, and Jacob.

For those who insist on an honest search for evidence in the biblical text rather than relying on an unseen and undefinable ideological "spirit" to anoint the text with pre-conceived ideas of truth, the Jesus of the NT does not appear in the Hebrew Scriptures. To the contrary, the radical re-assessment and portrait of Jesus offered to the world by the church has been drawn from the drastic historical revisionism of sacred writ.

---

theology including both testaments.

XI. The "I AM" Sayings of Jesus: Did Jesus Claim to be God?

Introduction

CHRISTIAN NT SCHOLARS UNIVERSALLY assume that the phrase *egō eimi* ("I Am") is the Greek translation of the Hebrew name of the God of the biblical Israelites. This leads them to presume that in several places where *egō eimi* occurs in the Gospel of John, Jesus is appropriating the sacred name of God as his own, thus declaring his divinity.[1] This essay examines the reasoning behind this mistaken Christian theory and surveys the evidence used to support it. Before beginning, it will be helpful to clarify some important facts about the language(s) and culture of Jesus, his apostles, the authors of the NT gospels, and their target audiences.

Preliminary Remarks

All four gospel authors wrote in Greek, and all but a few of their quotations of Jesus are cited in Greek. In the sixties, the Scottish scholar William Barkley wrote a multi-volume set of commentaries on the New Testament that achieved remarkable popularity.[2] Throughout twenty-seven volumes, Barclay expended virtually no effort in trying to analyze the Semitic wording that might have given birth to the Greek quotations of Jesus attested in the New Testament. His method was to analyze the NT with a sharp focus on the precise etymology and function of key Greek words in the text. His comments presumed a Hellenistic context and fostered the impression that Jesus and all the other actors in the NT stories chatted away effortlessly in Greek.

1. On this subject, see Kysar, *John, the Maverick*, "The Christological Meaning of the 'I AM Sayings,'" 56–60.

2. *Daily Study Bible*. Barkley, a Church of Scotland theologian, was trained in classical Greek, and his insights into the meaning and functions of various NT Greek words are fascinating.

But there are a few brief comments of Jesus cited in Mark 5:41, 7:34, and Matt 27:46 that permit a more accurate idea of what Jesus and his disciples spoke as a first language ("mother" tongue). That language was not the Greek in which the gospels are composed and into which the words of Jesus have been translated by non-Jewish authors. The mother tongue of Jesus was Aramaic, a Semitic dialect closely akin to Hebrew. It is a simple matter to demonstrate this assertion from within the gospel texts themselves.[3]

First, to command the resurrection of the small daughter of the Roman official Jairus, Jesus spoke in Aramaic (Mark 5:41 and parallels). This was a moment suffused with emotion, a time when thoughts would surely form much quicker in a mother tongue than in a second or a third language. Three disciples were present in the room when Jesus spoke to the young girl, and it may be inferred that they also were comfortable with the Aramaic language that came naturally to him.

Second, much later, waiting outside the hall where Jesus was on trial, Peter's Galilean Aramaic accent gave him away (Matt 26:73).[4] This further indicates that Aramaic was the language in which Jesus taught and in which Peter and the other disciples conversed with him during a normal day.

Third, as his life was ending on the cross, Jesus cited Psalm 22:1 in Aramaic rather than in Greek or even in its original Hebrew (Mark 15:34; Matt 27:46). The mother of Jesus was present at his crucifixion (John 19:25) and speaking in the language she spoke and had taught him as a child would have been natural.

Finally, an incident in the life of Paul illustrates the fact that Jesus and his disciples were far from the only Jews in Palestine who spoke Aramaic natively. In fact, because Aramaic was "the vernacular of [all] Palestinian Jews,"[5] when Paul was charged with being anti-Jewish (Acts 21:27–28), he convinced an unruly mob to listen to his defense because they heard him speaking Aramaic (Acts 22:2).[6]

---

3. Jesus spent a sizeable portion of his life in Galilee, especially Capernaum and his hometown of Nazareth, both of which were Aramaic-speaking villages

4. See Essay VIII, note 44. See also Mark 14:70 and Luke 22:59.

5. Bruce, *Acts*, 437–39.

6. The Greek text says that Paul spoke Hebrew to accomplish this, but most NT authorities follow the interpretation of F. F. Bruce (*Acts*, 437–39) who was certain that Paul was speaking Aramaic. The NIV is one of several modern translations that adopts this interpretation. Several other modern versions translate the Greek text as "Hebrew," but explain in a note: "that is, Aramaic." *The Jerusalem Bible* goes farther, translating "Hebrew," but noting that it means "Aramaic" and adding an additional explanation: "Hebrew was barely spoken after the return from exile."

Clearly, for daily conversation, teaching, and public speaking, Aramaic was the language used by Jesus and his disciples, as well as virtually all other Jews in the region.

But Luke's portrayal of Jesus reading from a Hebrew scroll in the synagogue in Nazareth (Luke 4:16–19) demonstrates that when he was praying or worshiping or when he studied the Bible (the "Scriptures"), Jesus was also comfortable to work from the Hebrew original. This competency of Jesus in Hebrew sheds light on an occasion chronicled in the Gospel of Mark. Jesus was asked by "a teacher of the Law" to name the most important commandment in Judaism. He answered without hesitation in a manner that emphasized his absolute commitment to monotheism: "The most important one is this: 'Listen, Israel. Yahweh is our God. Yahweh is *One*'" (Mark 12:29). On the surface, because Mark was writing in Greek, it may appear that this answer of Jesus was also delivered in Greek. But as a knowledgeable Jew responding to a Bible question from a well-educated "teacher," it is virtually certain that Jesus would have recited from the *Hebrew* Scriptures the verse that answered the Jewish teacher's question (Deut 6:4).

The Scholarly Misunderstanding of "I AM"

The author of the Fourth Gospel knew neither Aramaic nor Hebrew. But in their efforts to interpret John, virtually all modern NT scholars overlook the fact that John was limited to quoting Jesus in Greek because he lacked the ability to quote him in Aramaic or Hebrew. Then they assume that the Gospel of John describes Jesus accurately when he chooses the Greek phrase "I am" to claim for himself what they incorrectly presume to be the ineffable name of the God of Israel (Yahweh), the exclusive deity of the people of Israel. This reasoning flies in the face of the blunt affirmation of monotheism offered by Jesus just cited from Mark.

The standard procedure followed by these scholars is to imagine a multi-step linkage between the simple statement "I am" (Greek *egō eimi*) and the Hebrew divine name of God, Yahweh. But this procedure is indefensible grammatically. Here, it is important to note that biblical Hebrew does not have a word for the present tense of the verb "to be." This means that there is no Hebrew word for "am" and thus the entire argument about *egō eimi* in John is based upon Greek translation.

There are three fundamental problems with the idea that "I am" in Greek should be the cause of such an extreme claim about the name of Jesus. First, as will be demonstrated below, "I am" is not a name (a proper noun) but a short *verbal* phrase that introduces a proper name. To complete the process of self-identification or introduction, the verbal phrase must be completed by the addition of a name. This means, among other things, that "I am" is not one of the names of God.

Second, Greek was not the *native* language of Jesus or any other Jewish person in the Gospel of John. And although it is going beyond the evidence to assert that Jesus knew absolutely no Greek, there is no evidence that he ever used it to teach a lesson to his students or that he ever spoke Greek in public or in private. Neither is there any evidence to suggest that Jesus knew or ever referred to the Greek *Septuagint*, the only version of the Hebrew Scriptures John knew and cited.

Third, surely if Jesus were to have made an earth-shattering pronouncement about his own name, he would have chosen to make it either in his mother tongue (Aramaic) or in the holy language he used in worship and prayer (Hebrew).

Still, numerous NT scholars continue to accept the remarkable claim of John that Jesus chose the Greek language in which to appropriate the personal name of God for himself. The explanation of Professor Bart Ehrman is typical. After noting that *egō eimi* occurs just twice in Mark and Luke, and only five times in Matthew, Ehrman makes the following point, concluding with an exclamation: "Contrast this with the Gospel of John, where Jesus uses the verb to refer to himself a total of forty-six times!"[7] Later in the following paragraph, Ehrman asserts authoritatively that "by calling himself 'I am' he may actually be taking the name of God."[8] Not only did Raymond Brown agree with Ehrman, what Ehrman thinks *"may"* have been the case, Brown baldly asserted as *fact*, confidently citing John's depiction of Jesus using "the divine name 'I AM.'"[9]

To buttress his claim, Ehrman offers the following explanation: "In the Jewish Scriptures, when Moses is sent by God to assist the Israelites, he asks God his name. God replies, 'I am (Hebrew: *'Ehyeh*) who I am . . . This is what you shall say to the Israelites, I am has sent me to you'" (Exod 3:14).[10] Ehrman is assuming that his English translation of 3:14 is accurate. It is not! It is *a clumsy and inaccurate* translation of the Hebrew text. And it contorts a clear declarative Hebrew statement into a sentence that no fluent speaker of English would say: "I am has sent me to you." "I am" is not a *name* either in English or in Greek.

---

7. Ehrman, *New Testament*, 141, Box 10.4. And note that Ehrman assumes that Jesus spoke the phrase *egō eimi*, not that John placed the phrase on the lips of Jesus to support his own proto-ecclesiastical ideology.

8. Ehrman, *New Testament*, 141, Box 10.4.

9. Brown, *Community*, 114.

10. Ehrman (*New Testament*, 141, Box 10.4).

Again, it is more than a little bit curious that the single most important argument about the identity of Jesus (i.e, his divine name) revolves around a common phrase in a language he seldom if ever would have spoken. If Jesus or any of the other players in the drama of John's Gospel ever did speak Greek, they all would have needed to say "I am" (*egō eimi*) multiple times in the course of an ordinary day of conversation. In so doing, none of them would have been claiming the name of God.

"I AM" in Hebrew and Aramaic

Exodus 3:14, the verse which Ehrman chose to illustrate his theory about the divine name, is the correct starting point for analysis of the enigmatic name that God revealed to Moses during their burning bush conversation on the mountaintop. In that dialogue, God told Moses that he was sending him back to the Pharaoh to free the Israelites (3:10) and assured him that he (God) would be with Moses for the assignment. Moses expressed his reluctance to accept the assignment and posed a question in Exodus 3:13: "What if I go to the Israelites and tell them, 'the God of your fathers has sent me to you,' and they ask me, 'What is his name?' What shall I say to them?"

In the next verse (3:14), the divine response to Moses' question begins with the famous phrase translated "I am who I am" by Ehrman, a rendition found also in most modern published English versions. The Hebrew phrase is *'Ehyeh 'asher 'Ehyeh*. The word *'Ehyeh* is a verbal form that ordinarily should be translated as a future: "I will be who I will be." But neither in the present tense nor the future does this phrase used by God answer the question by Moses about the divine name. That is why God completes his answer by instructing Moses to tell the Israelites, "*Ehyeh* has sent me to you."

The first *'Ehyeh* is the Hebrew word that Ehrman translates as "I am." Because Ehrman identifies *'Ehyeh* as a verb, he assumes that it must be translated by a verb in English for accuracy. But this is a serious misperception. What Ehrman (and almost all other NT scholars) fail to understand is that a Hebrew word can take the *form* of a verb but perform the *function* of a noun. *'Ehyeh* is the most notable example of this grammatical anomaly in Biblical Hebrew.

When *'Ehyeh* functions as the *subject* in a biblical Hebrew verbal sentence, it becomes a proper noun that is an allomorph (alternate form) of the divine name *Yahweh*. This function is attested unequivocally in Exodus 3:14, where *'Ehyeh* is the subject of the verb *shelaḥani* ("has sent me"), and the

Hebrew sentence *'Ehyeh shelaḥani 'aleikhem* must be translated, "*'Ehyeh* has sent me to you"[11] instead of the meaningless "I am has sent me to you."

It is a simple matter to demonstrate that this is the case. In Exodus 3:14, the following sentence occurs: "*'Ehyeh* has sent me to you" (*'Ehyeh shelaḥani 'aleikhem*). Then in Exodus 3:15, the same sentence appears with only a single change: "Yahweh has sent me to you" *Yahweh . . . shelaḥani 'aleikhem*). These two examples together illustrate the exact parallelism of nominal *function* between *Yahweh* and *'Ehyeh*: the two words are alternate spelling of the same divine name.

There is no certain explanation as to why this alternate spelling of the divine name Yahweh should have been chosen in Exodus 3:14 (and elsewhere). One possibility is that *'Ehyeh* is the way in which God refers to Himself, while *Yahweh* is the way in which others refer to Him. But since *egō eimi* is not a noun and cannot function as a noun, it is incorrect to equate Greek *egō eimi* with Hebrew *'Ehyeh*.[12]

It is important to note that scholars from a broad spectrum of theological and ideological perspectives have recognized the nominal function of *'Ehyeh*. Those cited in the articles listed in footnote 12 include Ronald Youngblood who was a prominent American Conservative Christian, Hans Walter Wolff who was a liberal German Lutheran, and Rashi and Martin Buber who were Jewish. The issue involved is not liberal vs. conservative, Jew vs. Christian, or exegetical honesty vs. ecclesiastical loyalty. It is a simple linguistic fact about the way in which the Hebrew language functions. And that fact bears repeating: *'Ehyeh* is an alternate spelling of the divine name Yahweh.

Another aspect of the word *'Ehyeh* in Exodus 3:14 is the fact that it is first used as part of an unusual phrase known as an *idem per idem* construction ("the same for the same"). When *'Ehyeh* is recognized as a proper noun, *'Ehyeh 'asher 'Ehyeh*, is an idiomatic way of saying "*'Ehyeh* equals *'Ehyeh*," or "God is God," and he cannot be compared with any other entity. In other words, since *'Ehyeh* here is a noun in *function*, although it

---

11. The *JPS TANAKH* translates the phrase in 3:14 exactly this way.

12. Professor Ehrman may be aware of the nominal function of *'Ehyeh* but he does not consider it as a possibility in his discussion of Exodus 3:14. Surprisingly, Professor Marianne Thompson, a careful and accurate exegete, states categorically that, "the Hebrew verb form *'ehyeh* does not recur as a name for God" (*John*, 158). It is unclear from this statement whether Professor Thompson acknowledges that *'Ehyeh* is a noun in Exodus 3:14 but nowhere else or whether she does not acknowledge it at all. In either case, her statement is incorrect. In two previous articles I have laid out the case for the nominal function of *'Ehyeh* in multiple passages in the Hebrew Bible. See "Initial 'Alef-Yod Interchange and selected Biblical Passages" and "The Divine Name אהיה ['Ehyeh] As a Symbol of Presence in Israelite Tradition."

is not an easy idiom to translate into English, the Hebrew phrase means that the God of the enslaved Israelite ancestors can be compared only to himself and to nothing (or no one) else.

"I AM" in Greek

Because *'Ehyeh* is a significant divine title/name in the Hebrew Scriptures, it was imperative for Greek translators to understand the way in which it should be rendered properly. Pre-Christian Jewish translators of the *Septuagint*, thoroughly knowledgeable in both Hebrew and Greek, had no trouble with the phrase that modern scholars typically misunderstand. It is fitting that no ancient Greek version translates Hebrew *'Ehyeh 'asher 'Ehyeh* into Greek by *ego eimi hos ego eimi* to yield English "I am who I am."[13]

To the contrary, when the translators of the *Septuagint* needed to translate correctly what Moses was instructed in Hebrew to tell the Israelites, they did not use a grammatically impossible and nonsensical sentence in Greek. Because these translators knew that *'Ehyeh* was an alternate form of the name of God, their choices were brilliant. And in Exodus 3:14, their translations of Hebrew *'Ehyeh* in both phrases were correct.

Hebrew	Greek	English
'Ehyeh 'asher 'Ehyeh	*ego eimi ho on*	"I am the existing one."
'Ehyeh shelaḥani 'aleikhem	*ho on apestalken pros hymas*	"The existing One has sent me to you."

In other words, once the enigmatic Hebrew phrase *'Ehyeh 'asher 'Ehyeh* is translated correctly, it becomes clear that the Greek equivalent of the Hebrew *name 'Ehyeh* is not *ego eimi*, but *ho on* ("the existing one"). And *ho on* is a Greek participle that functions as a noun to match the Hebrew noun *'Ehyeh*. Since Greek cannot employ *ego eimi* as a noun of any kind, much less the name of God, even if God had been speaking to Moses in Greek instead of Hebrew, the divine *name* would not have been "I am".

This leads to a stark declaration: Because Hebrew *'Ehyeh* is a nominal allomorph (alternate name) of Yahweh and because Greek *ego eimi* is not and cannot be a name of any kind, the whole commotion about whether Jesus arrogated to himself the sacred name of the God of Israel simply by using the phrase "I am" is pointless.

---

13. An asterisk in linguistics denotes an impossible or not attested form or function.

An Actual Divine Name/Title: "The Existing One"

The great first century Jewish philosopher Philo of Alexandria did not think that God had a name, but that he was identifiable by his actions in history. For Philo, the basic truth about God, therefore, was his sheer existence. Philo's recognition of the fact that *ho ōn* ("the existing one") was the Greek equivalent of the Hebrew allomorph *'Ehyeh* underscored this aspect of the divine. In her discussion of Philo's understanding of *ho ōn* ("the existing one"), Professor Marianne Thompson recognizes correctly that "the LXX, and Philo's use of it, show that the revelation of God in Exod 3:14 was understood to emphasize God's sheer existence, the fact that God simply *is*."[14] Thompson is correct that Greek *ho ōn* connotes the idea of existence, perhaps to indicate that Yahweh exists while all other supposed "gods" do not. And she was correct to note that Philo believed *ho ōn* described the essence of God in Greek.

But Philo's opinion does not change the fact that *Exodus does assign a name to God (*'Ehyeh). And that Hebrew name is translated as *ho ōn* in Greek. *Egō eimi* does not function in the same way and cannot serve as a name of any kind. Interestingly, Thompson declines to mention that Jesus is not portrayed as using the name *ho ōn* in John or elsewhere in the NT.

In sum, because *egō eimi* cannot be a name or a title and the name *ho ōn* ("the existing one") is not used to refer to Jesus, neither Greek phrase supports the idea that Jesus attempted to take a divine name for himself.

This nominal function of *ho ōn* ("the existing one") as a divine title that describes the basic essence of God is the phrase that Exodus 3:14 introduces as the *name* of God. This may be tested elsewhere in Scripture, starting with the LXX of Exodus 3:14 just cited, where the declaration of Yahweh about Himself in Greek is "I am the existing one."

But *ho ōn* is also used as a divine name in the New Testament. Two clear examples in the Apocalypse of John attest this function.

First, shortly after the author of Revelation measured the temple of God (Rev 11:1) and a period of increasing "woe" had befallen the earth, a simple formula comes first from the mouth of the seventh angel. In gratitude to God who would now reign over His kingdom that had become "the kingdom of our Lord and of his Christ," the angel recites: "We give thanks to You, Lord God Almighty the existing one (*ho ōn*) (Rev 11:17). The same formula is repeated by the third in another series of seven angels, this one pouring out a bowl of divine wrath onto the world, while describing God as "the existing one" (*ho ōn*), the holy one" (Rev 16:5).

14. Thompson, *John*, 158.

Second, a longer formula is used in the opening chapter of Revelation as follows: "Grace to you and peace from him who is (*ho ōn*), who was, and who is to come" (Rev 1:4). Interestingly, the statement in the following verse then adds greetings from Jesus Christ, so that this ascription of *ho ōn* is describing God, but not Jesus. These examples show clearly that the author of the Apocalypse realized that the simple expression *ho ōn* connotes the name and thus the basic essence of God (his existence). No corresponding function is assigned to *egō eimi*.

This leads to a simple conclusion: Although the expression would have been syntactically and grammatically odd in Greek, if Jesus had referred to himself in the third person as *ho ōn* ("The existing One") forty-six times, perhaps the argument about the name and nature of Jesus might be different. As it stands, despite the special pleading of Thompson, Ehrman, Brown, and countless other NT interpreters of John about *egō eimi*, there is no "there" there.[15]

Still, despite all evidence to the contrary, the presumption among scholars that the Greek phrase "I am" is the *name* of God refuses to die. This yields the picture of serious scholars trudging through the *Septuagint* looking for other verses in which *egō eimi* might be interpreted as a divine name.

"I AM" as the Name of God in the Septuagint

The position of Gail R. O'Day[16] regarding *egō eimi* is representative. Commenting on John 8:34, she cited Exodus 3:14 which she viewed as the primary example of Greek *egō eimi* as the translation of the divine name. But since Hebrew *'Ehyeh* is the divine name in Exodus 3:14 and since it is translated into Greek as *ho ōn*, her claim for *egō eimi* is irrelevant. Then she turned to the LXX of Isaiah 43:25 and 51:12, both of which attest Greek *egō eimi, egō eimi* rendering Hebrew *'anokhi, 'anokhi hu'*. Since *'Ehyeh* is absent from these verses in Hebrew (the original text that is being rendered into Greek), neither contains the divine *name*. Hebrew *'anokhi* is simply the personal pronoun "I," which does not serve and cannot be viewed as an allomorphic name of God.[17] O'Day then added Isaiah 52:6 as

15. It is also important to remember that the allomorph *'Ehyeh* was rendered by the Greek future *esomai* ("I will be") in the second century BCE Greek versions of Aquila and Theodotion. This is a more slavish literal equation, but still does not present a Greek verbal form that could serve as a proper noun. It may signal the idea that the nature of God will become more evident via his actions on behalf of the Israelites. Hence the future tense.

16. O'Day, *John*, 634.

17. In Hebrew, neither two nouns nor two pronouns placed next to each other

a third example, where *egō eimi ho lalōn* translates *'ani hu' ha-mədabber* ("I am the one speaking"). But here again, *'Ehyeh* is absent from the MT, so *egō eimi* cannot be translating a name of God here either.

In these three references from LXX Isaiah, Greek *egō eimi* is *never* rendering Hebrew *'Ehyeh*, the alternative spelling of the name of God. What O'Day cites are complete sentences in Hebrew that do *not* require an expressed copula (a linking verb). Only when they are translated into complete sentences in Greek do they require a verb (in this case, *eimi*). But her argument does nothing to support the idea that *egō eimi* is an allomorph for the divine name in Greek as *'Ehyeh* is in Hebrew and *ho ōn* is in Greek.

In addition to Exodus 3:14 and the examples cited above from O'Day, Professor Marianne Thompson sees two additional OT places where "God's self-identification" is relevant. The first is Deuteronomy 32:39, part of the lengthy "Song of Moses" that purports to be the final message of Moses to the Israelites. The regnant scholarly view is that the Song originated "quite independently of Deuteronomy," and surely not from the hand of Moses at all.[18] The section of the poem in which verse 39 appears has been describing the inability of false gods to protect Israel or to rescue her from the hand of YHWH who intends to punish His own people. The statement, "there is no deity except Me" is a way of emphasizing that one deity has acted alone in all matters of Israelite history including punishment, vindication, death, and life. The deity claiming responsibility for those incidents identifies himself as follows: "I, I am He" (*'ani 'ani hu'*). But the deity does not disclose his divine *name* in the text. He links himself with the performer of the action being described.

Thompson's second contextual location of divine self-identification involves the book of Isaiah, although her choice of verses differs from that of O'Day. In Isaiah 43:10–11, the deity speaking through the prophet is claiming the same kind of exclusivity as that found in Deuteronomy 32. In Isaiah 45:3, Yahweh claims to have called the Persian ruler Cyrus the Great into existence, and he takes credit for the latter's military exploits, even though he remained unrecognized by Cyrus. YHWH had helped Cyrus, "for the sake of my servant Jacob" (Isa 45:4).

Two points are important. First, the fact is that a proper Greek translation of the Hebrew "I, I am He" (*'ani 'ani hu'* in Deut 32:39) and "I am He" (*'ani hu'* in Isa 43:10) is simply *egō eimi* (I am"). In neither case is God revealing His *name*, but in both cases, God is identifying His *action* on behalf

---

require an *expressed* copula to produce a complete sentence. But an appropriate expressed form of a verb is necessary to make a complete sentence in Greek.

18. See among numerous others, von Rad, *Deuteronomy*, 195.

of Israel. Apart from the contexts in which they appear, neither expression identifies the name of the actor involved.

A hypothetical modern conversation can illustrate this point. If an English speaker were asked, "Who are you," and the answer were, "I am," the reaction would surely be, "I did not ask *what* you are or what you have *done*, but *who* you are. What is your *name*?" If the language involved were Greek, the same reaction would be expected.

In fact, this hypothetical conversation parallels an actual account in Acts 9:4–5 in which Jesus identified himself to a person he was meeting for the first time. The following exchange occurs. Saul (later Paul), knocked to the ground en route to Damascus, heard a voice in the sky asking, "Saul, Saul, why are you persecuting me?" Saul was obviously shocked and perplexed. And his question was understandable: "*Who* are you?" The response of Jesus was not *egō eimi* because *egō eimi* was not his name and it would not have identified him. His answer was standard Greek: "I am Jesus" (*egō eimi Yēsous*). In other words, the name of the person speaking to Saul was "Jesus," not "I am." Had he said simply "I am," Saul still would not have known his name or his identity.[19]

Second, the interpretation of these incidents and their statements about the identity of the God of Israel as somehow confirming the divine identity of Jesus is not the result of textual exegesis, but of ideological accommodation. Either personal faith or loyalty to church dogma sometimes allows a scholar to presume that *John's* view of Jesus was the way in which Jesus viewed himself: "Jesus presents *himself* as God does: as the one in whom there is life for all and hence as the object of faith."[20] Or again, "Like the Father before him, the Son now reveals himself as the one who is."[21]

But these are the words of John, not of Jesus. And they had not been the earlier testimony of Mark, Matthew, or Luke either in his Gospel or in Acts 9:5. They attest to seven or eight decades of reflection *about* Jesus since his death, not the self-identification *of* Jesus about himself during his presence on earth. They are the first step in the direction of transforming the Jesus of history into the Christ of faith as the church ultimately would identify him.

John is an important book for the study of the way in which ecclesiastical doctrine *about* Jesus began to develop after his death. But it does not introduce readers to the person named Jesus of Nazareth who lived in the first third of the first century.

---

19. Additional references to the use of *ego eimi* as self-introduction are noted in Appendix E

20. Thompson, *John*, 160, emphasis added.

21. Thompson, *John*, 159. And notice the ideological capitalization of "son."

As essays IX and X demonstrate, interpreters who approach the Old Testament with such an unshakeable proto-ecclesiastical view of Jesus already in mind see the face of Jesus embossed on the page of innumerable OT verses. And it is not surprising that, in case after case, the ancient texts conjure up the image the church has insisted upon before the verses are read. Individual interpreters are of course free to "believe" whatever they wish to believe. But that is not the same thing as fighting against grammatical and syntactical reality to cling doggedly to the idea that Jesus thought he was the Yahweh of the Jewish Scriptures. One cannot be a monotheist and at the same time think himself also to be a deity in addition to God.

Two questions then arise: Are virtually all NT interpreters incorrect to believe that at least some of the forty-six occurrences of *ego eimi* placed on the lips of Jesus by John depict him as claiming divinity for himself? And is it reasonable to believe that the facts as John presents them are correct?

The Grammatical Function of "I AM"

"I AM" With a Predicate Nominative

To answer these questions, the Johannine "I am" (*ego eimi*) statements attributed to Jesus require additional analysis. As the gospel narrative advances, *ego eimi* is used in two different ways syntactically.[22]

When followed by a predicate nominative, the statements in which *ego eimi* occurs make grammatical sense, and readers can contemplate their theological import from the context and tenor of the narratives in which they occur. For Jesus to claim [I am] "the bread of life" (6:35), "the light of the world" (8:12), "the good shepherd" (10:11, 14), or even "the resurrection and the life" (11:25-26) is not equivalent to his saying "I am God Almighty," or "I am the Yahweh of the Scriptures," or the like. John also alleged that Jesus claimed to be "the way, the truth, and the life" (John 14:6). But even there Jesus pointed to God, not to himself, as the ultimate destination in the search for the divine, noting that "no one comes to the Father [God!] except via me."

Being an avenue, or even the *only* avenue of access to God is not the same thing as a claim to *be* God. Such an explicit claim about the divinity of Jesus did not develop until 150–200 years after John at the earliest, and

---

22. Thompson, *John*, 156–60) divides these functions into three categories. Her analysis is accurate as well as correct grammatically and syntactically. In what follows, two of her categories are considered together.

it is clearly a dogmatic decision rather than an exegetical position gleaned directly from the biblical text.

John also wished to portray Jesus as "the resurrection," an evocative way in which to describe and celebrate his belief that Jesus had been delivered from the grave. In this matter, a bit of grammatical attention to the Greek text of the gospels is informative. The Synoptic Gospels are clear in saying, "he was raised," emphasizing the idea that Jesus was raised by the power of God.[23] They do not say "He arose," and they do not record Jesus saying, "I raised myself." The idea appears to be that as a living and breathing example of the power of God to restore life, Jesus quite naturally would have been perceived as having attained the ultimate level of exaltation among his followers.

The image of God miraculously raising an individual from death back to life is attested in the Old Testament stories of two great prophets, Elijah and Elisha. Each man officiated at the resurrection of a deceased child.[24] In 1 Kings 17:22, the child's life returned when "Yahweh heard the plea of Elijah." The case involving Elisha is more detailed and explicit. Three times the text states flatly that the young boy was "dead" (2 Kings 4:20), did not "respond" (4:31), and "was laid out dead on his bed" (4:32). Only when Elisha had "prayed to Yahweh" (4:33) did the lad return to life. In both cases, full credit for the resurrection was accorded to Yahweh, and neither incident imagines that the child "arose" under his own power. Nor is there any indication that either of the two boys were deemed by their communities to have special power over death. To paraphrase the words that Paul would use to describe resurrection with reference to Jesus, they had been raised "by the glory of the Father" (Rom 6:4).

Paul's understanding of the resurrection of Jesus is also significant. In Paul's words, "he was raised on the third day" (1 Cor 15:4), using a passive form of the verb *egeirō*.[25] These repeated uses of the passive voice clearly express the idea that a subject (Jesus) is acted upon by another source (God) rather than the subject performing the action on his own.

23. As the frequent NT use of the passive form *ēgerthē* ("he was raised" [by God]) underscores. Note Matthew 27:64; 28:6; Mark 16:6; Luke 24:6. See also the numerous citations in BDAG, 214–215.

24. These two incidents are not the same thing as a "doctrine" of resurrection. In the OT, only the late passage in Daniel 12:1–2 may be interpreted as referring to the "awakening" of "many who sleep in the dust of the earth," some to everlasting life and others to reproaches and eternal contempt." This awakening in Daniel is slated to occur at the end of the present age.

25. Later in the same passage, the identical passive form is used seven more times (1 Cor 15:12–20). Both *ēgerthē* and *egēgertai* are passive forms; *ēgerthē* is an Aorist form implying punctiliar action, *egēgertai* is a Perfect form implying linear action.

Yet another clear expression by Paul is especially instructive. He not only asserted that Jesus "was raised," but that it had happened "by the glory of the Father" (Rom 6:4).

By the time of "John," decades after Paul, Jesus had become defined as the ultimate living and breathing example of resurrection. And John decided to describe his resurrection in a way that Paul and the Synoptic Gospels had not. Citing a nonexistent "Scripture" as having stated that "Jesus had to arise from the dead" (John 20:9),[26] John appears to be leading his congregation and readership to believe that Jesus might have raised himself.[27] By this subtle shift, John has been understood by later interpreters to have been headed in the direction of divinizing Jesus by attributing to him the power of resurrection that the earlier gospels had ascribed to God alone.

But again, for *John* to make an explicit claim for the divinity of Jesus is far different from asserting that Jesus had appropriated the sacred name and authority of God for himself long before his own death and seven decades before John began to write about him.

Among the more astonishing passages where John employs *egō eimi* is its appearance in chapter six. The larger context is crucial. The claim to be "the bread of life" (John 6:35) comes in the aftermath of a physical miracle during which 5,000 people were fed by Jesus. Then the repetition of the claim, "I am the bread of life" (John 6:45), introduces a longer narrative centered around "bread." John 6:48–51 quotes an oral teaching of Jesus to illustrate a clearly metaphorical mode of interpreting the well-known manna episode in Exodus 16:12–36, a story centered around food sent miraculously from God to the ex-slaves lost in the wilderness. The "food" was a substance that no one recognized and whose identification was unknown. "When the Israelites saw it, they said to each other 'What is it [*man hu*']? They did not know what it was" (Exod 16:15).[28] So, John depicts Jesus using this story as the basis for a lesson:

> I am the bread of life. Your fathers ate the manna in the wilderness, and they died. This is the bread which comes down out of heaven, so that one may eat of it and not die. I am the living bread that came down out of heaven; if anyone eats of this bread,

26. John attributes this idea to "Scripture," but does not cite any passage where such a statement occurs.

27. The expression is *dei auton ek nekrōn anastēnai*, implying an action taken under his own power as compared to the action of being raised that was carried out through another power, presumably God.

28. The expression *man hu'* in Exodus 16:15 may be either standard biblical Aramaic spelling of "what" [*man*]; or a dialectic variant of classical Hebrew *mah hu'*, used here as "folk etymology."

he shall live forever; and the bread that I give for the life of the world is *my flesh.*

That this was an incomprehensible position to the average Jew of the day is indicated by the following verses: "The Jews argued with each other, saying 'How can this man give us flesh to eat'?" (John 6.52), eliciting the following response from Jesus: "I tell you the truth, unless you eat the flesh of the son of man and drink his blood, you have no life in yourselves. Whoever eats my flesh and drinks my blood has eternal life; I [not God!] will resurrect them on the last day" (John 6.53–54).

Few modern NT scholars believe that Jesus spoke the words here ascribed to him.[29] Equally suspect is the accusation of John that "the Jews" believed he was advocating the eating of human flesh and drinking of human blood. It is not surprising that John's identification of the manna as Jesus made no sense to his hearers. For John to have Jesus offer *any* specific explanation of manna represented a radical reformulation of the original story that describes a substance so miraculous that it was *impossible* to identify. But a literal linkage between the physical Jesus and miraculous unidentifiable manna that had been sent from heaven 1,200 years earlier was (and is) quite incomprehensible.

Metaphorically, the eating of manna may be viewed as having sustained the Israelites long enough to make possible a later entry into the land of promise. Somewhat analogously, the Johannine interpretation here appears to identify Christian participation in the Eucharist as the guarantee of entrance into the Land of Canaan and perhaps even of resurrection to eternal life in the future. Thus, a one-time physical event in the wilderness may be linked metaphorically to a spiritual promise about the providence of God in this life and the hope of resurrection in the next. The manna story receives new life by depicting Jesus functioning in a way that recalls the ancient story.

But there is one big difference between the manna story in Exodus and the way in which John uses it to describe Jesus. When the Israelites were completely unable to identify the manna in the wilderness, they asked, "What is it?" The laconic answer of Moses was simply, "This is the bread YHWH has given you to eat" (Exod 16:15). He did not say, "this unidentifiable substance that has come down from heaven is YHWH himself." John offers a far more incredible answer when he has Jesus say, "I am the bread of life."

---

29. Thompson, *John*, 160, is one who does, affirming that Jesus "offers the bread of life because he himself is life (John 1:4)."

Professor Stephen Gunter offers a pertinent explanation of what is occurring here: "It seems to me that this is again a retrojection of later Christological dogma onto the first century biblical text. The best reading of the text is that 'John' is claiming that Jesus is God's chosen Actor in the divine drama, but that the injection of later dogmatic Christological/divine assertions into the narrative are not only anachronistic, but linguistic nonsense and theologically unwarranted from a fair reading of the text."[30]

Similarly, once it is understood within the realm of the metaphorical, the claim of Jesus to be "the light of the world" (John 8:12) makes sense. It is not the literal suggestion that Jesus was in fact a pharaonic equivalent of the sun in human form. But it was a terrific way for a teacher to challenge his students to learn the appropriate patterns for a correct Jewish life (*halakhah*) from him and not to remain in the darkness of ignorance. This is very much like the way in which Matthew 11:29 depicts Jesus challenging students to assume his "yoke" and "learn from" him rather than from another teacher.[31]

Routinely in the gospels, Jesus spoke metaphorically but those around him, including his own disciples, took his words literally and repeatedly failed to understand his true teaching. Two examples of this phenomenon are the dialogue between Jesus and Nicodemus (John 3:1–21) about the concept of becoming "born again" (literally "from above"), or his dialogue with the Samaritan woman (John 4:7–15) on the subject of "living water."[32]

But the crowning illustration of the fact that the disciples of Jesus failed to grasp the truth to which his metaphors pointed is offered by a question from his disciples recorded in Acts 1:6. Waiting with him for his transport back to heaven, they asked him, "Sir, are you going to restore the kingdom to Israel now?" Even after having studied with Jesus for three years, having witnessed the dramatic death and resurrection of their master, and having been in dialogue with him in his resurrected form, his closest followers still wondered when he planned to restore *political* independence to Israel, apparently with no thought of a kingdom that was "not of this world" (see John 18:36).

"I AM" Functioning Alone

The use of *egō eimi* without a predicate nominative is a different matter. A look at English translations shows the problem. John 8:24 cites Jesus

---

30. Personal correspondence from January 11, 2021.

31. Isbell, "Some 'Earthy' Dimensions of the Spiritual in Jewish Liturgy," 234–238.

32. My colleague Delbert Burkett suggested these two examples.

as follows: "You will die in your sins unless you believe that *egō eimi*." In English, the phrase, "unless you believe that I am" leaves the reader hanging, and surely wondering *what* or *who* it was necessary to believe Jesus to be. Was Jesus saying, "you must believe that I exist" or something more complicated? This is an awkward construction, signaled by the fact that modern translations need to add a predicate nominative ("I am [he]") that is absent from the Greek text. To cite only one of numerous examples, the NIV renders, "unless you believe that I am the one I claim to be," clearly recognizing the need to supply in English translation something that is missing from the Greek text.

But the widely used *New Jerusalem Bible* translated by modern Catholic scholars goes them all one better, reading "I am He" [capital H!] and appending an explanatory note: "'I Am' or 'I am He' is the divine name revealed to Moses." This explanation is directly contradicted by the syntactical facts of the matter, as shown above. The *Jerusalem Bible* also translates the Greek text of John 13:19 as it does 8:24 ("I am [He]"), but it leaves hanging the famous statement in 8:58: "Before Abraham ever was, I am." The construction in this case fails to recognize that Greek *egō eimi* standing alone needs a predicate nominative to complete its function. That John was arguing for the pre-existence of Jesus is clear, but the switch from the past tense ("was") to the present ("I am"), renders the Greek nonsensical. It is to be wondered why John did not have Jesus say simply, "I existed before Abraham." As it stands, absent major ideological surgery, John 8:58 is a statement that makes little sense either in Greek or in English.[33]

The Arrest of Jesus in the Garden

In John 18:1–6, the entire improbable scene of Jesus in the garden shortly before his crucifixion strains credulity. Following his moment of prayer in chapter 17, Jesus had repaired to an unnamed garden where his disciples and he often had gathered, John's geographical notation to explain how Judas knew the location (John 18:1–2). Shortly after the arrival of Jesus and his disciples, Judas arrived leading a 600-man detachment[34] of Roman soldiers plus some unidentified Jewish aides who served the chief priests and the Pharisees (John 18:3). This mixed group had formed a search party equipped with torches, lanterns, and weapons to look for Jesus. Such a group surely would have

33. John follows this awkward sentence by asserting that the response of the Jewish audience was "to pick up stones to throw at him," a depiction that has been discussed earlier. See Essay III, note 18.

34. The Greek word is *speira*, one-tenth of a Legion, or 600 men.

generated quite a commotion, but John does not credit their noise with attracting the attention of Jesus. Instead, because he "knew everything that was going to happen to him" (John 18:4), Jesus went out to meet the huge search party and asked a simple question: "Whom are you seeking?" To their answer, "Jesus of Nazareth," Jesus logically identifies himself directly and simply: "I am he" (John 18:5). This informed the soldiers that "I am the man whose name you just mentioned (Jesus of Nazareth)."

Because he was in fact Jesus of Nazareth, the only correct way in which Jesus could have answered this question in Greek was simply *egō eimi*. However, since Raymond Brown had already decided that *egō eimi* was the *name* of God, he interpreted the response of Jesus as anything but simple, exulting that "Roman soldiers and Jewish police fall to the earth of the garden before him as he utters the majestic 'I AM.'"[35] This ideologically motivated assertion by Brown is nothing short of astounding.

First, it is hard to imagine a phalanx of 600 armed Roman soldiers requiring the assistance of a gaggle of assistant lower-level Jewish priests to arrest a single Jewish dissident. Nor is it credible to believe that Roman soldiers would have been placed under the leadership of Judas or Jewish aides serving the local priesthood.

Second, Jesus was doing nothing more than responding to the group seeking the person named "Jesus of Nazareth," identifying himself by telling them, "I am he." He was identifying himself as Jesus of Nazareth, the subject of their search, not as divine. And since the soldiers had already used his name, he did not even need to give them the complete answer that he used in meeting Saul for the first time (*egō eimi Yēsous*, "I am Jesus").[36] All Jesus needed to do was link himself with the name used by the soldiers. And the soldiers were not looking for someone named *egō eimi*, they were looking for someone named Jesus.

Third, it is another impossible stretch of credulity to assume that Roman soldiers were conversant with Exodus chapter three in Hebrew, where *'Ehyeh* functions as an allomorph of Yahweh. And these soldiers would have known as little about the LXX version of Exodus three as they did about the Hebrew original. But if they had known both the Hebrew Scriptures and

---

35. Brown, *Community*, 118. The text says simply that accompanying Judas at the head of the 600-man detachment of Roman soldiers were "some officials (Greek: *hyperetas*) from the chief priests and the Pharisees." The phrase "Jewish police" is not in the Greek text. Apparently, Brown imagined that adding Jewish police to the arresting contingent made the situation even more dire and Jesus even more courageous. John 18:3 says simply "servants of high priests and Pharisees."

36. See above on this account from Acts 9:4–5.

the LXX, they would have known that *egō eimi* is not the Greek nominal equivalent of the Hebrew divine name *'Ehyeh*.

Fourth, the original scene would have involved Aramaic-speaking Jewish priestly assistants and Pharisees, Aramaic-speaking Jesus, and Latin-speaking Roman soldiers. More than seventy years after the fact, all the dialogue of the scene was inserted into the Gospel by John writing in *Greek*, a language that would have been foreign to all the three parties to the original incident.

To be sure, Greek was a commonly spoken second or third language for many people in the region, and it is quite possible that many of the people involved in the garden scene could understand simple conversational Greek. But if Jesus did use Greek to identify himself to the Roman soldiers as the person they were seeking, nothing in his answer was unusual. In short, it is a linguistic reality that Jesus would have identified himself as the individual whom the soldiers were seeking with a simple statement that had no connection to the divine name of God (either *'Ehyeh* or *Yahweh* in Hebrew and Aramaic or "the existing one" in Greek.). It is thus unclear how anyone present on the scene might have perceived a straightforward response by Jesus to a simple question to be "magisterial."

There is absolutely no reason to believe that Roman soldiers might have thought Jesus was responding to their search by announcing, "I am Yahweh the God of Israel." Had that been his intention, and had he been speaking Greek, he could have said "I am Yahweh" (*egō eimi Yabe*), "I am the Lord" (*egō eimi ho kyrios*), or "I am the One who exists" (*egō eimi ho ōn*). Had he made such a claim to the soldiers, they might have fallen to the ground in the garden laughing rather than believing they were in the presence of Almighty God.

In this regard, it should be noted that the soldiers recovered quickly from whatever sense of awe they might have experienced in the presence of Jesus in the garden. Before he was sentenced by Pilate, they flogged him, they twisted together a crown of thorns that they jammed onto his head, they clothed him in a purple robe mocking him again and again as "King of the Jews," and they slapped him in the face (John 19:1–3). After he was sentenced, they took him into custody (John 19:16b), they crucified him (19:18), they stole his clothes (19:23), they gambled for his undergarment leaving him hanging totally naked (19:24), and they thrust a spear into his side to make certain he was dead (19:34).

To avoid the emotional overreaction of Brown, the *egō eimi* statement attributed to Jesus in the garden should be compared to other instances of *egō eimi* in the Gospel of John: three people other than Jesus are reported to have used *egō eimi* to identify themselves.

The first example involves the blind man whose sight had been restored by Jesus. Acquaintances who had known him throughout his life asked, "Is this not the man who used to sit and beg?" (John 9:8). The man replied simply: *egō eimi* ("I am he"), exactly what Jesus in the garden said to the mob searching for him. No one who was present thought their healed fellow worshiper was arrogating to himself the name of God.

The second example involves Peter. As he warmed himself by a fire in the courtyard outside the room in which Jesus was being interrogated, Peter denied being a disciple of Jesus three times (John 18:25). Although Matthew 26:73 certifies that Peter was speaking Aramaic at the time, John translates two of his denials to include the simple phrase *ouk eimi* ("I am not.").[37] John surely realized that in neither case was Peter denying that he was God. He was denying his connection with Jesus.

Example number three is in John 1:19–20, where John the Baptizer is asked by Jewish emissaries from Jerusalem, "Who are you?" His answer requires the negative form of *egō eimi* ("*egō ouk eimi ho christos*"), and it is categorical: "I am not the christ [messiah]."[38] He then repeats this denial to his own disciples in John 3:28 ("*ouk eimi egō ho christos*").[39]

The significance of these denials by John the Baptizer becomes apparent in John 4:26 when Jesus responds to a Samaritan woman wondering about the messiah with a frank confession: "I am he (*egō eimi*), the one speaking to you." She soon thereafter reported to the people of her village how deeply impressed she had been by the stranger with whom she had conversed at the city well, even musing that he might have been the messiah (John 4:29). But the Samaritan woman did not identify Jesus as divine, and she did not "fall to the ground" upon hearing his self-identification. To the contrary, she understood his answer as normal human language used in a normal human conversation because she knew that claiming to be a messiah was not the same thing as claiming to be divine.

---

37. The omission of the expressed pronoun "I" (*egō*) is not linguistically significant; the form of the verb *eimi* carries the first-person singular marker with or without the added *egō*.

38. The definite article implying only one messiah is quite confusing to students of Scripture who know about the anointment of multiple Israelite and Judahite kings, high priests, and prophets, and even read of the Persian monarch Cyrus being designated in the Book of Isaiah (45:1) as Yahweh's messiah.

39. The change in word order does not affect the meaning of the sentence. It merely shifts the emphasis from "*I* am not the christ" to "I am *NOT* the christ."

In all these cases, it would be difficult to find a different way to express in Greek what the healed blind man, Peter, and John the Baptizer all said. None of them was claiming the divine name for himself.[40]

Final Thoughts About "I AM"

Innumerable times in the OT, the God of Israel is cited by a prophet as introducing a message or a commandment by saying, "I am Yahweh," or "I am Yahweh your deity." Perhaps the most well-known occurrence of the phrase is its use to certify that the Ten Commandments came directly from God who alone had the authority to demand obedience from his people: "I am Yahweh your deity who brought you out of the land of Egypt, the house of slavery" (Exod 20:2). The influential German OT scholar Walther Zimmerli analyzed the function of this description of God and dubbed it "The Self-Revelation Formula."[41] Only the one true God could use this expression. No Jew would make such an outlandish statement about himself.

Jesus was certainly familiar enough with the Old Testament to have known this formula and its frequency. Linguistically, it would have been a simple matter for Jesus to identify himself as Yahweh had he wished to do so. In Hebrew or Aramaic, he could simply have said, "I am Yahweh" or "I am 'Ehyeh." To choose a name of God in Greek, he could have said "I am the Lord" (ho kyrios), "I am the Existing One" (ho ōn), or even "I am Yahweh" (ego eimi Yabe). In short, it would have been a simple matter for Jesus to identify himself as Yahweh. He did not. The 46-fold repetition of the phrase egō eimi in John reveals nothing about the man whose name was Jesus.

The attempt to turn the simple phrase, "I am," into "I am God," misses the larger point of the Fourth Gospel. In multiple contexts throughout John, the true meaning of Jesus' answer to a variety of questions or accusations from "the Jews" was not that he claimed to be almighty God and could do whatever he wished. Instead, even John admitted that Jesus repeatedly underscored the fact that he did nothing on his own, that his authority was derived from a greater Another.[42]

40. Even recognizing that John the Baptist, Jesus, the Samaritan woman, the formerly blind man, and Peter all thought and spoke in Aramaic before John translated their conversations into Greek, in no case would the Semitic thoughts (either Aramaic or Hebrew) being translated into oral Greek have included the word 'Ehyeh, a possible allomorph of Yahweh.

41. Zimmerli, I Am Yahweh.

42. For example, (a) "The words that I say to you I do not speak on my own authority, but the Father who dwells in me does his works" (John 14:10); (b) "The son can do nothing of his own accord, but only what he sees the Father doing" (John 5:19); (c) "I

Why Not "Send?"

If one were seeking a way to describe the mission of Jesus to a Jewish audience, there is no better word than "send." Prophet after prophet in the Jewish Scriptures was "sent" by God and tasked with a message for Israel. The commission of Moses was described in Exodus 3:10, where God spoke to Moses the simple declarative sentence: "I will *send* you to the Pharaoh." It was confirmed in 3:12: "I have *sent* you."[43]

Other human emissaries of God in "the Scriptures" who were commissioned or "sent" (Hebrew: *š-l-ḥ*) include Gideon (Judg 6:14), Isaiah (Isa 6:8), Jeremiah (Jer 1:7), and Ezekiel (Ezek 2:3). In each case, God was choosing a human partner to serve as his spokesman. Never was the one being sent considered the equal of the One who had the authority to send. And multiple passages in John highlight exactly this point. To the contrary, John consistently describes two separate-but-not-equal entities with different levels of authority. In John 7:16, Jesus states bluntly: "My teaching is not mine, it is from the One who *sent* me." In John 8:28, Jesus refers to "just what the Father has taught me." Similar are John 7:28, "I have not come of my own accord;' John 7:29, "I come from Him [God], and *He sent me;*' and John 8:18, "my other witness is the Father who *sent me.*"

These statements make it impossible to conclude that Jesus viewed himself as God or as the equal of God. Professor O'Day grasped the point perfectly: "God, not Jesus, 'makes' something of Jesus."[44]

Indeed! And neither in the OT nor in the NT is the person who is "sent" equal to the One doing the sending.

---

can do nothing on my own . . . I seek not my own will but the will of him who sent me" (John 5:30); (d) "I have not come of my own accord" (John 7:28).

43. In the context of the Johannine emphasis on the miraculous "signs" of Jesus, it is worth remembering that Moses had been sent to Egypt empowered by God to perform special signs to procure the deliverance of the Hebrew slaves. But John does not make that connection.

44. O'Day, *John*, 645.

XII. Conclusions and Future Directions

Preliminary Remarks

OFFERING A JEWISH PERSPECTIVE on the Gospel of John is fraught with difficulties. John is the favorite NT gospel for millions of Christians, and it is perhaps the best loved book of the entire Christian Bible. As such, it is read and received as an integral component of the authentic and divinely inspired sacred canon for those who comprise the church. I am an outsider. I do not speak as a Christian and I do not view John as a gospel whose veracity I have a responsibility to defend for the sake of church ideology, whether Catholic, Protestant, liberal, conservative, or fundamentalist.

For me, John is an interesting text to be examined like any other piece of religious literature using the tools of historical-critical and linguistic analysis. In this endeavor, I understand that the sound of my outsider voice may enter some Christian ears as nothing beyond unwelcome cacophony. In fact, many Christians may deem it inappropriate for a non-Christian to speak at all about their sacred text.

My response to such an objection, delivered as gently as possible, is to note that the Gospel of John exerts an inordinate amount of energy opining about issues that are integral to my life as a Jew and my career as a scholar of Judaism. For those who view it as an inspired book, the Fourth Gospel has been granted official ecclesiastical (canonical) authority to teach the Christian dominant culture in which I reside not only what Christianity is and what Christians should believe, but also what Judaism is, what Jews believe, why Jews are dangerously wrong, and why Jews must be granted no option except to agree with John. It is this Johannine determination to define Jews and Judaism that I and so many of my students and congregants find disheartening and frightening.

My responses in these essays are not intended to serve as a Jewish *quid* to the Jew-bashing *quo* of John. Modern interpreters continue to reduce the number of anti-Jewish passages in John. They then create theories designed to explain the reduced number of passages that remain. But if John's opinions of Judaism could somehow be interpreted objectively and his anti-Judaism acknowledged openly, I would gladly surrender the privilege of expressing an opinion about his gospel.

But John continues to be taught and preached in the church. And since his definition of Jews and Judaism is accepted by the church as authoritative, I believe it is not only my privilege but also my *duty* to answer what I perceive to be his historically untrue and factually incorrect indictments of Judaism.

My responses to John will not sound strange to most Jews. What I hear when I read John is much the same message that Jews around the world hear. We are still the bull's eye in the center of the target field outlined in the Gospel of John to guide attacks on "the Jews," the group that some interpreters believe has been denied all possibility of fellowship with God. I find it troubling that the most influential Christian NT scholar of the twentieth century believed Jews to be excluded by John and his followers from being loved.[1] This viewpoint that has now endured for two millennia is heartbreaking, slamming the door on any possibility of a co-operative joint Jewish-Christian partnership with each other and with God.

This modern iteration of John 14:6 ("*the* way") leaves nothing to the imagination. "When outsiders (*sic!*) come to the light and believe, they become children of God and can be loved as brothers."[2] Obviously, then, when "outsiders" do *not* come to the light and do *not* believe to the satisfaction of John and the church, they cannot be children of God and they cannot be loved. "A passage such as I John 2:15, 'Have no love for the world,' is tantamount to 'Hate the world.'"[3] There is no other path, no possible alternative. John's way, Raymond Brown's interpretation of that way, the way of the church, or nothing. Not the right to be loved by fellow humans, not even the right to be loved by God: "It is not clear that the Johannine God loves the sons of darkness."[4] And it cannot be denied that "the Jews" are the "sons of darkness" in the thinking of John.

---

1. Recall here the blunt assessment of Raymond Brown: "the Fourth Gospel articulates no demand to love all human beings or to love one's enemies." See Essay I, note 26.

2. Brown, *Epistles*, 272 and *Epistles*, 85: "Only true believers in Jesus are the children of God."

3. Brown, *Epistles*, 272.

4. Brown, *Epistles*, 272.

The Painful Words of John and the Image of Jesus

But while, as the saying goes, "words can never hurt us," Jews are always aware that we are never out of the range of Johannine ideas pressed upon us second hand by our friends, neighbors, and colleagues. Their understanding of John informs their approach to us, assuring them that there is only one pathway to God (John 14:6), and it is assuredly not the route we have chosen. And this Johannine message about "the Jews" has all too often been accompanied by "sticks and stones" which have indeed broken our bones—and worse.

In addition, many self-appointed lay missionaries, often parroting only what they have been taught by their clergy and scholars, routinely camouflage their messages as concern for our eternal destiny. Presuming to introduce us to the loving Jesus who offers us redemption as their brand of Christianity defines it, they turn away from the clear teaching of the "Scriptures" to pay homage to the ideology that serves as the foundation for John's presentation of Jesus to the world. Here is a shocking example. One of the most important commandments of Scripture is "Love your neighbor as yourself" (Lev 19:18).

Even though he is not known for respecting "Law" (*torah*), Paul, writing about forty years earlier than the Gospel of John, cites this specific commandment as the ultimate fulfillment of the entire Law (Gal 5:14; Rom 13:9). The three Synoptic authors, all earlier than John and closer to the lifetime of Jesus, reflect Jesus as approving this pivotal text of loving your neighbor in Leviticus 19:18 (Matt 19:19 and parallels). They even have him expanding the definition of the word "neighbor" to include more people, not fewer.[5]

But Father Raymond Brown, the most famous and copied NT scholar of the past one-hundred years, admitted openly that "Jesus' teaching about neighbourly love came to be altered [in John],"[6] and he did not appear to worry that this alteration negating one of the most important commandments of Scripture was authored by John rather than Jesus. In other words, Brown chose a saying from John to replace the original commandment reported to have been uttered by God: "I am Yahweh" (*ego eimi kyrios*).

Every reader of John must bear in mind the fact that Jesus already had been crucified seventy years before John took stylus in hand. Then John (followed by his selectively literal interpreters) decided to compress the neighborhood and expand the ranks of the "Other" by reversing the teaching of

5. See Luke 10:25–37.
6. Brown, *Epistles*, 273.

Jesus about loving one's neighbor as oneself. It is regrettable that the church has chosen to follow the one gospel writer who personifies the ultimate "not one of us" path rather than to follow the Levitical commandment about love that Paul, Mark, Matthew, and Luke all thought Jesus honored. Either these other NT authors were wrong or John's caustic gospel teaches us nothing about what Jesus may have believed.

There is broad scholarly agreement that scarcely a word in the Gospel of John is from the mouth of Jesus.[7] This means that what current Christian readers of John believe about eternal matters of truth is based upon what *John* said *about* Jesus. But the words *attributed* to Jesus originated with and were owned by John. After noting the numerous instances of disagreement among NT authors, Bart Ehrman states the matter succinctly and accurately: "Each author is a human author and needs to be read for what *he* (assuming they were all men) has to say."[8] After adding the fact that the human words of John have become inextricably linked to the ways in which successive generations of Christian interpreters have augmented his Gospel, it is clear that modern readers are not being introduced to Jesus but to John. We do not know what Jesus thought of "the Jews" nor they of him. We are told only what John thought things must have been like seven decades before he wrote his opinion about those things. The worst aspect of this realization is that John's opinions were based on false and historically skewed interpretation.

The church has never hidden the fact that the Gospel of John is the work of a human writer designated as "John." Nor has the church been able to avoid the fact that this human author admits to having picked and chosen only some of the "signs" performed by Jesus—some but not all (John 20:30–31). And John's "pick and choose" method of exegesis has been the characteristic of John most often mimicked by his interpreters.

Naturally, the church holds the idea that the divine spirit so guided and inspired John that his choices were wise and his words true. But the reader of John who does not subscribe to the idea that the church can so anoint the words of "John" as to transform them into the words of Jesus has the right to be skeptical. This is especially important in cases where

---

7. The famous "Jesus Seminar," a group of Catholic and Protestant NT scholars, met multiple times over a period of more than ten years seeking to determine the authenticity of the words of Jesus in the gospels. They concluded that the only possibly authentic saying of Jesus in the Gospel of John was 4:43, which they described merely as "probably" from Jesus. For details, see Robert Funk, Editor, *The Five Gospels*.

8. Ehrman, *Misquoting Jesus: The Story Behind Who Changed the Bible and Why*, 12. The book is an extremely useful introduction to the complicated field of biblical textual criticism.

John overturns the teachings of other biblical authors. Once the authority of the church is removed from the equation, it becomes clear that what modern readers encounter in John is not Jesus, but the joint creation of a fully human object of faith proposed by a human author backed by the human authority of the church.

From a Jewish perspective, this creation is a figurehead that is neither real nor believable. Since the words in John can ring true only when viewed through the eyes of faith, it seems clear that the gospel writer has it backwards. His words do not inculcate or inspire belief; they require that readers of John must *begin* with the proper dosage of the appropriate prescription of faith. Such faith thus ingested must then be married to the claims of John *before* they can acquire meaning. In other words, a specific brand of faith is a *prerequisite* to make sense of the Gospel of John, not just "faith," but "adequate" faith that only John and his followers, ancient and modern, can define—"*the* way."

In the crucible of history, the words of John, read honestly but lacking this prior faith commitment, are one man's opinions that have been ratified through two millennia by millions of fellow believers. But despite the huge number of interpreters who echo the party line of "John," in the end, all that remains are multiple individuals who come to John already as staunch believers and find exactly what they want desperately to find— confirmation of their own pre-judgment. In this context, it is inevitable that anyone standing outside the circle of believers should come to be defined as the enemy. But it is terrifying to imagine that the Jesus of "John" would approve the hateful conclusions toward which the *words of John about him* have been dedicated over the centuries.

Why is this important? In the first place, if rapprochement ever is to become possible, it must be admitted that current missionary targets (including "the Jews" of today) are being asked to accept and worship a human creation issuing forth from the church rather than a divine messenger sent directly to earth by God. If the Jesus of John and the church really said and did the things reported in the Gospel, and if he approves the ends to which citations of his words have been put, then no one should be surprised that Jews find such a Jesus "weighed in the balances and found wanting." If, as conservative Christians insist, the Jesus of John *is* the Jesus of history, and if the Jesus of John is the *God* of Christianity, then John has done Jews the great favor of issuing a clear warning that neither this deity nor his "children" can love or accept them if they persist in continuing to be Jewish.

This is not another anodyne call for "religious tolerance." People tolerate an uncomfortable rash, hoping it will go away quickly with the administration of proper medication. So, the idea that Jews should hope only to be tolerated by their Christian neighbors has no attraction. Said bluntly, no Jew has any incentive to abandon the God of Abraham in favor of the imaginary human deity created by a gospel writer who deems Jews to be the children of the devil.

Respect is a different matter. Can the modern Christian *respect* Judaism as an authentic pathway to God with its own independent integrity? And is the teaching of John a help or a hindrance to achieving that respect? Insistence that John remains worthy of retaining its lofty status as divine truth makes it difficult to believe that either of these two questions can be answered to the satisfaction of either the Jew or the informed Christian. This may result finally in mutual agreement that mutual agreement is unattainable and the best anyone can expect is that holders of these mutually exclusive perspectives will at least forego the impulse to engage in open warfare. But an uneasy truce is not the same thing as an alliance of partners dedicated to shared common values.

Parallel Lines of Faith

Before abandoning the hope of a joint Jewish-Christian partnership with God in the reparation of the world, perhaps another possibility can be explored. Parallel lines do not meet to form a perfect merger from two into only one. "Parallel" means that both lines continue to remain viable and identifiable without the merger that decrees one the winner and the other the loser. In this instance, parallelism can serve as an authentic pattern if both sides agree that Jews and Christians worship the same God, the father of Abraham, Isaac, and Jacob; that this God cannot not renege on the covenant with Israel and still be God; and that faithful Jews are no more in danger of final expulsion from God's presence than are faithful Christians. Differing conceptual structures that define the meaning of salvation remain, and the entrances into that salvation are not identical. But if lives shaped by godness are the common goal, Christians may celebrate the significance of Jesus in their lives, while God's Jewish children will not need to convert hoping Jesus will help them find the God who is already their Father. Both Jews and Christians can rejoice in the fact that they are already sons and daughters of God.

Christians need to continue cultivating their relationship to Jesus as their consciences dictate. Jews need to be faithful to their Scriptures, their prophets, their sages. The parallel lines need not intersect, for as both branches of the children of God follow faithfully, they both may arrive at a shared destination, authentic relationship with the one true God.[9]

Such a concept applied to Judaism and Christianity has been attempted before, and as the world continues to become smaller, there must be an increasing sense of urgency about defeating the impulse to destroy iterations of faith, culture, and humanity that differ from one another. Here is a look at the latest attempt at creative co-existence between Judaism and Christianity. As with all partnerships, it is not without rough spots, but neither is it without hope for success.[10]

We Jews and You Christians

On December 3, 2015, a large group of Orthodox rabbis signed a statement[11] on the relationship between Christianity and Jews, and they released it to coincide with the golden anniversary of the famous papal *Nostra Aetate*[12] declaration of 1965. Hailed as the most significant Jewish statement on Jewish-Christian relations in fifteen years,[13] the statement is noteworthy in three respects.

First, the Jewish statement celebrates the decision in *Nostra Aetate* to reject all forms of anti-Semitism, including deicide. The single most damaging accusation leveled by Christians against Jews for 2,000 years is easily that the Jews killed Jesus. Surely all Jews can rejoice in the rejection of such an odious, and factually incorrect, charge.

Second, the rabbis acknowledge Christianity as "the willed divine outcome and gift to the nations." Such a stance by Jews, coupled with Catholic statements about the enduring covenant between God and Israel, indicates that the authors of the statement believe it is now safe to "acknowledge the ongoing constructive validity of Christianity as our partner

9. This concept was suggested to me by Professor Stephen Gunter in a private conversation. Shortly after the conversation, Professor Gunter shared this explanation and expansion of his idea. His verbal and written remarks are the foundation of this and the preceding paragraph.

10. The following paragraphs are a revision of remarks posted originally in May 2016 on *Bible and Interpretation, accessed at* www.bibleinterp.com.

11. http://cjcuc.com/site/2015/12/07/groundbreaking-orthodox-rabbinic-statement-on-christianity/

12. www.vatican.va/archive/hist_councils/ii_vatican_council/documents/vat-ii_decl_19651028_nostra-aetate_en.html

13. In 2002, *"Dabru Emet"* ("Speak the truth"), also available online by its title, was prepared by leading scholars involved in the National Jewish Scholars Project. It offered eight general statements "about how Jews and Christians may relate to one another."

in world redemption without any fear that this will be exploited for missionary purposes." Here the pregnant phrase "missionary purposes" raises a note of alarm (see further below).

Third, the rabbis underscore the elements of commonality between the two faith systems, and they stress the importance of Christianity's efforts to bring ethical monotheism to the world, a fact noted first by Maimonides in the twelfth century. Here too, surely all Jews can celebrate the world-wide impact of the ethical teachings of the Church, freely adopted from and shared with Judaism.

One week after the statement of the rabbis, the Vatican released its own statement in honor of *Nostra Aetate,* focusing on the fourth article that deals with the relationship between Catholics and Jews.[14] A cursory reading of the statement relates the Catholic perception of missiology in a manner that appears to justify the high-sounding words of the rabbis: "The Catholic Church neither conducts nor supports any specific institutional mission work directed towards Jews." In other words, we Jews can now relax about conversion attempts aimed at us by Catholic Christians.

But the continuation of the Church statement quickly indicates a substantial impediment to the application of this concept: "While there is a principled rejection of an institutional Jewish mission, Christians are nonetheless called to bear witness to their faith in Jesus Christ also to Jews." In short, this "nonetheless" makes it clear that Catholics will indeed continue to evangelize Jews, but that whatever evangelization takes place should be accepted as nothing more than individual Catholics (priests? laity?) responding faithfully to their divine calling. Jews in business or personal relationships with individual Catholics will continue to be selected as the evangelization targets that allow their Catholic friends and acquaintances to live up to their divine "calling."

Students of the history between Jews and the Church should be reminded that the controversy involving conversion has been around for a long time, illustrated best by the issue of forced baptism, the ritual entrance into Christianity. For centuries, the *official statements* of the Church were in sharp contrast to the *practices* of individual clergymen throughout Europe, and the history of those practices is a series of despicable actions.

The first known instance of mass forced baptism occurred on the island of Minorca in 418 CE. Bishop Severus of Minorca led a series of mass conversion ceremonies that lasted eight days. During the campaigns, the island synagogue was burned to the ground, and more than 500 Jews were

---

14. "The Gifts and the Calling of God are Irrevocable," available online by its title.

converted.[15] Over one-hundred years later, Pope Gregory I (590 to 604) wrote to the Bishop of Naples[16] that baptism (= conversion) should not be imposed upon Jews by force and was not valid unless it was accepted willingly. That this opinion became the official stance of the Church in 1199 is indicated by the fact that one of the clauses in the *Constitutio pro Judaeis* declared categorically that violence could not be used to force a Jew to convert. This papal bull represented the official position of the papacy regarding Jews throughout the Middle Ages and beyond. Its function as the official position of the Church had also been confirmed in an updated papal bull, *sicut Judaeis* ("To/concerning the Jews")[17] repeating the actual paragraph heading used by Pope Gregory in his letter to the Bishop of Naples six centuries earlier. The wording of the *Sicut Judaeis* is unambiguous: "For We make the law that no Christian compel them, unwilling or refusing, by violence to come to baptism."[18]

The response of priests throughout Europe was a great debate about the correct interpretation of the term "willingly." If a Jew chose baptism when force was not actually applied, was this a willing choice? Because no clause in the *Constitutio* addressed the question about the validity of a baptism administered under the *threat* of violence or expulsion, the common practice was to assume that the Jewish convert had agreed "willingly." Because the consequences of refusing to convert were clear, the result, as Norman Zacour notes, was predictable: "To put it bluntly, conversions to Christianity were rarely wholehearted."[19]

Actual baptism/conversion practices were abetted by a concomitant idea in medieval Christianity that apostasy from the true faith was considered heresy, punishable by death. Thus, in a letter of 1199, Pope Innocent III, perhaps the most influential pope of the Middle Ages, put into words what had often been true in actions, writing that any Jew who submitted to baptism under the threat of force, *if no force had actually been applied*, automatically expressed a *conditional* willingness to accept Christianity and could not renounce his baptism after the fact without triggering the punishment of heresy and death.[20]

15. These incidents were documented by Bishop Severus in *Epistula Severi*. See *Severus of Menorca: Letter on the Conversion of the Jews*.

16. Either Fortunatus II (593–600) or Paschasius (600–610).

17. First issued in 1123.

18. For a translation of the oft-repeated Bull, see "The Papal Bull Sicut Judaeis" in *Studies and Essays in Honor of Abraham A. Neuman*, 243–80.

19. Zacour, *Jews and Saracens*, 14.

20. For the full text of the letter, see Thatcher and McNeal, *A Source Book for Medieval History*. Innocent also convoked the Fourth Lateran Council in 1215. One of

This decision of Innocent III ratified and approved the conditions that had already produced a series of tragic events. On May 14, 576, Bishop Avitus of Clermont-Ferrand had made the following speech to the Jews of his town after a Christian mob had destroyed the local synagogue: "If you are ready to believe as I do, become one flock with us and I will be your pastor. If you are not ready, depart from this place."[21] Under this threat of expulsion, about five hundred Jews chose to convert, and the Jews who did not convert left for Marseilles. A Christian celebration ensued. That this incident was considered an example of "willing" conversion was certified in 938 when Pope Leo VII told the archbishop of Mainz, Germany, that he should expel local Jews if they refused to convert, citing the earlier action in Clermont-Ferrand as a precedent.[22] Other documented instances of forced baptism occurred repeatedly throughout Europe.

Children were a special problem. At what age was a child deemed competent to make a "willing" decision to convert? To cite only one of numerous examples, in ca. 825, Bishop Agobard assembled the Jewish children of Lyons, France, and baptized all who *appeared* to him to be agreeable.[23] Then, as late as 1747, Pope Benedict XIV ruled that once a child had been baptized, even illegally, he or she was to be considered a Christian and reared in a Christian home. Under this ruling, large numbers of Jewish children were taken away from their own parents and placed in another home to be reared as Christians.

Two well-known examples are illustrative. In 1762, the son of the rabbi in Carpentras in the Provencal region of France was captured in a rural area just outside the city and immediately baptized in ditch water. He was never allowed to see his family again.[24] In 1858, six-year-old Edgardo Mortara was abducted from his family home in Bologna, Italy, by papal police and taken to the House of Catechumens. The boy had been baptized secretly five years earlier by a teen-aged domestic servant who feared he was about to die. The boy had been only one year old at the time, he had been baptized by a young girl rather than an ordained priest, and his parents neither knew about nor gave consent to the baptism. But the Church ruled that his baptism was valid and could not be revoked. Since canon law

the 72 canons issued by the council ratified his earlier letter and imposed additional restrictions on Jews.

21. *Encyclopedia Judaica*, "FRANCE, History of."

22. *Catholic Encyclopedia*, "Pope Leo VII."

23. Langenwalter, *Agobard of Lyon: An Exploration of Carolingian Jewish-Christian Relations*, 2009. Note especially her Chapter Two: "Agobard's Anti-Judaism," 105–143. See also Heil, "Agobard, Amolo, das Kirchengut und die Jüden von Lyon," 48.

24. Lunel, "The Jews of the South of France," 125.

forbade a Christian child to be reared in a non-Christian home, Edgardo was taken away from his family and never returned.[25]

A new chapter in the history of forced baptism had begun in 1543, with the establishment of the "House of Catechumens" in Rome. Any person who was perceived to have even a slight inclination towards Christianity could be imprisoned in the House of Catechumens while his intentions were explored by Christian examiners. In popular thought, it was believed that any person who secured the baptism of an unbeliever was assured of paradise, and this belief led to innumerable instances of forced captures and imprisonment, as one might expect. Then "in 1554, Pope Julius III imposed a tax of ten gold ducats on each of the 115 synagogues in the Papal States to cover the cost of maintaining residents in the House who had converted and were not allowed to return to their Jewish homes."[26]

Protestants Respond

The discussion to this point has focused on Catholic Christianity because it was the source from which the statements of the rabbis and the Church were generated. When attention turns to non-Catholic Christian responses, concern about proselytism is heightened. *Christianity Today*, the leading evangelical Christian magazine, addressed this very issue in December 2015.[27] The article presents two very different Protestant responses. Professor Marv Wilson of Gordon College (an evangelical but not fundamentalist Christian school) has noted: "For Jews, the words 'mission' or 'conversion' are historically connected with the Crusades, the Inquisition, Jewish expulsion from Spain in 1492, and the silence of many Christian churches during the Holocaust."[28]

In sharp contrast, the same article notes that other non-Catholic Christians are not at all worried about the Jewish reaction to missiology or conversion pressure. Nor are they willing to accept the idea of abstaining from evangelization of Jews even in an overtly organized manner. *Christianity Today* cites Joel Hunter, co-convener of the Jewish-Evangelical Leader Dialogue:[29] "While we can certainly agree that the Jews are participants

25. The standard treatment of the affair is by Kertzer, *The Kidnapping of Edgardo Mortara*.

26. "Catechumens, House of," *Encyclopedia Judaica*.

27. "Orthodox Rabbis Say Christianity Is God's Plan, Vatican Says Stop Evangelizing Jews." Hereafter, *Christianity Today* refers to this same article.

28. *Christianity Today*.

29. Hunter is the pastor of the largest evangelical church in Florida, and best known

in God's [unfolding] salvation, and we can affirm that they are complete in that role, it is more difficult for us not to want to share with them our deepest joy."[30] Hunter goes on to affirm that it is "difficult for evangelicals to avoid" what he considers the clear New Testament commission to witness to Jews as well as everyone else in the world. Leaving little room for misunderstanding, Hunter concludes that "my desire to be personally close to [Jews] will involve my sharing Christ by word or deed." There is little room for dialogue with the person who holds such a position. And he and his group are not unique.

David Brickner is the executive director of "Jews for Jesus," a particularly obnoxious group whose mission statement is clear: "We exist to make the messiahship of Jesus an unavoidable issue to our Jewish people worldwide."[31] In other words, they are bent on their self-appointed task of turning every Jew in the world into their own quite peculiar kind of Christian. It is not surprising that Brickner pointedly dubs the statement from the Vatican "egregious." In his opinion, the Vatican has completely misinterpreted Paul, who, Brickner is certain, "would be horrified at this repudiation of the words with which he started his letter in Romans: 'For I am not ashamed of the gospel, because it is the power of God that brings salvation to everyone who believes: *first to the Jew*, then to the Gentile.'"[32] This position signals Brickner's confidence that, even among other Christians, no one possesses divine truth except his tiny splinter group.

Also cited by the same article in *Christianity Today* is Jim Melnick, the international coordinator of the Lausanne Consultation on Jewish Evangelism, a second group whose very name signals its refusal to accept Judaism under any circumstance. He makes his position clear to *Christianity Today* by noting that Jews are beloved by God, but he insists that they *cannot* "find salvation without faith in Yeshua" (his idea of the name "Jesus").

It must be admitted that these fundamentalist followers of Paul have the better of the New Testament interpretation argument here. There is little doubt that Paul believed Jews should become Christians, and his personal method of procuring such conversions bears repeating: "To Jews, I acted like a Jew in order to convert Jews. To people following Torah, I acted like I too was Torah observant in order to convert those who are Torah observant. To the weak, I became weak that I might convert the weak. I have become all

---

as a spiritual advisor to President Obama. He is generally considered to be quite progressive on a wide range of social issues. See https://www.charismanews.com/us/40153-megachurch-pastor-joel-hunter-pays-price-for-political-activism?tmpl=component

30. *Christianity Today.*

31. http://jewsforjesus.org/about-jews-for-jesus/categories

32. Statement in *Christianity Today* citing Romans 1:16, emphasis added.

things to all people, in order that I might by all methods save somebody."[33] "Jews for Jesus" adherents have adopted this attitude of trying to appear Jewish, wearing kippahs, hijacking Jewish rites and rituals, and frequently insisting that they should be allowed to enter synagogues to explain to those unenlightened among us that to be a real Jew is to become a Christian.

But is Paul truly the model modern Christians wish to emulate in every regard? It is striking that following the only debate about *kashrut* (dietary laws) recorded in the New Testament, both sides agreed to retain modified guidelines about meat with blood still in it.[34] But immediately thereafter, Paul simply decided unilaterally to change the agreement to which he had been a party. Noting that persons would "do well to avoid" non-kosher food is not equivalent to a binding ecclesiastical law. And Paul's subsequent career indicates that his attitude to *kashrut* was quite cavalier (Acts 15:29).

Further, when Paul writes to the Corinthians about rules of sex, marriage, divorce, and remarriage, he openly admits that he had "no command from the Lord"[35] and that the one issuing instruction about this broad topic is "I not the Lord" (1 Cor 7:10, 12). So, confirmed bachelor Paul simply followed his own judgment. If Paul is the model, modern Christians might consider the possible benefits of using their own judgment in the realm of decency, respect, and common courtesy *vis-à-vis* the necessity of pressing their own personal interpretation of faith on Jews.

Evangelization and the Essence of Christian Faith

A fundamental tenet of most forms of Christianity is at stake. The reigning concept of what constitutes a true Christian is founded upon the idea that there is only one pathway to obedience, John's "*the* way." And since that pathway to God places the Christian under *obligation* to seek the conversion of the Jew, real dialogue will remain impossible and the parallel lines will be broken forcibly and tragically again and again.

It is important to note that this idea is an integral part of the faith followed by many conservative Christians. Here, for example, is a statement by the largest Protestant denomination in the nation taken from the Southern Baptist website:

> A resolution adopted by messengers to the 1996 Southern Baptist Convention annual meeting in New Orleans called on

33. First Corinthians 9:20–22.
34. See Acts 15:20.
35. First Corinthians 7:25 and see also 7:40.

Southern Baptists to pray for the salvation of Jewish people and to direct energies and resources toward proclaiming to Jewish people the good news of salvation in Jesus, the Messiah. That resolution drew national attention and was denounced as intolerant by critics, some of whom said efforts to evangelize Jews amounted to "spiritual genocide." A Southern Baptist leader at the time responded that the intent was not to convert Jews into Gentiles, but *"to convert them from being Jews who do not have a relationship with the God of their fathers to Jews who do."* Christians, however, have little choice when it comes to sharing their faith with Jews, said Don Kammerdiener, executive vice president of the International Mission Board. "Many Jewish leaders reject such efforts as being wrongheaded, arrogant or even contributing to the spiritual and cultural equivalent of the Holocaust," Kammerdiener said. "But the Bible is clear regarding *the necessity of sharing the gospel with Jews."* Jesus and the apostles were Jews. Jesus stated clearly that His followers were to begin their witness to Him in Jerusalem, the heartland of the Jews. Jesus is the Messiah promised to the Jews, the Savior of all who believe in Him. He is the fulfillment of the Old Covenant promises. "The Bible is explicit in saying, in Romans 1:16, that Jews are not only included in the gospel invitation, but that the gospel is to go to the Jew first and also to the Gentile." *"Obedient Christians have no choice except to invite Jews and all other peoples to come to faith in Christ."* [emphasis added]

Clearly, evangelizing Jews to bring them to Christ is assumed to be the duty of every obedient Christian. This statement, along with those cited above from organizations whose very existence is geared towards evangelization of Jews, vividly underscores the heart of the difficulties facing all relationships between Jews and Christians. If Christians continue to believe that their way is the only way, and that they alone can offer to Jews a true "relationship with the God of their fathers," the concept of a partnership with Christians "without any fear that this will be exploited for missionary purposes" will remain a naive dream.

From Catholics, the wording of the latest official statement seems directly on target until it adds the "nonetheless," a word that can function remarkably like an escape clause akin to the opening provided by the elastic concept of *willingness* used by individual priests of earlier times. Thus, regardless of how open to parallel lines of mutual respect any specific official Catholic statement may sound, Jews must continue to insist that these official pronouncements of the Church be translated into reality in the lives of individual Christians.

Individual Christians must come to believe that it is wrong for a teacher to "witness" to a Jewish student attending a Catholic (or Baptist or Episcopal) high school. It is wrong for a priest to baptize a patient who lies suffering and perhaps dying in the hospital.[36] The visit of a friend to a Jew dying of pancreatic cancer that produces a triumphant announcement of the man's conversion at his Jewish funeral is equally inappropriate and wrong. Such an act cannot be dismissed as the lifelong concern of a friend and business partner who wanted to be certain that his Jewish colleague would not miss heaven, acting as a friend who was merely doing what Christians are "called" to do.[37] Even if these kinds of actions were all done "in a humble and sensitive manner" (as prescribed by the official statement), both Christians and Jews must label them wrong.

Final Thoughts on a Path Forward

Perhaps someday every Christian denomination will issue a clear statement that forswears all attempts, organized, disorganized, haphazard, or even accidental, to convert Jews. But the current defiant stance of conservative/fundamentalist Christians and the persistent intractability of the Catholic theological position on Jesus indicates clearly that no respite is in sight for Jews who will remain targets of evangelization by those who believe their own Christianity cannot be authentic unless they harangue others. Whether in Catholic Christianity or Protestantism, mere words are not sufficient to heal the breaches between Jews and Christians. But words can become the impetus for a broad attitude adjustment throughout Christendom. And if, please God, the official stances of an enlightened Church can become reality in the daily lives of average Christians, then, and only then, Jews will be able to embrace full partnership with our younger sister in the faith.

36. Sarna, *American Judaism*, 222, has shown that the earliest Jewish hospitals in America were founded "in response to attempts on the part of well-meaning Christian nurses to convert Jews on their deathbeds."

37. This was the exact occurrence at a funeral conducted by the present writer for a lifelong member of our local synagogue. The man's business partner rose at his funeral to announce that only two days before his death our Jewish brother heavily drugged and nearing the end of his life, had converted to Christianity. This private conversion took place quite conveniently when no one else was in the room to witness the event. But the friend was confident that his action had assured our brother of his place in heaven. The man's family as well as all of us in attendance were outraged. In all fairness, it must be noted that three Catholic priests, the man's own Protestant pastor, and several lay Christians apologized to the family for what they too recognized as inexcusable behavior.

Only when the task of co-opting the faith of the "other" comes to a halt can the task of becoming partners of the one true God begin, bringing to its mission the correction of a world that is thrashing around blindly in its arid wasteland of human greed, anger, hatred, intolerance, and dreams of supremacy.

Postscript

As I HAVE DONE in previous published works, so in this analysis of the Gospel of John, I want to affirm that I do not intend to show disrespect either to Christianity or to her sacred texts. I do not pretend to be a New Testament specialist current in all the technical details and the latest arguments about the precise meaning of specific passages. I make no claim to have produced a comprehensive survey of NT scholarship or to have interacted with everything being published in the field of NT interpretation. But I have read carefully and cited numerous pertinent books by many of the more prominent NT scholars of our age. The NT specialists I have chosen to cite most frequently are those who have influenced legions of other less well-known interpreters. I have learned most from those whom I cite most often.

Raymond Brown was a giant of a scholar, and I am in awe of his erudition and thoroughness. I have tried to avoid criticizing Brown (and others) simply because his exegetical judgment does not match mine. But I differ from him strongly whenever he writes as a theologian whose loyalty is to the church rather than as a scholar following rigorous exegetical results wherever they may lead. And I believe careful analysis of his voluminous works indicates that his loyalty was to the church rather than to the text.

Bart Ehrman's *Introduction to the New Testament* is one of the most informative and best written books on the subject I have found. My disagreements with him arise chiefly from his perception of the Hebrew Scriptures or the customs and practices of Judaism. He too is sometimes more ideological than I would prefer and his not infrequent forays into speculation detract from his more informed opinions. But his treatment of the NT and other early Christian literature is superb, and he has taught me a lot.

Other Christian scholars for whom I have only admiration and whom I have cited quite often include Alan Culpepper, Robert Kysar, Louis Martyn, Marianne Meye Thompson, Gail O'Day, Pheme Perkins, and D. Moody Smith.

Rabbi Michael Cook, Amy-Jill Levine, and Adele Reinhartz are fellow Jews with whose methods of thinking and interpretation I am most comfortable. They have all spent far more time studying John than I have, and they are all able to put into words better than I can much of what I sense in reading John.

Special notice is due to my own erudite colleague, Professor Delbert Burkett, whose *Introduction to the New Testament* has taught me more than I have been able to show with only a few notes and from whom I have learned much more in many a private conversation.

These essays are related to questions that congregants, students, and fellow Jews have asked me. My views are based on what I experience when I read the Gospel of John with their questions in mind. I appreciate the ways in which modern Christian scholars attempt to interpret the words of "John" gingerly, seeking to minimize his anti-Jewish rhetoric. I also note with appreciation their sensitivity to the tragic *results* that John's harsh language about "the Jews" has produced over two millennia. These scholars often appear to be searching to find a less offensive interpretation of things that appear to me to have been said quite plainly by John, and their opinions are necessarily sprinkled with theories—plausible theories in some cases, but still theories. It is perhaps inevitable that my admiration and respect are not matched by complete agreement with many of the theoretical positions to which they appeal. In most such cases, my judgment is that the exegetical foundations for these attempts at a wholesale re-interpretation of John simply do not account adequately for the raw facts that are the text of John. Sometimes the solutions they offer seem to me to raise more questions than they answer.

My attempt to read the text of John points to three potential problems. First, in some cases, I believe that the clearly hateful and historically false teachings of John continue to harm modern Jews in much the same way that they have poisoned Jewish-Christian relations for two millennia. Second, by creating a uniformly negative impression of "the Jews" in his gospel, John created the image of a Christian Jesus opposing and deriding these troublesome and uncomprehending Jews that feels "normal" to many modern readers. I do not find the Jesus portrayed in these squabbles compelling or believable. Third, in other Johannine narratives, the attempt to communicate a Christian gospel of love for all humankind is obscured by unwarranted and divisive language. Taken together, these three foci do not augur well for the future of Jewish-Christian relations.

Jewish readers will determine if my responses address Jewish issues in ways that are on point and relevant to modern Jewish life. Christian readers and scholars will decide if I have mishandled the facts of the matter and whether anything I have said is helpful to them. All readers will judge whether my positions are an honest accounting of the evidence or merely one Jew's expression of discomfort at John's consistently negative characterization of "the Jews."

There is one special person to whom I am the most deeply indebted. Professor Stephen Gunter and I have been friends since our days together in college. I have always loved him like a brother, and I have always had utmost respect for the way he lives life as a Christian. As he developed his academic career in textual studies and Christian missiology at Emory and Duke, I came to admire him also as a scholar. His willingness to read this entire manuscript and to share emails and numerous long telephone conversations with me have made the final product far better than I could have made it by working alone. I have noted his opinions several times, but no one will know how many other places are markedly better because of his advice. The mistakes, of course, are mine.

Stephen, thank you. And Ruth Ann, thanks for allowing Stephen and me to play together. The length of our telephone conversations was entirely my fault—every time!

I continue to benefit from the love sent to me in countless ways every day by my wife, Leslie. As an experienced editor, she has read through all of the essays multiple times, and she has made multiple suggestions that have improved the manuscript on almost every page. As a trained journalist and brilliant writer in her own right, Leslie understands my frequent struggles to find the right word or phrase. Should a reader find an apt expression or a particularly compelling turn of phrase in this manuscript, the odds are good that they were suggested by her. Leslie, I love you. Thanks for everything.

Many of the questions that prompted these essays came from my favorite Jew, my son Baraq. Some of these questions originated in childhood as he sat on my lap during story time. With his scintillating intellect and the penetrating honesty of a young person, Baraq regularly pierced the outer layer of words and insisted that I confront the innermost meanings of biblical narratives. As an adult, his uncanny ability to penetrate beneath the surface of a text continues to startle me. I am convinced that his approach to life is typical of the way many Jewish readers around the world respond to "John." He has listened, he has responded with helpful suggestions on many an occasion, and he has helped me improve. Thank you, son. I love you.

Charles David Isbell
01/13/2022
Baton Rouge, Louisiana

Appendix A: The *Shemoneh 'esreh*

The *Shemoneh 'esreh* (*'Amidah*) may be charted as follows:

Section One: Praise and Thanksgiving

#	Subject
1	The Patriarchs who were created by God, their Helper, Savior, and Shield.
2	God who "resurrects the dead"
3	Praise for the holiness of God

Section Two: Petitions

4	Prayer for "insight" (*binah*)
5	Prayer for restoration to God: "bring us back" (*hashivenu*)
6	Prayer for forgiveness (*selaḥ lanu*)
7	Prayer for redemption (*ge'ulah*)
8	Prayer for healing (*refu'ah*)
9	Prayer for agricultural abundance (*kol mineh tevu'atah le-tovah*)
10	Prayer for the ingathering of Exiles (*leqabetz galuyotenu*)
11	Prayer for justice (*shofṭenu*)[1]
12	*Birkat ha-minim*
13	Prayer for compassion for the Righteous (*tzadiqim*)
14	Prayer for the rebuilding Jerusalem (*boneh yerushalayim*)
15	Prayer for the restoration of Davidic reign (*beyt david*)

1. The Hebrew root means both "justice" and "judgment."

Section Three: Gratitude and Confidence

---

16   Request for the acceptance of our prayer (*shemaʿ qolenu*)

17   Gratitude for worship (*ʾavodah*)

18   Thanksgiving: *modim ʾanakhnu lakh.*

19   The Priestly Blessing[2]

---

2. Numbers 6:24-26, well known from its use as a benediction both in synagogue worship and in many Christian churches: "May the Lord bless you and guard you. May the Lord shine His face on you and deal graciously with you. May the Lord lift His face in your direction and grant you *Shalom.*"

Appendix B: The Apocalypse of John

A BRIEF COMMENT ABOUT a fifth piece of literature that later Christian tradition linked to the name of John the son of Zebedee and the Johannine community is also instructive. As we have seen, the author of the gospel declined to identify himself within his narrative, and the author of the three epistles twice used his title of "Elder" but never his name. But the author of The Revelation (Apocalypse) opens his book with a clear self-identification. In Revelation 1:1, "John" is the "servant" of Jesus Christ who was visited by a heavenly messenger ("angel"); in 1:4 and 1:9 he is identified as the person addressing "the seven churches that are in Asia;" and in 22:8, he underscores his involvement: "I, John, am he who heard and saw these things." Then in 22:18-19, the angel who had showed "these things" to John describes them as a "book."

This internal identification of the author as "John," caused the early church to link the final book of the New Testament with the Johannine community via the man they deemed to be the author of all five works, John the son of Zebedee. Although this identification has not been accepted by scholars, there are literary links that call for comment.

Both contain significant descriptions of Jesus that appear only in the Gospel of John and the Revelation. First, the well-known designation of Jesus as the "word" (*logos*) of God is found only in John 1:1 and Revelation 19:13. Second, the phrase "water of life" (*hydōr zōēs*) is attested only in John 7:38 and Revelation 22:17. Two such distinctive and theologically pregnant appellations suggest that John and Revelation shared a common origin within a community (the "Johannine") that venerated similar traditions about the specific wording of at least some of the teachings of Jesus.

Thus it is not surprising that the accusation of slander (literally "blasphemy," *blasphēmian*) from "those who say they are Jews and are not, but are from a synagogue of Satan" (Rev. 2:9; 3:9) strikes a tone quite similar to the invective hurled at the Jews in John 8:44–47, especially when the reference to "the devil" (*ho diabolos*) is added to the mix in Revelation 2:10. This is additional evidence of the absolute schism between the Johannine community and anything Jewish.

Appendix C: Rabbinic Disagreement

Two specific examples illustrate the flexibility of rabbinic debates about serious theological issues. The first involves the question of capital punishment.

Capital Punishment

Biblical legislation prescribes capital punishment for a variety of offenses, providing various methods of carrying out a death penalty.

Crime or "Sin"	Punishment
apostasy (Lev 20:2; Deut 13:11; 17:5)	Stoning
blasphemy (Lev 24:14, 16, 23; 1 Sam 21:10)	
sorcery (Lev 20:27)	
violation of Shabbat (Num 15:35–36)	
misappropriation of חרם (Josh 7:25)	
a disobedient son (Deut 21:21)	
adultery (Deut 22:20–24: *both* man and woman)	
rape (Deut 22:25)	
incest (Lev 20:14)	Death by Fire
fornication by the daughter of a priest (Lev 21:9)	
the perceived adultery of Tamar (Gen 38:24–26)	
an apostate city (Deut 13:15; 1 Kgs 18:40)	Death by Sword
homicide (Num 35:9)	

If one is limited to a literal interpretation and allows the debate about capital punishment to be determined by the Bible alone, the "biblical" position plainly champions the view that capital punishment was an acceptable and necessary aspect of criminal procedure.

In fact, the Bible not only favors but *commands* the death penalty in more than a few places, as the chart above indicates. However, when the death penalty came under discussion among the Talmudic sages, an interesting shift began to occur. Numerous places in the Mishnah refer to the death penalty as if it were taken for granted by the Tanna'im just as it had been by the biblical authors. For example, *Makkot* 1:10 (*Sanhedrin* 7:1) reads: "The court has power to inflict four kinds of death-penalty: stoning, burning, beheading, and strangling." Both preceding and following this summary statement are a series of paragraphs describing exactly how each of these methods was to be carried out. But one short paragraph of this intriguing Mishnaic debate about capital punishment sheds light on the whole process and exemplifies the spirit of openness among scholars whose theological views differed, a spirit that the Gospel of John is anxious to illustrate was absent among the Jews who met and interacted with Jesus.

In *Makkot* 1:10: (7a), a general principle is enunciated and placed on the docket for discussion. "A Sanhedrin (Jewish High Court) that votes a death penalty one time in seven years is called reckless." Reactions among the rabbis to this broad statement are mixed and far from unanimous agreement.

First, Rabbi Elazar the son of Azaryah says, "One time in seventy years" would also be reckless.

Then Rabbi Tarfon and Rabbi Akiva weigh in: "If we were on the Sanhedrin, it would never impose the death penalty." This opinion is especially significant because a unanimous Sanhedrin vote was necessary for a death penalty, at least two witnesses must have testified under oath that they witnessed the act of murder, and the eyewitnesses whose testimony resulted in conviction are required to participate in the act of execution. Even one member, voicing the intensity of complete opposition expressed by Tarfon and Akiva, could almost ensure the fact that no death penalty would ever be issued.

The extreme nature of opposition from Tarfon and Akiva prompted a sharp response from Rabban Shimon the son of Gamliel: "Well then, we would multiply capital crimes (lit., "the shedding of blood") in Israel."

This was a debate carried out during the era of Roman hegemony, when Jews did not have the legal authority to execute a death penalty for any reason. In other words, the entire discussion could not have been simply about when or whether to apply a death penalty. It served as an exercise intended to instruct scholars about the complexity involved in the taking of a human life even with appropriate biblical justification. To do this, in the brief report of what surely must have been a heated debate, virtually every position represented in the modern debate about capital punishment is found:

> General principle: death penalty acceptable only rarely
> (once in seven years).
>
> Death penalty acceptable only in *exceptional* cases
> (once in seventy years, Elazar).
>
> Death penalty is an improper sentence in *every* case
> (Tarfon and Akiva).
>
> Death penalty necessary as a deterrent to crime (Shimon).

After setting forth these various points of view, the Mishnah makes no attempt to declare which position was determined to be *the* correct Jewish interpretation. The point of such an example is clear. There was no central agency dictating *the* Jewish view of capital punishment. As their discussion of the issue demonstrates, men who were both learned and honorable disagreed among themselves about capital punishment so sharply that they were unable to arrive at a consensus, and thus no student of the Mishnaic masters could simply hide behind blind acceptance of a specific rabbinic opinion endorsed uncritically. Whatever an individual Jew might decide about the death penalty, he or she would have to face the fact that credible and serious rabbinic scholars had disagreed with that conclusion. No one could read their debate, vote "I agree," and be relieved of the responsibility of personal reflection and involvement in a complex moral issue. Both in the Mishnaic era and in all subsequent periods, the biblical information had to be transvalued, i.e., subjected to interpretative decisions that moved beyond the Bible from the outset. And all opinions proffered by respected scholars were included in the "Final Report," with no hint of violence or recrimination against anyone who dissented.

Rabbi "Zero"

The second example involves a man named "Rabbi Ephes" of Antioch. Commenting on Genesis 2:1, he is quoted as declaring that *va-yǝkhûllû* could refer only to total destruction, meaning that God destroyed his initial creation (in Genesis chapter 1) and then started over with a second creation in the next chapter. Now the majority opinion was that *va-yǝkhûllû* meant simply, "they [the heavens and the earth] were *completed*." I wrote to my former doctoral advisor, the incomparable Cyrus Gordon, asking which of the two interpretative options was correct. He answered as follows: "actually *va-yəkhŭllŭ* means both: retrospectively 'completed,' and prospectively 'destroyed.'" In other words, both sides of this disagreement about the interpretation of an important biblical teaching were possible, even plausible.

The salient point here is that the opinion of Rabbi Ephes stood in isolated disagreement with all the other rabbis whose opinions we possess. And while this theological chasm is not as wide as the Gospel of John wishes to make between Jesus and "the Jews," the doctrine of creation is not an insignificant issue. For a single rabbi to offer an opinion about creation that differed sharply from all other participating Jewish authorities was quite remarkable.

In fact, the name "Ephes" ("Zero") is clearly an odd one, given the penchant among the rabbis for assigning names that reflect the character or profession of certain individuals. When I asked Dr. Gordon if the name Zero might have meant the other rabbis viewed Rabbi Ephes as an atheist, he said he did not think so. And he suggested another possibility: "Perhaps 'Zero' was the rather humorous nickname by which he became known in recognition of the fact that so many of his opinions went against the norm," and thus his batting average for being on the winning side of a debate was "zero!" But not one of his theological opponents hinted that the good dissenting rabbi should be killed, and he is cited ten or eleven more times in rabbinic literature, although never on the winning side of a debate.

In addition, despite his odd name and his penchant for voicing alternative or dissenting points of view, his opinion was sought about matters of liturgy and Scriptural interpretation, and he was accorded great respect by his peers. The Talmud records one example of this respect. As the patriarch of the academy in Sepphoris lay dying, he appointed Hanina ben Hama to succeed him. But Hanina ben Hama refused to accept the appointment because to do so would supersede Rabbi Ephes and would not show proper respect for the fact that Ephes was his senior by two and one-half years.

The number of similar examples could be increased one hundredfold, and they offer clear illustration of the atmosphere of collegiality that typified rabbinic disagreements and debates. The repeated insistence in the Gospel of John that Jewish scholars who disagreed with something Jesus was teaching or claiming would have been determined to forego discussion and leap immediately to a plot to kill him does not accord with what is known about rabbinic debate in the general period.

Appendix D: Early Christian Anti-Judaism

It has been a standard feature of Christian preaching through the ages that the Roman destruction of Jerusalem in 70 was really God's decisive punishment of the Jewish people for their rejection of Jesus, who had died around the year 30. The earliest Christian sermon that we possess, outside of the NT, is largely a tirade against the Jews for their treatment of Jesus. Melito, bishop (apparently) of Sardis in the mid-100's, declares that the Jewish people and its Scripture became an "empty thing" with the arrival of Christianity and the gospel (*Pascha* 43); only those Jews who believe in Jesus have any ongoing religious validity. Melito accuses the Jews as a nation of having "murdered" Jesus and asserts that their current suffering (after 70 and a further failed revolt in 132-135) is a consequence: "You cast the Lord down, you were cast down to earth. And you, you lie dead, while he went up to the heights of heaven" (*Pascha* 99-100).

EVEN IF ONE ACCEPTS the New Testament version of the passion narratives depicted in the Synoptic Gospels and John, it is certain that no one hearing the sermons of Christian preachers from the second century on had been alive at the death of Jesus. Yet, the addresses in the sermons of the early church fathers are made in the singular as if "the Jews" were a single corporate personality throughout their centuries of history. Even a cursory reading of the Hebrew Bible, which was the only Bible of early Christendom, shows that the whole idea of collective responsibility is repugnant, more like revenge than anything else. It is an idea implying that "anybody with certain religious or genetic characteristics becomes morally responsible for the actions of any others with those features." It is also an idea that is expressly denounced by Ezekiel [18.20!].

Anti-Jewish Sermons and Statements

Among the countless examples that could be adduced, the following are only a tiny representative sample.

The early second century *Epistle of Barnabas* adds a scathing denunciation of sacrifices, fasting, Shabbat, and the Temple, all of which the author believed the Jews had misunderstood because an evil angel had misled early Israel to interpret incorrectly what God really requires [9:4].

Justin Martyr [ca. 100–165] referred to the "general silliness, and deceit and fussiness and pride of the Jews." Yet another early second century father, *Polycarp Bishop of Smyrna*, labeled anyone who did not accept Jesus as the messiah an "anti-Christ." Less than a century later, these types of statements produced the ultimate charge of "Christ Killers:" In his treatise titled *Against the Jews*, bishop *Hippolytus* (d. 235 CE), declares:

> Why was the temple made desolate? Was it on account of the ancient fabrication of the calf? Or was it on account of the ancient idolatry of the people? Was it for the blood of the prophets? . . . By no means, for in all these transgressions, they always found pardon open to them. But it was because they killed the Son of their Benefactor, for He is coeternal with the Father (*Against the Jews*, Paragraph 7).

The first non-Jewish Christian scholar to study Hebrew was the second-century church father *Origen*, who used his knowledge of the biblical language to argue that the Jews had disrespected their own Bible and had interpreted it incorrectly. Their misinterpretation had caused them to substitute trivial religious observances for the practice of true religion and that led to their punishment and exile. Here is an example of the way Origen emphasized the three most important points for his hearers to know about Judaism:

> I challenge anyone to prove my statement untrue if I say that the entire Jewish nation was destroyed less than one whole generation later, on account of these sufferings which they inflicted on Jesus. For it was, I believe, forty-two years from the time when they crucified Jesus to the destruction of Jerusalem . . . for they committed the most impious crime of all, when they conspired against the Savior of mankind, in the city where they performed the customary rites which were symbols of profound mysteries. Therefore, that city where Jesus suffered these indignities had to be utterly destroyed. The Jewish nation had to be overthrown, and God's invitation to blessedness transferred to others, I mean

to the Christians, to whom came the teaching about the simple
and pure worship of God (*Cels.* 4.22).

Here are the words of Cyprian, an early third century Church father:
"the Jews are those whose peoplehood has been canceled, whose holy city
has been destroyed, and whose status as the people of God has been trans-
ferred away from them to the Christians."

Eusebius, an early fourth century Christian author, made the same sort
of claims in his *Ecclesiastical History* (3.5.3), which became an extremely
influential document for subsequent generations of Christians. His work defined many aspects of the Christian understanding of history until the modern period. Speaking of the fall of Jerusalem in 70, he asserts that Christians
fled the city so that "the judgment of God might at last overtake them [Jews]
for all their crimes against the Christ and his Apostles, and all that generation
of the wicked be utterly blotted out from among men."

Appendix E: EGO EIMI as Self-Introduction/Identification

THE MOST COMMON WAY for Greek-speaking persons to introduce themselves was to employ the simple phrase *egō eimi*. But *egō eimi* standing alone was not a name and it furnished no clue to the identification of the person saying it. As shown in Essay XI, *egō eimi* was used by Jesus to introduce himself to Saul. But his self-introduction was not *egō eimi* alone. To help Saul know whom he was encountering, *egō eimi* had to be followed by his personal name Jesus (*egō eimi Yēsous*). In short, the name of the person addressing Saul was not *egō eimi* because *egō eimi* is not a name.

Simply telling someone *egō eimi* does nothing to identify the speaker. Either *egō eimi* must be followed with the name of the person or with an explanatory phrase of some kind, or a contextual marker like "[I am] the person you seek," or "[I am] the lady you requested." But *egō eimi* standing alone explains nothing and identifies no one.

In addition to the examples in Essay XI, there are three interesting NT incidents outside the Book of John that illustrate the appropriate use of *egō eimi* in Greek.

1. In the Gospel of Luke, a Jewish priest named Zechariah heard an unidentified angel announce that his childless wife Elizabeth was soon to bear him a son whom they would name John. Because Zechariah and his wife were both old, Zechariah was understandably skeptical, and asked the anonymous angel, "How can I be sure of this?" (Luke 1:18). "The angel said to him, 'I am Gabriel'" (1:19). This response to Zechariah was in simple Greek: "*egō eimi Gabriēl*." This was not an angel claiming to be divine. To the contrary, Gabriel immediately explains that the veracity of his pronouncement is certified by the fact that "I stand in the presence of God, and I have been dispatched to speak to you."

2. In Acts 10:2, a Roman centurion named Cornelius sent messengers to the house in Joppa where Peter was staying as a guest. He wanted to

quiz Peter about a dream of his that had puzzled him. When the envoys arrived at the house in Joppa, Peter was in the process of pondering his own vision when "the spirit" told him that three men were looking for him and instructed him to accompany them to the residence of their employer, Cornelius (10:19–20). Peter went to the front door and informed them, "I am (*egō eimi*) the one you are seeking" (10:21).

3. Romans 11:1–32 is a lengthy and detailed segment of a letter from Paul to the churches in Rome. Using a well-known format designed for a scholarly presentation of his views, Paul begins with a question about the possible salvation of the Jews: "Did God reject his people?" His simple answer is: "God did not reject his people" (11:1–2), followed by a more detailed explanation of the relationship between the Jews and God (11:3–10). Then he repeats his question: "Did they stumble and fall beyond recovery?" His answer is again direct and to the point: "Not at all" (11:11). This short answer is also followed by more details in the next two verses.

In Romans 11:13, Paul appears to stop and catch his breath before asserting his identity and credentials on the subject at hand: "I am speaking to you, Gentiles, because I am (*eimi egō*) the apostle to the Gentiles."

In each of these examples, *egō eimi* by itself would be meaningless. The name Gabriel and the assignment he was given from God, Peter's linkage of himself to the name of the person being sought by the servants of Cornelius, and the official designation of the letter writer explaining theology to Gentiles are all necessary to complete the thoughts expressed in their respective contexts.

A final example of the function of *egō eimi* when it serves to help someone self-identify is found in the Greek translation of Genesis 27. The story is familiar. Esau the older, hairy twin is dispatched by his aged and sightless father to go out hunting wild game with which to prepare the father's favorite meal (27:1–4). After that meal, the father intended to transmit to Esau his final, deathbed blessing.

When Jacob's mother (Rebecca) overheard her aged husband promising his final blessing to Esau (her husband's favorite), she devised a plan to help Jacob (her favorite) cheat Esau. Since Jacob was not a hunter, she instructed him to kill two choice kids from the family flock for her to prepare as the aged Isaac's favorite dish. (27:5–10). But there was a small problem. Jacob was smooth skinned, while Esau was hairy. Thus, even though the sightless father could not see which boy was bringing him the meal, a simple touch would reveal Jacob as a trickster and call forth from the father not a blessing but a curse (27:11–12). The mother solved the problem in short order. When Jacob brought back the two tame kids, she slaughtered the kids and prepared the meal for Isaac, dressed Jacob in some of Esau's clothes, and covered his smooth hands and neck with the pelts of the kids (27:14–17). She then sent Jacob to Isaac carrying the food she had prepared.

Two times, the imposter assured his father that he was Esau (27:19, 24). Even though the old father was suspicious, touching the hairy animal pelts that covered the hands of Jacob and catching the scent of Esau's hunting clothes convinced him that Esau was the son in the room with him. Then he gave his final, irrevocable blessing to Jacob.

Immediately thereafter, Esau returned from the hunt, prepared his father's favorite dish from the wild game he had killed, and brought it to Isaac to ask for his promised blessing. The confused Isaac asked, "Who are you?" And Esau identified himself to the old man: "I am (*egō eimi*) your firstborn son, Esau" (27:30-32), both he and his anguished father realized that the misapplied blessing could not be recalled and the damage could not be undone.

Both boys had self-identified using the name Esau. One was a lying cheater whose devious plan began when he stole the name of his older brother. One spoke his name truthfully.

Bibliography

Anderson, Bernard W. *Out of the Depths, the Psalms Speak for Us Today*. Philadelphia: Westminster, 1983.

Arndt & Gingrich, *A Greek-English Lexicon of the New Testament and Other Early Christian Literature*. 2nd ed. University of Chicago Press, 1958.

Barclay, William. *Daily Study Bible*. 17 vols. Glascow: Saint Andrews, 1965.

Barrett, C. K. *The New Testament Background: Writings from Ancient Greece and the Roman Empire that Illuminate Christian Origins*. Revised and Expanded Edition. San Francisco: Harper, 1989.

Bauckham, Richard. *Jesus and the Eyewitnesses: The Gospels as Eyewitness Testimony*. 2nd ed. Grand Rapids: Eerdmans, 2017.

Ben-Horin, et al., eds. *Studies and Essays in Honor of Abraham A. Neuman*. Leiden: Brill, 1962.

Black. C. Clifton. *The First, Second, and Third Letter of John*. The New Interpreter's Bible 12. Nashville: Abingdon, 1998.

Blumhofer, Christopher M. *The Gospel of John and the Future of Israel*. Society for New Testament Studies Monograph Series 177. Cambrige University Press, 2020.

Brown, Raymond E. *The Community of the Beloved Disciple*. New York: Paulist, 1979.

———. *The Death of the Messiah: From Gethsemane to the Grave*. London: Doubleday, 1994.

———. *The Epistles of John*. Garden City, NY: Doubleday, 1982.

———. *The Gospel According to John*, Anchor Bible 29. Garden City, NY: Doubleday, 1966.

———. *The Gospel of John and the Johannine Epistles*. Collegeville, MN: Liturgical, 1960.

———. *An Introduction to the New Testament*. New York: Doubleday, 1997.

Bruce, F. F. *The Book of the Acts*. The New International Commentary on the New Testament. Grand Rapids: Eerdmans, 1954.

Brueggemann, Walter. "From Hurt to Joy, From Death to Life." *Interpretation* 28.1 (1974) 3–19.

———. "The Formfulness of Grief." *Interpretation* 31.4 (1977) 263–75.

Bultmann, Rudolph. *Essays, Philosophical and Theological*. London: SCM, 1955.

Burkett, Delbert. *An Introduction to the New Testament and the Origins of Christianity*. Cambridge University Press, 2002.

Chilton, Bruce. "Caiaphas." In ABD 1:803–6.

Cook, Michael. *Modern Jews Engage the New Testament: Enhancing Jewish Well-Being in a Christian Environment*. Woodstock, VT: Jewish Lights, 2012.

Cronin, Sonya. *Raymond Brown, "the Jews," and the Gospel of John: From Apologia to Apology.* London: T. & T. Clark, 2015.

Crossan, John Dominic. *Who Killed Jesus? Exposing the Roots of Anti-Semitism in the Gospel Story of the Death of Jesus.* San Francisco: Harper, 1995.

Culpepper, R. Alan. *The Johannine School,* SBL Dissertation Series 26. Missoula: Scholars, 1975.

———. "Preaching the Hostile References to 'the Jews' in the Gospel of John." In *The Gospel of John and Jewish-Christian Relations,* edited by Adele Reinhartz, 49–69. New York: Lexington, 2018.

Earle, Ralph, et al., eds. *Exploring the New Testament.* Kansas City: Beacon Hill, 1961.

Ehrman, Bart D. *Lost Christianities: The Battles for Scripture and the Faiths We Never Knew.* New York: Oxford University Press, 2003.

———. *Misquoting Jesus: The Story Behind Who Changed the Bible and Why.* San Francisco: Harper, 2005.

———. *The New Testament: A Historical Introduction to the Early Christian Writings.* New York: Oxford University Press, 1997.

Elbogen, Ismar. *Jewish Liturgy, A Comprehensive History.* Translated by Raymond P. Scheindlin. New York: Jewish Publication Society, 1993.

Freed, Edwin D. *The New Testament, A Critical Introduction.* 3rd ed. Wadsworth, 2001.

Freedmann, Lillian C., *Antisemitism in the New Testament.* Lanham, MD: University Press of America, 1994.

Frend, W. H. C. *The Rise of Christianity.* Philadelphia: Fortress, 1984.

Fried, Lisbeth S. "Cyrus the Messiah? The Historical Background to Isaiah 45:1." *Harvard Theological Review* 95.4 (2002) 373–93.

Greenspoon, Leonard J., and Ronald A. Simkins, eds. *Studies in Jewish Civilization.* Vol. 13, *Spiritual Dimensions in Judaism.* Omaha, Nebraska: Creighton University Press, 2003.

Hauck, Friedrich. "*Ekballo.*" In TDNT 1:527–28.

Heil, Johannes. *Agobard, Amolo, das Kirchengut und die Jüden von Lyon.* In *Forschungen zur westeuropäischen Geschichte* 25:1. Francia, 1998.

Isbell, Charles David. "The Divine Name היהא As a Symbol of Presence in Israelite Tradition." *Hebrew Annual Review* 2 (1978) 101–18.

———. "Emic or Etic: Interpreting the Hebrew Scriptures." *www.bibleinterp.com* (July, 2015).

———. "Essays Introducing a Jewish Perspective on the Gospel of John." *Socio-Historical Examination of Religion and Ministry* 2.1 (2020) 17–26.

———. *God's Scribes: How the Bible Became the Bible.* Warren Center, PA: Marco Polo Monographs, 1999.

———. *How Jews and Christians Interpret Their Sacred Texts: A Study in Transvaluation.* Eugene, OR: Resource, 2014.

———. "Initial 'Alef-Yod Interchange and Selected Biblical Passages." *Journal of Near Eastern Studies* 37 (1978) 227–36.

———. "The *Limmûdîm* in the Book of Isaiah." *Journal for the Study of the Old Testament* 34.1 (2009) 99–109.

———. "The Musical Notations in the Book of Psalms." *Studies in Jewish Civilization* 19:11–26.

———. "'The Orthodox Rabbinic Statement on Christianity, 'To Do the Will of Our Father in Heaven': Toward a Partnership between Jews and Christians." *www.bibleinterp.com* (April, 2016).

———. "Paul and Judaism." *www.bibleinterp.com (July, 2017).*

———. "Persia and Yehud." *The Old Testament in Archaeology and History*, 529–56.

———. "Saul the Sadducee? A Rabbinical Thought Experiment." *Socio-Historical Examination of Religion and Ministry* 1.2 (2019) 85–119.

———. "Some 'Earthy' Dimensions of the Spiritual in Jewish Liturgy." In *Studies in Jewish Civilization* 13:227–38.

———. "Zoroastrianism and Biblical Religion." *Jewish Bible Quarterly* 34/3 (2006) 143–54.

Jastrow, Marcus. *A Dictionary of the Targumim, the Talmud Babli and Yerushalmi, and the Midrashic Literature*. Peabody, MA: Hendrickson, 2005.

Jewish Encyclopedia. New York & London: Funk & Wagnalls, 1905.

"John, Gospel of." *Jewish Encyclopedia* IX. New York & London. Funk & Wagnalls, 1905.

Katz, Steven T. "Issues in the Separation of Judaism and Christianity after 70 CE: A Reconsideration." *Journal of Biblical Literature* 103.1 (1984) 43–76.

Kee, Howard Clark, and Irvin J. Borowsky, eds. *Removing the Anti-Judaism from the New Testament*. Philadelphia: American Interfaith Institute/World Alliance, 1998.

Kegley, Charles W., ed. *The Theology of Rudolf Bultmann*. New York: Harper & Row, 1966.

Kertzer, David. *The Kidnapping of Edgardo Mortara*. Vintage Books, Random House, 1997.

Kimelman, Reuven. "Birkat Ha-Minim and the Lack of Evidence for an Anti-Christian Jewish Prayer in Late Antiquity." In *Jewish and Christian Self-Definition*, 2:226–44. Philadelphia: Fortress, 1981.

Kysar, Robert. *Voyages with John: Charting the Fourth Gospel*. Waco: Baylor University Press, 2005.

———. *John, the Maverick Gospel*. 3rd ed. Louisville: Westminster John Knox Press, 2007.

Langenwalter, Anna Beth. *Agobard of Lyon: An Exploration of Carolingian Jewish-Christian Relations*. University of Toronto PhD thesis. University Microfilms: Michigan, 2009.

Langer, Ruth. *Cursing the Christians? A History of the Birkat Haminim*. Oxford University Press, 2011.

Levine, Amy-Jill. "Christian Privilege, Christian Fragility, and the Gospel of John." In *The Gospel of John and Jewish-Christian Relations*, edited by Adele Reinhartz, 87–110. New York: Lexington, 2018.

Levine, Amy-Jill and Marc Zvi Brettler, eds. *The Jewish Annotated New Testament*. 2nd ed. Oxford University Press, 2017.

———. *The Bible with and without Jesus: How Jews and Christians Read the Same Stories Differently*. New York: HarperOne, 2020.

Levine, Baruch A. *The JPS Torah Commentary: Leviticus*. New York: Jewish Publication Society, 1989.

Lizorkin-Eyzenberg, Eli. *The Jewish Gospel of John*. Privately published, Copyright 2015–2019.

Lunel, Armand. *The Jews of the South of France*. Translated by Samuel N. Rosenberg, *Hebrew Union College Annual* 89 (2018).

MacIntyre, Alasdair. *Three Rival Versions of Moral Enquiry.* Notre Dame: University of Notre Dame Press, 1990.

Martyn, J. Louis. *History and Theology in the Fourth Gospel.* 3rd ed. Louisville: John Knox, 2003.

Mason, Steve. *Josephus and the New Testament,* 2nd ed. Peabody, Mass: Hendrickson, 2003.

Midrash Rabbah. Freedman and Simon eds. Ten Volumes. New York: Soncino,1983.

Milgrom, Jacob. *Leviticus 1–16.* New York: Doubleday, 1998.

Moore, Daniel F. *Jesus, An Emerging Jewish Mosaic.* New York: T & T Clark, 2008.

Neusner, Jacob. *Jews and Christians: The Myth of a Common Tradition.* SCM, 1991. Reprint, Eugene, OR: Wipf & Stock, 2003.

Nicholls, William. *Christian Antisemitism: A History of Hate.* Northvale, N. J.: Jaxon Aronson, Inc, 1993.

O'Day, Gail R. *The Gospel of John: Introduction, Commentary, and Reflections. The New Interpreter's Bible* 9:491–865. Nashville: Abingdon, 1995.

Perkins, Pheme. *The Gospel of Mark. The New Interpreter's Bible* 8:507–733. Nashville, Abingdon, 1995.

Perrin, Norman, *The New Testament: An Introduction.* New York: Harcourt, Brace, Jovanovich, 1974.

Von Rad, Gerhard. *Deuteronomy, A Commentary. The Old Testament Library.* Philadelphia: Westminster, 1966.

Redford, Donald. *Akhenaton, the Heretic King.* Princeton, NJ: Princeton University Press, 1984.

Reinhartz, Adele, *Befriending the Beloved Disciple: A Jewish Reading of the Gospel of John.* New York: The Continuum International Publishing Group Inc., 2001.

———. *Cast Out of the Covenant: Jews and Anti-Judaism in the Gospel of John.* Lexington Books/Fortress Academic, 2018.

———, ed. *The Gospel of John and Jewish-Christian Relations.* New York: Lexington, 2018.

Rivkin, Ellis. *What Crucified Jesus? Messianism, Pharisaism, and the Development of Christianity.* Cincinnati: Behrman House-URJ, 1997.

Roberson, Carroll. *John: The Jewish Gospel.* Bloomington, Indiana: Westbow, 2017.

Roth, Cecil. *A History of the Jews.* New York: Shocken, 1970.

Sampley, J. Paul. *The First Letter to the Corinthians: Introduction, Commentary, and Reflection.* The New Interpreter's Bible 9. Nashville: Abingdon, 2020.

Sanders, James A. "The Hermeneutics of Translation." In *Removing the Anti-Judaism from the New Testament,* edited by Howard Clark Kee and Irvin J. Borowsky, 43–62. Philadelphia: American Interfaith Institute/World Alliance, 1998.

Sandmel, Samuel. "Bultmann On Judaism." Charles W. Kegley, ed. *The Theology of Rudolf Bultmann.* New York: Harper & Row, 1966, 211–35.

———. *A Jewish Understanding of the New Testament.* 3rd ed. New York: Jewish Lights, 2005.

———. "Pilate, Pontius." IDB 3:811–13.

Sarna, Jonathan A. *American Judaism: A History.* New Haven and London: Yale University Press, 2004.

Schaff, Philip. "Alogi." In *A Dictionary of Christian Biography and Literature to the End of the Sixth Century A.D., with an Account of the Principal Sects and Heresies,* by Henry Wace. Grand Rapids: Christian Classics Ethereal Library, 2000.

Schniedewind, William. *How the Bible Became a Book*. Cambridge University Press, 2004.

Schuller, Eileen. "The Gospel of John in the Catholic Lectionary." In *The Gospel of John and Jewish-Christian Relations*, edited by Adele Reinhartz, 71–85. New York: Lexington, 2018.

Schürer. Emil. *A History of the Jewish People in the Time of Jesus Christ*, 3rd ed. Peabody, MA: Hendrickson, 1998. First issued in 1890 by T. & T. Clark.

Singer, Isidore and Isaac B. Broydé. "Pilate, Pontius." *Jewish Encyclopedia* 5:34.

Smiga, George M. *The Gospel of John Set Free*. New York: Paulist, 2008.

Smith, D. Moody. *John Among the Gospels*. 2nd ed. Columbia: University of South Carolina Press, 2001.

Spong, Shelby. *Liberating the Gospels: Reading the Bible with Jewish Eyes*. San Francisco: Harper, 1996.

Taaunon, Gwendly. *The Path of Shadows: Chthonic Deities, Oneiromany, and Necromancy in Ancient Greece*. Australia: Manticore, 2018.

Tanakh: The Holy Scriptures. The New Jewish Publication Society Translation According to the Traditional Hebrew Text. Philadelphia: Jewish Publication Society, 1985.

Thatcher and McNeal. *A Source Book for Medieval History*. New York: 1905.

Thompson, Marianne Meye. *The God of the Gospel of John*. Grand Rapids: Eerdmans, 2001.

———. "'They Bear Witness to Me': The Psalms in the Passion Narrative of the Gospel of John." J. Ross Wagner et. al, eds. *The Word Leaps the Gap: Essays on Scripture and Theology in Honor of Richard B. Hays*, 267–83. Grand Rapids: Eerdmans, 2008.

———. *John, A Commentary*. Louisville: Westminster/John Knox, 2015.

Treat, Jay Curry. "Barnabas, Epistle of." *ABD* 1:613.

Westermann, Claus. *Isaiah 40–66*. Translated by David M. G. Stalker. *The Old Testament Library*. Philadelphia: Westminster, 1969.

———. *The Praise of God in the Psalms*. Richmond: John Knox, 1965.

Wylen, Stephen M. *The Jews in the Time of Jesus: An Introduction*. New York: Paulist, 1996.

Zacour, Norman. *Jews and Saacens in the Consilia of Oldradus de Ponte*. Rome: Pontifical Institute of Mediaeval Studies, 1990.

Zimmerli, Walther. *I Am Yahweh*, Edited by Walter Brueggemann. Atlanta: John Knox, 1982.

Subject Index

Scripture Index